PATRICE PETRO

JOYLESS
STREETS

WOMEN AND MELODRAMATIC

REPRESENTATION IN

WEIMAR GERMANY

■

Princeton University Press
Princeton, New Jersey

Copyright © 1989 by Princeton University Press

Published by Princeton University Press, 41 William Street,
Princeton, New Jersey 08540
In the United Kingdom: Princeton University Press, Chichester, West Sussex

Library of Congress Cataloging-in-Publication Data

Petro, Patrice, 1957—
Joyless streets : women and melodramatic representation in Weimar, Germany /
Patrice Petro.
p. cm. Bibliography: p. Includes index.
ISBN 0-691-05552-1 (alk. paper) ISBN 0-691-00830-2 (pbk.)
1. Motion pictures—Germany—History. 2. Silent films—Germany—History.
3. Motion picture audiences—Germany—History. 4. Photojournalism—Germany—
History. 5. Women in mass media—Germany—History. 6. Sex role in mass media—
Germany—History. 7. Women—Germany—History—20th century. 8. Feminist
criticism. I. Title. II. Title: Title: Women and melodramatic representation in Weimar.
PN1993.5.G3P435 1989 791.43´0943—dc19 88—22684 CIP

This book has been composed in Linotron Caledonia and Bauhaus

Princeton University Press books are printed on acid-free paper and
meet the guidelines for permanence and durability of the Committee on
Production Guidelines for Book Longevity of the Council on Library Resources

Printed in the United States of America by Princeton Academic Press

Designed by Laury A. Egan

3 5 7 9 10 8 6 4 2

For my parents,
Helen Marie Gill and
Anastas Thomas Petro

It is an irretrievable image of the past which threatens to disappear in any present which does not recognize its common relation with that image.

—WALTER BENJAMIN, "Eduard Fuchs, der Sammler und der Historiker"

· CONTENTS ·

· LIST OF FIGURES ·

· ACKNOWLEDGMENTS ·

I would like to thank the Deutsche Akademischer Austauschdienst for providing me with the research grant that enabled me to study in Germany during the academic year 1985–1986. For their very specific contributions to my research, I am indebted to Dr. Peter Bucher of the Bundesarchiv in Koblenz, Diethart Kerbs of the Akademie der Künste, Hans Helmut Prinzler of the Stiftung Deutsche Kinemathek, and the staff of the Landesarchiv and the Institut für Publizistik in West Berlin. I would also like to acknowledge a special debt of gratitude to Aronold H. Crane, who allowed me to reproduce the Moholy-Nagy photocollage which appears on the cover of this book. Most importantly, I would like to express my profound thanks to those individuals in Berlin who supported my studies in fundamental ways, giving freely of their time, their personal resources, and their practical guidance: Elfi Bettinger of the Freie Universität, Clara Burckner of Basis-Film Verleih, Detlef Oesterreich of the Max Planck Institut, and Eva Schulze of the Institut für Zukunftsstudien.

Many of the ideas presented in this book were first given shape and direction in discussions with Nataša Ďurovičová and Charles Wolfe, whom I first met while I was a student at the University of California–Santa Barbara. I am deeply grateful to Nataša and Chuck for their unwavering support and intellectual generosity over the years, and for their painstaking attention to numerous drafts of this work. My initial research on the Weimar cinema was developed and refined during my years as a doctoral candidate in the Department of Communication Studies at the University of Iowa. To Rick Altman, Dudley Andrew, Ed Ball, Dana Benelli, Ava Collins, Jim Collins, Greg Easely, Caryl Flinn, Ursula Hardt, Ana Lopez, and Shari Zeck I am especially grateful for making my years at Iowa so intellectually stimulating and personally rewarding. My warmest thanks go to Tania Modleski, who first encouraged me to undertake a book-length study of women in Weimar, and who read an earlier draft of the manuscript with interest and great care. I would also like to acknowledge the Center for Twentieth Century Studies at the University of Wisconsin–Milwaukee, and its director, Kathleen Woodward, for providing me with the time and institutional support to put the finishing touches on this book. Special thanks to Meaghan Morris, and to my colleagues and friends in Milwaukee in the departments of English, German, and Art History: Jamie Daniel, Roswitha Mueller, Patricia Mellencamp, and Priscilla Camilli. Last, but certainly not least, I would like to thank Andrew Martin, who not only read and commented on every word and every draft of this manuscript, but who also accompanied me on the various journeys that contributed to its writing.

A version of Chapter 2 was first published as "Modernity and Mass Culture in Weimar: Contours of a Discourse on Sexuality in Early Theories of Perception and Representation," *New German Critique*, no. 40 (Winter 1987): 115–46.

PATRICE PETRO
Milwaukee, Wisconsin September 1988

It would be difficult to name any other period or nation in film history that has sustained such elaborate and sophisticated analysis as the Weimar cinema. Siegfried Kracauer's *From Caligari to Hitler* and Lotte Eisner's *The Haunted Screen*, although written over thirty years ago, remain pioneering works in film studies and are of continuing importance to contemporary analyses of film history, national cinema, and film spectatorship.[1] If recent scholarship on filmmaking during the silent era is any indication, the Weimar cinema will not only continue to generate important studies of cinematic representation and spectatorship particular to Germany, but will also serve as a model for the ways in which these issues are taken up in film theory more generally.[2]

I undertake the present study in the tradition of previous work on the Weimar cinema, and with the desire to pose new questions about the historical nature of spectatorship and representation. But my approach to the history of the German film differs significantly from a number of previous approaches. It is my contention that even the most sophisticated analyses of the Weimar cinema remain caught within what Luce Irigaray has called "the blind spot of an old dream of symmetry,"[3] or what I would describe as a reasoning

[1] Siegfried Kracauer, *From Caligari to Hitler: A Psychological History of the German Film* (Princeton, N.J.: Princeton University Press, 1947); Lotte Eisner, *L'Ecran Démoniaque* (Paris: Le Terrain Vague, 1952), translated with new material as *The Haunted Screen: Expressionism in the German Film and the Influence of Max Reinhardt*, trans. Roger Greaves (Berkeley and Los Angeles: University of California Press, 1969).

[2] Janet Bergstrom, "Sexuality at a Loss: The Films of F. W. Murnau," *Poetics Today* 6, nos. 1–2 (Spring 1985): 185–203; Thomas Elsaesser, "Social Mobility and the Fantastic: German Silent Cinema," *Wide Angle* 5, no. 2 (1982): 14–25; Elsaesser, "Film History and Visual Pleasure: Weimar Cinema," in *Cinema Histories/Cinema Practices*, ed. Patricia Mellencamp and Philip Rosen, The American Film Institute Monograph Series, vol. 4 (Frederick, Md.: University Publications of America, 1984), 47–84; Elsaesser, "Lulu and the Meter Man: Louise Brooks, Pabst and *Pandora's Box*," *Screen* 24, nos. 4–5 (July–October 1983): 4–36; Miriam Hansen, "Early Silent Cinema: Whose Public Sphere?" *New German Critique*, no. 29 (Spring–Summer 1983): 147–84.

[3] According to Irigaray, this "blind spot" consists of a male vision or perspective which is trapped in an Oedipal trajectory, and therefore unable to *see* woman's difference in terms other than that of man's complementary other—the mother. This assessment of

which makes distinctions without difference by repeatedly conflating narrative with national identity, national identity with subject, and all three terms with male subjectivity and male identity in crisis.

The now familiar reading of "crisis" in Weimar culture and society, a crisis culminating in fascism and commonly described in terms of a breakdown of male identity, in fact provides the "master plot" for analyses of representation and spectatorship in the Weimar cinema. There exists a wealth of historical evidence to support an assessment of Weimar society as a society in crisis: the lost war with its legend of an undefeated German army "stabbed in the back" on the home front; the growing strength of political reaction and the instability of democratic party politics; the chronically destabilizing effects of inflation, unemployment, and depression. It is nevertheless symptomatic that analyses of crisis in Weimar almost always return to questions about male subjectivity: unresolved Oedipal conflicts serve to symbolize the political and economic situation of Germany in the 1920s, and narrative is said to enact the drama of male passivity and symbolic defeat which supposedly organizes both the history of Weimar and its cinema.

The discovery in Weimar narratives of unsuccessful challenges to patriarchal authority, for instance, has led to extended speculation about the historical spectator to whom these narratives were addressed. Often with complete disregard for the stylistic and formal devices which render many Oedipal narratives unstable, critics and theorists have traditionally presumed the historical spectator of the Weimar cinema to be male. Drawing on Kracauer's now classic study, even cultural historians have endorsed a circular reasoning, ostensibly reaching a conclusion about Weimar culture while actually assuming this conclusion as a founding premise: the Oedipal logic of Weimar narratives, it is claimed, reflects German social history, because it refers to the disturbed development of male

male vision has obvious implications for Weimar film history, which I explore more fully in chapter 1. For a more detailed discussion of male vision's blind spots, see Luce Irigaray, *Speculum de l'autre femme* (Paris: Les Éditions de Minuit, 1974). This book is available in English translation as *Speculum of the Other Woman*, trans. Gillian C. Gill (Ithaca, N.Y.: Cornell University Press, 1985).

subjectivity, which is in turn made evident by the Oedipal logic of Weimar narratives.[4]

While most writing on the Weimar cinema has tended to recycle similar conclusions, post-Freudian critics have recently attempted to get beyond the problems posed by this approach. In contrast to Kracauer, these critics celebrate the formal instability of Weimar narratives for constructing a subject position which can no longer be fixed within the terms of Oedipal logic or gendered spectatorship: neither active (masculine) nor passive (feminine), this subject position is said to mark the site of an ambiguity regarding gender definition and sexual orientation. Where historians and theorists once viewed the loss of stable male identity with considerable nostalgia and regret, today some see this loss of identity as testifying to the mobility of subjectivity in Weimar. Leaving aside the novelty of its claims, this new approach returns us almost inevitably to familiar terms and debates. Not only does it come suspiciously close to the Nazi view of "Weimar decadence" in its preoccupation with an allegedly ineffectual patriarchal authority; it also continues to assume a male spectator, only now this spectator is one whose male identity is released from rigid demarcations of sexual difference, transforming gender definition. Whether nostalgic or laudatory about the crisis of male identity in Weimar, many historians and theorists thus engage in similar reasoning, where claims regarding subjectivity, textuality, and national identity are universalized through reference to a male spectator and subject alone.[5]

That the male spectator has served as the unquestioned model for analyses of spectatorship in Weimar suggests an indisputable

---

[4] Peter Gay's monograph on Weimar culture is exemplary in this respect. See his *Weimar Culture: The Outsider as Insider* (New York: Harper and Row, 1970).

[5] Peter Sloterdijk makes a similar point in his *Kritik der zynischen Vernunft*, 2 vols. (Frankfurt am Main: Suhrkamp, 1983), which has recently been translated into English as *Critique of Cynical Reason* (Minneapolis, Mn.: University of Minnesota Press, 1987). Sloterdijk writes of two easily distinguishable points of access to Weimar historiography: a nostalgic-archaeological one and an apologetic-political one. This distinction roughly corresponds to what I have called the "laudatory" and "nostalgic" approaches to Weimar film history, although, as I have suggested, both approaches evidence an equal amount of nostalgia for that moment in the Weimar past when, as Sloterdijk writes, "an uninterrupted tradition . . . discovered to its surprise that everything had already been there once before—our entire intellectual 'identity' [I would add, a specifically *male* identity] under the rubble."

historical and theoretical blindness. Contrary to the assumption that the historical audience of the Weimar cinema was composed primarily of men, an assumption implied in the tendency to read social history from Oedipal configurations in Weimar narratives, audience research has made it clear that a vast number of filmgoers in Germany were women.[6] It is not simply the empirical existence of a female viewing audience, however, that leads me to question prevailing accounts of representation and spectatorship in this period. Close analysis of a wide spectrum of textual practices in Weimar also reveals that a female spectator was indeed assumed and addressed by such popular forms as the cinema and the illustrated press, and that these forms, particularly in their most inflated, unstable, and melodramatic expressions, refer to something other than male identity and male symbolic defeat.

The critical emphasis on the male spectator has nevertheless ensured that all modes of representation in Weimar are interpreted merely as variations on the same theme. In a recent essay on the social history of the Weimar cinema, for example, one critic refers to a popular, and often highly melodramatic, cinematic genre and implies that its representation of social conflict and economic ruin illustrates the terms of male subjectivity in crisis:

> [Karl Grüne's *Die Strasse*, 1923] portrays the life of a dissatisfied lower middle class man who longs for excitement. His search leads him to the street where he is seduced by a prostitute and framed for a murder. He barely escapes and returns to the security of his home. Life there no longer seems unbearable. One of the most successful films of this type was Bruno Rahn's *Dirnentragödie* (*Tragedy of the Street*, 1927). In this film, a prodigal, middle class son ventures into the street, falls prey to its corruption, and returns to the arms of his mother.[7]

[6] See Emilie Altenloh's 1914 study, *Zur Soziologie des Kino: Die Kino-Unternehmung und die sozialen Schichten ihrer Besucher*, diss. Heidelberg (Jena: Eugen Diederichs, 1914), reprinted in facsimile by Medienladen, Hamburg, 1977. Although there are obvious difficulties in using a 1914 study to support claims about a postwar cinema, Altenloh's dissertation does serve, at the very least, to cast doubt upon the assumption of an exclusive address to male audiences in later years.

[7] Bruce Murray, "*Mutter Krausens Fahrt ins Glück*: An Analysis of the Film as a Critical Response to the 'Street Films' of the Commercial Film Industry," *Enclitic* 5–6, nos. 1–2 (1981–1982): 46.

In this passage, the formulation of an address to a male spectator is central to the meaning of the street film, which is summarized as a genre that displaces male anxieties about class identity onto anxieties about women and sexual identity. The male figure's search for sexual excitement, which ends in defeat and regression, thus sets up an allegory about male subjectivity that stresses both psychic and social defeat: impotent, passive, apparently an object of pity, the male subject in Weimar fails to achieve the kind of mastery necessary for the legitimate functioning of the political, economic, and social order.

As persuasive as this reading may be for Grüne's *Die Strasse*, it not only universalizes the implied subject of several street films; it also offers an impoverished view of the genre by measuring all street films against an assumed generic "norm."[8] The translation of *Dirnentragödie* as "Tragedy of the Street," for example, conveniently fixes the film within a dominant narrative tradition in Weimar, but eliminates in the process the film's specific subject suggested by the original German title, "Tragedy of the Whore." To be sure, as in other street films, the narrative clash of bourgeois and criminal elements becomes an allegory for subjectivity which comments on the film's anticipated spectator. In *Dirnentragödie*, however, the anticipated spectator is imagined to be female, and the film's fixation on the city street as a *new* place for women endows each woman who appears there (and, by extension, in the cinema) with criminality as part of her desire, given that her very presence threatens both male authority and bourgeois morality. It is important to note that the popularity of the street genre rendered identifiable certain recurrent narrative conventions. However, with the release of *Dirnentragödie* in 1927, many of these

---

[8] In this regard, Janey Place's remarks about attempts to categorize *film noir* (or what might be called American film expressionism) are especially relevant. The conventions of film style, she explains, "are not 'rules' to be enforced, nor are they necessarily the most important aspects of each film in which they appear; and no attempt to fix and categorize films will be very illuminating if it prescribes strict boundaries for a category. This leads to suppression of those elements which do not 'fit,' and to exclusion of films which have strong links but equally strong differences from a particular category. Often the most exceptional examples of these films will be exceptional precisely *because* of the deviations from the general 'norms' of the movement." Janey Place, "Women in film noir," in *Women in Film Noir*, ed. E. Ann Kaplan (London: British Film Institute, 1978), 39.

conventions had been displaced, called into question, or rendered unstable. The narrative convention of the prodigal son's venture into the street and his resigned return home, for instance, serves only to frame the story of the aging prostitute whose struggle for economic autonomy and sexual mobility lies at the center of the narrative. The ultimate failure of this struggle, as suggested by the narrative's conclusion, moreover, merely reinforces what is for this film (and, indeed, for many street films) a gender-specific interpretation of tragedy: the tragedy of a woman who excessively speaks her desire within an order she knows to exceed her—to speak for her.[9]

That most critics have chosen to interpret *Dirnentragödie* as merely another drama of male regression, and thus repeated the gesture of repression the film sets out to expose, speaks of the limitations and outright distortions in our current understanding of representation and spectatorship in the silent era. And not only *Dirnentragödie* and the street film are misrepresented in the process. More important, it is the existence of a female spectator, and the function of representation for mobilizing her desires and unconscious fantasies, that analyses of the Weimar cinema have repressed or ignored in order to reproduce the same story—the story of male subjectivity in crisis—which is then taken to be the story of German history or culture itself.

My approach to the Weimar cinema attempts to challenge what has traditionally passed as a historical or cultural explanation of that cinema. Turning first to issues raised by film historiography in the

[9] Alain Corbin provides an interesting historical reading of the prostitute's position in European culture, which has implications similar to those I have been making about the street film. He writes, for instance, "The development of the modern theory of congenital syphilis between 1860 and 1865, and its subsequent propagation between 1885 and 1910, was to charge the prostitute's image with new anxieties in learned discourse. The commercial woman henceforth threatens the genetic patrimony of the dominant classes. As the bearer of virulent syphilis, she infects the male bourgeois, who then transmits, as a risk of diseased inheritance, a still more terrifying hereditary disease that will devastate his posterity. The virus incubated by the prostitute sets in motion a process of degeneration that threatens to annihilate the bourgeoisie. The alcoholic, syphilitic, and often consumptive prostitute, herself a victim, it is said, of a morbid heredity, represents woman's criminal inclination. . . . In short, she becomes the symbolic synthesis of the tragedy of the times." Alain Corbin, "Commercial Sexuality in 19th Century France," in *The Making of the Modern Body: Sexuality and Society in the Nineteenth Century*, ed. Catherine Gallagher and Thomas Laqueur (Berkeley and Los Angeles: University of California Press, 1987), 212.

opening chapters, I reconstruct the debates about mass culture and modernism which have dominated discussions of the visual arts in Weimar since the 1920s. Although my aim is to suggest reasons for the sustained indifference to questions of female subjectivity in histories of Weimar cinema and culture, I also want to draw out the theoretical implications of other, inextricably related issues, propose ways to redefine the contours of gendered spectatorship and the perception and representation of women more generally, and argue the necessity of writing (film) history from an explicitly feminist perspective.

The first part of this book therefore adopts a theoretical and historiographic approach; the second part is devoted almost entirely to textual analysis. In an effort to map out the discursive field within which the Weimar cinema operated, I focus on the illustrated press, surveying the institutional and artistic interchanges between press and film in the 1920s, and exploring the shared concern of both with issues of female sexuality and gender identity. Weimar photojournalism has much to tell us about Weimar film, since the illustrated press offers an instance of an unambiguous address to female audiences and thus provides an invaluable point of reference for considering questions of gender, representation, and address in the Weimar cinema.

Most of the images and texts to which I refer date from the "stabilization period" of the Weimar Republic: the years between 1924 and 1928, when the German economy temporarily recovered from the multiple crises resulting from war, revolution, and inflation. Although most art historians characterize this period in terms of a *Neue Sachlichkeit* or "new objectivity" in the cinema and visual arts, I attempt to locate a different aesthetic in film and photography, one which is indebted less to stability and machine-culture than to instability, theatricality, and an expressive play of mourning and pathos.[10] While I make reference to several popular genres of the period (the fantastic film, the social problem film, the mu-

[10] My decision to focus on the film melodrama derives from my interest in the Weimar cinema in its aesthetic delay vis-à-vis the cutting edge of high modernism and the rationalization of mass culture. In this regard, I have benefited from a rereading of Walter Benjamin's *Ursprung des deutschen Trauerspiels*, which appears in *Gesammelte Schriften*, ed. Rolf Tiedemann and Hermann Schweppenhäuser, vol. 1, part 1 (Frankfurt am Main: Suhrkamp, 1974), 203–430. This study is also available in English. See *The Origin of German Tragic Drama*, trans. John Osborne (London: New Left Books, 1977).

sical comedy), I concentrate on the film melodrama and the conventions adapted from the *Kammerspiel* (chamber play) drama and the street film which represent women in a decidedly melancholy key. I am interested in looking at how the Weimar melodrama anticipates a female audience, and how it enables us to see the crises of the Weimar years (political, economic, psychic) as they came to figure differently for women, for those spectators whose experience of modernity was in no way equivalent to the experience of the male spectator so often analyzed by historians and theorists. No one film genre, of course, can stand for the entirety of German film culture. However, in trying to specify the appeal of the Weimar cinema to female viewers, I hope to widen the parameters of film historical debate so that other film genres may be explored for the ways in which women were addressed as spectators at the time.

Although I pursue the "subject" of Weimar film history in the next chapter, it is important to emphasize that every theory of spectatorship is based on a conception of subjectivity which it either posits or implies. My emphasis on women in Weimar is meant to make a historical conception of female subjectivity explicit. However, I do not aim to "correct the balance" of film historiography, as it were, or simply to provide an account of the female subject to match existing accounts of the male subject during this period. Such an approach would not only wrongly assume women's history to be separate or distinct from the history of men, but would also reproduce women's history as a marginal history, a suppressed but hermetic alternative to official accounts. Rather than provide a separate or alternative history, then, I aim to suggest ways to shift the focus of Weimar film history, to account for the address to women—as spectators, as subjects, as part of a national audience—in such a way that no aspect of that history can remain quite the same. Admittedly, this project is an ambitious one. But unless we are willing to ask difficult historical questions about gender and spectatorship, we will be forced to remain content with the old questions, and with their predictably limited answers.

JOYLESS STREETS

ON THE SUBJECT OF WEIMAR FILM HISTORY

·

> For the man who accompanies her, "she" is osten-
> sibly more the object of observation than what is
> happening on the screen. "She is always touched
> to tears," and psychological studies of the specta-
> tor—especially of the female spectator—are for
> many much more amusing than the films them-
> selves and much more of a reason to spend an
> hour in the movie theater now and then.
> —EMILIE ALTENLOH
> *Zur Soziologie des Kino* (1914)[1]

It is hardly coincidental that the earliest study of the female spectator in Germany was written by a woman.[2] Exploring the com-
plexities of audience expectation and response, Emilie Altenloh's
1914 dissertation *Zur Soziologie des Kino* surveys crucial differences among spectators, who are distinguished according to gender, age, and class. Notwithstanding its empirical approach, Altenloh's study takes up issues that remain remarkably up-to-date, and
many of her conclusions seem directly applicable to current devel-

---

[1] Emilie Altenloh, *Zur Soziologie des Kino: Die Kino-Unternehmung und die sozialen
Schichten ihrer Besucher*, diss. Heidelberg (Jena: Eugen Diederichs, 1914), 94, reprinted in facsimile by Medienladen, Hamburg, 1977, and quoted in Schlüpmann, "Kinosucht," *Frauen und Film* 33 (October 1982): 45.

[2] It is also not surprising that this quotation from Altenloh's study was first cited in an
essay on spectatorship, also written by a woman. I am referring here to Heide Schlüpmann's brilliant essay "Kinosucht."

opments in film studies. What Altenloh observes with a wry sense of humor remains as pertinent today as it was in Imperial Germany: men at the movies have often seemed aroused as much by the sight of women in the audience as by the image of woman on the screen.

Altenloh's study, however, is most compelling in the manner in which it invites us to ask a different question about subjectivity and desire in the German film. If, as she suggests, the challenge for the male critic has often been to make the female spectator's desire mirror his own, then the challenge for the female critic certainly consists in shifting the terms of the debate—to describe her pleasure in looking and thereby make that pleasure her own.

But to effect such a shift of focus, it is necessary first to reconsider the recurrent and unresolved debate pertaining to a wider aspect of Weimar film history: the status of the Weimar cinema as popular or avant-garde, realist or experimental, mass cultural or modernist. Indeed, while the subject in Weimar film history has inspired very little controversy, the object of that history has been the topic of an intense and protracted debate. However, it is symptomatic that the opposing views emphasizing either mass culture or modernism start out by defining radically different objects of analysis, only to insist on a remarkably similar subject—the male subject whose identity is seen either as confirmed by mass culture or as destabilized by modernist practices.

To summarize the debate over Weimar film history in terms of such polarized, mutually exclusive options may raise objections which have little to do with issues of gender or spectatorship. One could reasonably claim, for example, that the mass culture/modernist debate is really a pseudodebate to the extent that it denies the diversity and pluralism of film culture in Weimar.[3] Or one could take issue with the terms and categories suggested by the associations implicit in the mass culture/modernist opposition. Modernism and the avant-garde, for instance, constitute distinct aesthetic and political responses to the status and function of art in the twen-

---

[3] Such an objection to the mass culture/modernist debate in Weimar film history was voiced by several participants at a colloquium held on German cinema at Clark University, July 1985, sponsored by the Goethe Institute, Boston, and organized by Eric Rentschler and Anton Kaes.

tieth century. Thus, as several theorists have argued, to conflate one with the other is to perpetuate the use of imprecise, sweeping terminology and to ignore the need for concrete historical analysis.[4]

In response to the first objection, which dismisses debates over mass culture and modernism and argues instead for historical diversity, I would suggest that by simply pointing to the multiplicity of film practices in Weimar (where, as this approach usually claims, various "mass cultural" and "modernist" forms existed side by side), one makes the serious error of taking the conventional opposition between mass culture and modernism at face value. While Weimar clearly supported a lively and heterogeneous film culture, it should be equally clear that when historians choose to characterize the Weimar cinema as either mass cultural or modernist, they are not merely choosing among cinematic practices. Rather, they are specifying the historiographic stakes in returning to Weimar film culture in the first place, using polarization as a strategy to define an aesthetic which often conceals its implications for gendered spectatorship. For this reason, we must examine the assumptions behind claims favoring mass cultural realism as well as those emphasizing modernist experimentation in Weimar, and then indicate the ways in which this opposition represses textual differences so as to promote an equally dubious notion of spectatorship and sexual difference.

It seems to me that the second objection, which questions the mass culture/modernist debate on grounds of insufficient historical specificity, poses the correct challenge, though from a slightly skewed perspective. To be sure, arguments for Weimar cinema as either mass cultural or modernist are rife with ill-chosen analogies and imprecise associations. But rather than dismiss these confusions out of hand, we would do better to attend to the historical determinants that facilitate such confusions. In the case of the Weimar cinema, an analysis of historical determinants becomes only

---

[4] See, for example, Peter Bürger, *Theory of the Avant-Garde*, trans. Michael Shaw (Minneapolis, Mn.: University of Minnesota Press, 1984); Andreas Huyssen, *After the Great Divide: Modernism, Mass Culture, Postmodernism* (Bloomington, In.: Indiana University Press, 1986); and Jochen Schulte-Sasse, "Foreword: Theory of Modernism versus Theory of the Avant-Garde," which prefaces the English translation of Bürger's book.

slightly more complex, since issues of mass culture and modernism frame contemporary debates over the history of Weimar cinema in as high a degree as they did the historical debates over the nature and meaning of the cinema that were waged in Germany in the teens and twenties.

In his introductory essay to *Kino-Debatte*, Anton Kaes explains how the commercial expansion of the cinema in Imperial Germany posed a threat to the cultural leadership assumed by literary and artistic modernists. "The power claims of the new medium," Kaes writes, "threatened the monopoly position of literature and caused within the cultural system a moment of insecurity. With the extent of the threat grew tensions between old and new mediums and, simultaneously, the pressure for dismantling these tensions."[5] As Kaes points out, the tensions between dominant and emergent forms, between literature and theater on the one side and cinema on the other, were only temporarily eased in the 1920s when an institutional place was cleared for cooperation and interchange between modernism in the arts and mass cultural practices. Prior to the 1920s, however, these tensions were often highlighted and exacerbated by a prolonged debate in which artists and intellectuals attempted to come to terms with the nature and meaning of cinematic spectacle.

When defining the cinema's peculiar "nature," German artists and intellectuals elaborated comparisons and contrasts between mass cultural practices and the traditional arts. Extended analogies between the aesthetics of the cinema and the aesthetics of the metropolis, for example, served to construct a correspondence between reception conditions in film and reception conditions in city life. As one critic proposed in 1910, "The psychology of the cinematic triumph is metropolitan psychology. Not only because the metropolis constitutes the natural focal point for all radiations of social life, but especially because the metropolitan soul—that always hurried soul, curious and unanchored, tumbling from fleeting

---

[5] Anton Kaes, "Introduction," in *Kino-Debatte: Texte zum Verhältnis von Literatur und Film, 1909–1929*, ed. Anton Kaes (Tübingen: Max Niemeyer Verlag, 1978), 1. A revised version of this introduction is available in English translation as "The Debate about Cinema: Charting a Controversy (1909–1929)," trans. David J. Levin, *New German Critique*, no. 40 (Winter 1987): 7–33. Unless otherwise indicated, all translations that follow are my own.

impression to fleeting impression—is also the soul of cinematography."[6]

An ambivalent and often openly hostile attitude toward the metropolis in German literature and philosophy (extending from Schopenhauer and Nietzsche to Spengler, Heidegger, and Thomas Mann), the product of political underdevelopment and intensive modernization in turn-of-the-century Germany, was thus quite easily translated into ambivalence and hostility toward the cinema. Franz Pfemfert, editor of the expressionist journal *Aktion*, remarked in 1911, "Edison is the battle cry of a culture-murdering epoch; the war cry of barbarism. . . . The torch bearers of culture hasten to new heights while the people listen below to the rattling of the cinema and place a new record on the phonograph."[7] Pfemfert's polemic against the cinema, Kaes suggests, not only serves to confirm the cultural value of modernism; it also reveals a defensive reaction and a fundamentally ambivalent attitude toward the mass cultural audience—an audience much despised by modernist artists but also much needed as their customer in the cultural marketplace.

It was not simply the cinematic spectacle, however, that provoked such scorn or elicited such intense reaction. It was also the appearance of a new, and equally threatening, mass cultural audience that commonly became the subject of extended description and debate. In 1910, for example, Alfred Döblin wrote:

Inside the pitch-black, low-ceilinged space, a rectangular screen glares over a monster of an audience, a white eye fixating the mass with a monotonous gaze. Couples making-out in the background are carried away and withdraw their undisciplined fingers. Children wheezing with consumption quietly shake with the chills of evening fever; badly smelling workers with bulging eyes, women in musty clothes, heavily made-up prostitutes leaning forward, forgetting to adjust their scarves. Here you can see "panem et circenses" fulfilled: spectacle as essential as bread, the bullfight as popular need.[8]

[6] Herman Kienzl, "Theater und Kinematograph," in *Der Strom* 1 (1911–1912); quoted in Kaes, *Kino-Debatte*, 6.

[7] Franz Pfemfert, "Kino als Erzieher," *Die Aktion* 1 (19 June 1911); quoted in Kaes, *Kino-Debatte*, 10.

[8] Alfred Döblin, "Das Theater der kleinen Leute," in *Kino-Debatte*, 38; translated by

In a recent essay on the silent cinema in America and Germany, Miriam Hansen remarks of this particular passage, "It is no coincidence that literary intellectuals, fascinated by the whiff of Otherness that emanated from the movies, hardly ever failed to mention the presence of prostitutes in the audience."[9] As Hansen explains, the prostitute came to serve as an emblem for the cinema as a whole, typifying literary intellectuals' simultaneous contempt for and fascination with an openly commercial (and hence "venal") form.

Of course, hostility and defensiveness toward the mass cultural audience was not the prerogative of literary intellectuals alone, nor was it manifested only in metaphorical or textual forms. The high percentage of women in early film audiences was in fact perceived as an alarming social phenomenon, one which confirmed the breakdown of traditional values elsewhere evidenced by the declining birthrate, the rising marriage age, and the influx of women into the industrial labor force.[10] The presence of a female audience, in other words, not only represented a threat to traditional divisions between public and private, cultural and domestic spheres; it represented a threat to the maintenance of social legitimacy, to the distinctions preserving traditionally defined male and female gender roles and responsibilities. It is not surprising, then, that mass culture itself was commonly personified as "feminine," as having the capacity to induce passivity, vulnerability, even corruption. And, as mass culture's opposite, modernism was often construed as "masculine," as providing an active and productive alternative to the pleasures of mass cultural entertainment.[11] In this respect, we

Miriam Hansen and quoted in her essay, "Early Silent Cinema: Whose Public Sphere?" *New German Critique*, no. 29 (Spring–Summer 1983): 147–84.

[9] Hansen, "Early Silent Cinema," 174.

[10] On the history of Weimar women, see Renate Bridenthal, Atina Grossmann, and Marion Kaplan, eds., *When Biology Became Destiny: Women in Weimar and Nazi Germany* (New York: Monthly Review Press, 1984); Atina Grossmann, "The New Woman and the Rationalization of Sexuality in Weimar Germany," in *Powers of Desire: The Politics of Sexuality*, ed. Ann Snitow, Christine Stansell, and Sharon Thompson (New York: Monthly Review Press, 1983), 153–71; and Claudia Koonz, *Mothers in the Fatherland: Women, the Family and Nazi Politics* (New York: St. Martin's Press, 1987), especially chapter 2, "Weimar Emancipation."

[11] For a discussion of gendered metaphors in American and German mass cultural criticism, see my "Mass Culture and the Feminine: The 'Place' of Television in Film Studies," *Cinema Journal* 25, no. 3 (Spring 1986): 5–21. See also Andreas Huyssen's

might tentatively suggest that while such associations clearly reinforced the stereotype of female passivity, they also signaled an attempt to delay the loss of male cultural authority, to preserve the
illusion of male activity.

While issues of gender are clearly a historical ground or "absent
cause" of early debates over the cinema in Germany, this historical
dimension becomes accessible to us in textual forms—in the metaphors, analogies, and slippages—which point beyond issues of
mass culture and modernism to reveal another, implicit debate
over subjectivity and sexual difference. In chapter 2, I consider this
debate and its historical determinants more fully. I would merely
like to suggest here that the discourse on sexuality informing debates over mass culture and modernism in early German film theory reemerges in contemporary histories of the Weimar cinema,
where we find a similar preoccupation with issues of activity and
mastery, passivity and loss.

Mass Culture, Modernism, and the Male Spectator in Weimar Film Histories

Siegfried Kracauer's *From Caligari to Hitler* (1947) and Thomas Elsaesser's recent series of essays on the Weimar cinema are to date
the most sustained arguments concerning subjectivity in the German silent film. Kracauer's study remains the most thorough attempt to formulate large-scale claims about representation and spectatorship in Germany. And Elsaesser's work has done more than
any other study to redefine Kracauer's thesis in order to bring to
the attention of contemporary film scholars the central relevance of
the Weimar cinema to problems of history, subjectivity, and visual
pleasure. While Kracauer and Elsaesser demonstrate a remarkably
similar concern for issues of subjectivity and representation in Weimar, they nevertheless differ significantly when defining the object
of their study: for Kracauer, the Weimar cinema is mass cultural;
for Elsaesser, it is incontestably modernist. In the analysis which

excellent essay on this topic, "Mass Culture as Woman: Modernism's Other," in *Studies
in Entertainment: Critical Approaches to Mass Culture*, ed. Tania Modleski, Theories
of Contemporary Culture, vol. 7 (Bloomington, In.: Indiana University Press, 1986),
188–207.

follows, I scrutinize these views, both for what they claim about representation in Weimar and for what they often presume about the textual and historical nature of spectatorship.

In his introduction to *From Caligari to Hitler*, Kracauer writes, "Behind the overt history of economic shifts, social exigencies, and political machinations [in Weimar] runs a secret history involving the inner dispositions of the German people."[12] This "secret" history, Kracauer goes on to explain, reveals itself strikingly in the cinema of the period, a mass cultural cinema whose mechanisms of psychological repression under the guise of artistic experimentation blocked its proper social function and contributed to an ideological one.

As Kracauer insists, popular cinematic practices (or, to use his terminology, popular or recurrent "screen motifs") lend themselves to a historical reading of aesthetic form and symbolic content. "Of course," he remarks in passing, "popular magazines and broadcasts, bestsellers, ads, fashions in language and other sedimentary products of a people's cultural life also reveal valuable information about predominant attitudes, widespread inner tendencies."[13] For Kracauer, however, the cinema exceeds these other mass cultural forms in what he calls its "inclusiveness," its ability to render faithfully the contours of the "inner world" of subjectivity and the "outer world" of social reality.

Kracauer maintains that the archaic period of film production in Germany (1895–1918) did in fact fulfill a social function, since it attended to "unobtrusive" social phenomena that were "normally neglected":

> During that whole era [roughly 1895–1911] the film had the traits of a young street arab; it was an uneducated creature running wild among the lower strata of society. Many people enticed by the movies had never attended artistic spectacles before. . . . An attraction for young workers, salesgirls, the unemployed, loafers and social non-descripts, the movies were in rather bad repute. They afforded a shelter to the poor,

[12] Kracauer, *From Caligari to Hitler: A Psychological History of the German Film* (Princeton, N.J.: Princeton University Press, 1947), 11.
[13] Ibid., 6.

a refuge for sweethearts. Sometimes even a crazy intellectual would stray into one.[14]

According to Kracauer, this cinematic address to those usually neglected (the working class, women, even crazy intellectuals) served a positive social function, but was nevertheless soon abandoned. In his view, the artistic pretensions of such producers as Paul Davidson and Erich Pommer, and the almost missionary zeal of reform-minded associations (*Kinoreformbewegung*), ensured that the mass cultural cinema would be made to serve a different ideological function. Appealing to the authority of the established arts, and supported by the government and conservative institutions, the cinema "yielded to the truly German desire to serve the established powers."[15] The cinema, in other words, turned away from social reality, from the realm of the everyday, and inscribed itself within an abstract realm of cultural value and authority. The result, in Kracauer's view, was a "mental forlornness" among mass cultural spectators, an inability to choose between two equally limiting options: identifying with cultural authority or lapsing into passivity, self-destruction, and despair.

Although he describes it in a way similar to recent feminist analyses of the classical narrative cinema in America, the problem of identification and self-identity in the Weimar cinema has for Kracauer a very specific historical source in pre-Hitler Germany. "In pre-Nazi Germany," he proposes, "middle-class penchants penetrated all stratas: they competed with the political aspirations of the Left and also filled the voids of the upper-class mind. This accounts for the nation-wide appeal of the German cinema—a cinema firmly rooted in middle-class mentality."[16] Kracauer thus posits a correspondence between the cinema's pretensions to art and the middle-class pretensions to cultural respectability. Both groups, in his view, had lost all basis in reality: "Although . . . lower middle-class people could no longer hope for bourgeois security, they scorned all doctrines and ideals more in harmony with their plight, maintaining attitudes that had lost any basis in reality. . . . Small shopkeepers, tradesmen and artisans were so full of resentment that

[14] Ibid., 16.
[15] Ibid., 18–19.
[16] Ibid., 8.

they shrunk from adjusting themselves. Instead of realizing that it might be in their practical interest to side with democracy, they preferred . . . to listen to Nazi promises. Their surrender to the Nazis was based on emotional fixations rather than the facing of any facts."[17]

These various petit bourgeois types—small shopkeepers, tradesmen, and artisans—are also the historical audience Kracauer names for the Weimar cinema. This historical audience or historical spectator is located in the narratives traced by the films as well. Kracauer gives the following example from the film *Sylvester* (1923):

> Unable to make his decision, the man breaks down, and while his mother caresses him as if he were a child, he rests his head helplessly upon her bosom. This gesture, followed (and corroborated) by the suicide of the man, betrays his intense anxiety to return to the maternal womb. . . . It is noteworthy that, far from being repudiated, his singular gesture of capitulation reappeared, almost unchanged, in various German films, indicating that his instinctive reluctance to attempt emancipation might be considered a typical German attitude . . . an attitude which results from a prolonged dependence of the Germans upon a feudal or half-feudal military regime—not to mention the current social and economic motives enforcing the perpetuation of this attitude within the middle class.[18]

In his reading of *Sylvester*, Kracauer suggests that the instability of male identity, so pronounced in the gesture of the male figure's regression to the maternal womb, serves to displace issues of class and national identity in the film. He then re-places this relationship by drawing a homology between fictional character and national audience, each of which is said to occupy an unstable, dependent, or (perhaps more precisely) powerless position, one without mastery, protection or control.

This homology between fictional and national "character" raises the larger issue of Kracauer's representation of history itself. The very title of his book, *From Caligari to Hitler*, indicates a narrative

[17] Ibid., 11.
[18] Ibid., 99.

version of German history, proposing a vast interpretive allegory in which a sequence of historical events (the unification of the Reich, the expansion of industry, the lost war, inflation, stabilization, and Nazi rule) is rewritten in terms of a deeper and presumably more fundamental narrative, a narrative of male passivity and symbolic defeat that organizes both the history of Weimar and its cinema. In this regard, Kracauer's history of the German film offers a remarkable illustration of what Fredric Jameson calls an "expressive causality" in the narrative representation of the past. As Jameson explains, if there remains a constant temptation to construct the past in terms of expressive causality or of allegorical master narratives, "this is because such master narratives have inscribed themselves in texts as well as in our thinking about them."[19] These master narratives, he continues, "reflect a fundamental dimension of our collective fantasies about history and reality."[20]

While Jameson raises issues of vital importance here, particularly with respect to the place of subjectivity in narrative and in history, it is crucial to question his insistence that allegorical narratives reveal "our collective thinking" or "our collective fantasies" about history and reality. Indeed, although it is clear that "master narratives" exert considerable influence in our culture and our discourses, the claim that such narratives account for the totality of social experience elides their real function in repressing different experiences and different desires. Kracauer's history of the Weimar cinema is a case in point, for as a "master narrative" it reveals a specific (if pervasive) fantasy and collective vision, one of male subjectivity in crisis and male symbolic defeat. It should be noted that Kracauer was aware of different audiences and different kinds of desires, as his remarks about the archaic period in the German cinema suggest. But by establishing a homology between fictional and national male character, and by constructing an absolute break between "archaic" and "classical" German cinema, he effectively closes off any discussion of these other audiences, these other desires. For Kracauer, the story of the mass cultural cinema in Weimar remains that of an essentially failed Oedipal drama; perhaps

---

[19] Fredric Jameson, *The Political Unconscious: Narrative as a Socially Symbolic Act* (Ithaca, N.Y.: Cornell University Press, 1981), 34.
[20] Ibid., 34.

unwittingly, he thus implies that German fascism might have been averted if only the male subject had achieved the mastery necessary for political and symbolic order.

While Kracauer's study constructs mass culture as its object and the male spectator as its explicit subject, Thomas Elsaesser's work on the Weimar cinema calls these assumptions into question. In a highly complex argument that spans several articles written in the early 1980s, Elsaesser engages in an extended dialogue with Kracauer's study so as to reformulate questions of spectatorship, representation, and visual pleasure in Weimar film history.[21]

Elsaesser claims in each of these essays that Kracauer's argument about spectatorship suffers from a number of distortions and generalizations. However, Elsaesser does not completely dismiss Kracauer's postulation of the petit bourgeois male as the historical subject or spectator for Weimar films. In fact, Elsaesser himself names this subject as the historical audience for early fantastic films in Weimar, and as the spectator-in-the-text for a later film like *Die Büchse der Pandora* (*Pandora's Box*, 1928).[22] What Elsaesser actually takes issue with, then, is not so much Kracauer's historical argument about the male spectator as Kracauer's tendency to collapse this conception of spectatorship into a much more complex and uncertain textual system. As Elsaesser explains in "Film History and Visual Pleasure" (1984), the very instability, excess, and foregrounding of specular relations in Weimar films would suggest

[21] Thomas Elsaesser, "Social Mobility and the Fantastic: German Silent Cinema," *Wide Angle* 5, no. 2 (1982): 14–15; "Lulu and the Meter Man: Louise Brooks, Pabst and *Pandora's Box*," *Screen* 24, nos. 4–5 (July–October 1983): 4–36; "Film History and Visual Pleasure: Weimar Cinema," in *Cinema Histories/Cinema Practices*, ed. Patricia Mellencamp and Philip Rosen, The American Film Institute Monograph Series, vol. 4 (Frederick, Md.: University Publications of America, 1984), 47–84.

[22] In his essay "Social Mobility and the Fantastic," Elsaesser claims that fantastic films in Weimar "open up a perspective towards a class of spectators whose precarious *social* position—'students,' clerks, young men with frustrated ambitions and vague resentments—make them members of the petite-bourgeoisie, whose engagement with the class struggles takes the form of avoiding class struggle by imagining themselves above and outside" (25). In "Lulu and the Meter Man," Elsaesser similarly invokes Kracauer's reading of spectatorship and Weimar film history when he analyzes the opening sequence of the film. Elsaesser writes, "by placing the spectator in the fiction, via the meter man . . . the episode [turns into] a parable of movie watching as paid for pleasure. With his exit, the petite-bourgeoisie, Kracauer's *Angestellten*, exit from the fictional space of the film, and yet, they are the historical audience that the film addresses" (18).

14

that "the textual systems of German cinema cannot be approached solely via a spectator-based film history."[23] In other words, structures of identification in the German cinema are so unstable that no spectator position—outside of the traditional categories of nation and class—can be deduced or analyzed with any degree of certainty.

This uncertainty of textual systems in Weimar also leads Elsaesser to criticize Kracauer's reading of history and his analyses of individual films. In Elsaesser's estimation, Kracauer not only reduces the complexity of German film history; more questionably, he reduces the narrative and formal complexity of Weimar films. "The desire to see the films as elaborating analogies with social and national history," he explains, "means that Kracauer has to fill in the gaps, smooth out the narrative logic, invert the causal chains, level off intensities, and thereby deny or put aside the very resistances and ambiguities that make these films different from realist-illusionist narrative."[24] In short, Elsaesser argues that Kracauer ultimately constructs Weimar films as classical Hollywood narratives and therefore elides the marks of stylization, excess, and ambiguity which define the Weimar cinema as formally and historically distinct from classical narrative traditions.

In marked contrast to Kracauer, Elsaesser claims that the Weimar cinema was not mass cultural or realist but was instead a self-conscious art cinema. Although Elsaesser's label for this cinema varies—sometimes it is an "art cinema," other times an "avant-garde cinema," and still other times a "counter-cinema"—his general point becomes clear when he explains what the Weimar cinema was *not*. "The Weimar cinema has never been a particularly popular cinema," Elsaesser writes. "It has always been something of a filmmaker's or a film scholar's cinema. . . . The specific features of German cinema cannot be understood in terms of some essence, some typical national character or particular obsession, but as the moment when in retrospect something became apparent."[25]

[23] Ibid., 72.
[24] Ibid., 62.
[25] Ibid., 81.

To say that the Weimar cinema has been a film scholar's cinema in recent film historiography is one thing, but to claim that it was merely a film scholar's or a filmmaker's cinema in the 1920s is surely to elide its appeal to contemporary German audiences. And yet, as the second part of Elsaesser's statement makes clear, his interest does not lie with the historical audience or the historical German spectator, whether defined in terms of a "national character or particular obsession" (as Kracauer puts it), or in terms of some "essence" (a formulation to which I will return shortly). Instead, Elsaesser is interested in the Weimar cinema insofar as it marks "the moment when in retrospect something became apparent." This leads him to suggest that "perhaps the properly ideological role of the cinema and its sweeping popularity only began when this particular imaginary was elided in favor of family melodrama and family romance, when the oscillation and the hesitation ceased and classical narrative became the veritable imaginary of both history and the subject."[26]

One could certainly challenge the presumption that the effects of melodramatic narrative and visual pleasure are inevitably stabilizing.[27] But it seems more important to question Elsaesser's general understanding of ambiguity, particularly where this has implications for sexual difference and spectatorship in the Weimar cinema. Elsaesser speaks directly to these issues in his essay "Lulu and the Meter Man" (1983), where he analyzes the construction and apparent deconstruction of masculine visual pleasure in G. W. Pabst's *Pandora's Box*. For Elsaesser, *Pandora's Box* raises fundamental issues about gender and identification, where "male obsessions—repressed homosexuality, sado-masochism, an urge to possess, capture, limit and fix—confront feminine androgyny and feminine identity."[28] But, he contends, this particular representation of sexual difference serves merely to reveal the fascination exerted by the cinema itself:

[26] Ibid., 81.

[27] Elsaesser himself has challenged this conventional view of the family melodrama, and has underscored the genre's fundamentally destabilizing effects. See Elsaesser's earlier and extremely influential essay "Tales of Sound and Fury: Observations on the Family Melodrama," *Monogram*, no. 4 (1972): 2–15.

[28] Elsaesser, "Lulu and the Meter Man," 35.

Sexuality in the cinema, in *Pandora's Box* at any rate, is the infinitely deferred moment of, the constantly renewed movement away from, identity. . . . The achievement of Pabst's film . . . is to have presented sexuality *in* the cinema as the sexuality *of* the cinema, and to have merely used as his starting point the crisis in the self-understanding of male and female sexuality that characterizes his own period.[29]

Having opened his analysis by posing questions of history and sexual difference, Elsaesser concludes by asking what he believes to be a more urgent question: "What is desire, sexuality and fascination in the film?"[30] But this question, particularly in light of Elsaesser's remarks about "male obsessions" and "feminine identity," begs the *truly* urgent question: desire, sexuality, and fascination for whom? Elsaesser concludes by dismissing the problem of gendered spectatorship in the cinema altogether, since the fascination and ambiguity of Weimar textual systems are, in his view, irreducible to the "place of femininity in the realm of the sexual," to what he might call the search for an elusive "essence." In this way, Elsaesser is able to sidestep questions of sexual ambiguity and androgyny as they relate to the female spectator, in favor of a sliding or unstable identification, one that remains bound to a male spectator position.

As the examples of Kracauer and Elsaesser suggest, whether the object of Weimar cinema is assumed to be mass cultural or modernist, the subject of that history remains the same. At this point, there would thus seem to be little reason to return to issues of unstable masculinity in the Weimar cinema, unless we begin to address these issues historically and with a female spectator in mind. For example, we might ask, what did the destabilization of male identity mean for female viewers in Weimar, especially given the perceived crisis in conventionally defined male and female gender roles? If traditional notions about gender were in crisis as a result of social, economic, and cultural changes, how did changing representations of sexual difference function for female viewers?

[29] Ibid., 33.
[30] Ibid., 30.

WOMEN IN WEIMAR:
THEORIZING THE FEMALE SPECTATOR

In returning to the subject of Weimar film history, feminist scholars have recently proposed new ways of looking at certain time-
honored views of subjectivity and sexual difference in the German
cinema. In her 1982 essay "Kinosucht" (literally, "Cinema Addiction"), for instance, Heide Schlüpmann scrutinizes the assumption,
common to early writings on film spectatorship, that women were
so emotionally involved with events on the screen that they were
"distracted" from political action and manipulated by mass cultural
practices. The preoccupation with cinematic "distraction," Schlüpmann points out, was in fact bound up with sexual difference, and
with discussions about a new and thoroughly modernized form of
perception. Quoting from Emilie Altenloh's 1914 study, she makes
this point especially clear:

> [T]he cinema and its spectators are typical products of our
> time in that both are characterized by a continuous preoccu-
> pation and a nervous restlessness. During the day, in their
> jobs, people cannot free themselves from their haste, they
> cannot recover. Temporarily they seek in the cinema short
> term distraction and diversion and yet in the middle of the
> screening they are already thinking of how to fill the approach-
> ing hours. In order to immerse oneself in a work of art—in
> drama, music, or painting—one needs certain leisure and at-
> tention. This concentration the cinema does not demand.[31]

Altenloh's remarks here suggest that forms of industrial production have permeated leisure activities. Yet, as Altenloh demonstrates elsewhere, female viewers' emotionally absorbed gaze—a
gaze which was neither "restless" nor "distracted"—in fact resisted
such rationalized mass cultural reception, revealing an attention
that failed to keep pace with industrial patterns in the realm of
leisure. The reasons for this, Schlüpmann argues, must be located
in the web of social processes which accompanied rapid industrial
development in Germany, such as the fragmentation of social experience and the growing isolation of the domestic sphere. Female

---

[31] Altenloh, *Zur Soziologie des Kino*; quoted in Schlüpmann, "Kinosucht."

viewers' absorbed or intensely concentrated gaze, in other words, cannot be explained solely by referring to strategies of mass cultural domination. Indeed, as Altenloh's study and Schlüpmann's analysis suggest, female viewers' peculiar "addiction" to the cinema reveals that popular culture often served a crucial function in mediating women's experiences of modernity.

Prompted by Schlupmann's analysis, Miriam Hansen's essay "Early Silent Cinema: Whose Public Sphere?" (1983) returns to the Altenloh dissertation in an effort to discern the social context of audience reception in the silent era. "With all due skepticism to empirical studies," Hansen remarks, "Altenloh's close analysis of theater statistics and two thousand four hundred questionnaires has to be considered one of the most differentiated sources on spectator stratification available."[32] Perhaps most interesting to Hansen, however, is Altenloh's suggestion that female viewers of varying class and marital status tended to express a remarkably homogeneous attitude toward the cinema. Romances and social dramas featuring such stars as Asta Nielsen, for example, were indisputable favorites with female audiences and, as Hansen points out, these preferences take on special meaning when seen in the context of the social and economic situation of female viewers and the role of filmgoing in their everyday lives:

In her chapter on working-class women . . . Altenloh remarks on the comparative lack of interest in educational and political (primarily social-democratic) activities such as occupied the leisure time of their male counterparts: "In this context [Altenloh writes,] the cinema plays an important role, especially for women who do not have a job of their own. Once they are done with their housework, they have very few options for filling out their free time. More often they will go to the cinema because they are bored than for any real interest in the program. . . . Gradually, however, this stop-gap activity becomes an essential part of their daily lives. Before long, they are seized by a veritable passion for the cinema, and more than half of them try to gratify that passion at least once a week. During the screening, they live in another world, a world of

---

[32] Hansen, "Early Silent Cinema," 176.

luxury and extravagance which makes them forget the monotony of the everyday."[33]

It is noteworthy that Altenloh attributes a degree of leisure time to working-class women that seems a projection of her own class position. (As several historians have pointed out, and as I will suggest in greater detail in chapter 2, working-class women were subjected to an intensification of household labor in times of inflation and depression and thus could hardly have found the time to be completely "finished" with domestic chores.) When Altenloh goes on to consider the responses of upper-class women, those "who supposedly had access to this other world by virtue of their socioeconomic status,"[34] she nevertheless finds a commonality among women of various social classes, stemming from specific and discernible operations within the broader social sphere. Notwithstanding the differences between them, Altenloh argues, bourgeois and working-class women seemed to share a remarkably similar "passion" for the cinema in its ability to provide a heightened sensory experience which transformed the monotony of everyday life.

That women's absorption in the cinema may be traced to certain gender-specific experiences of cultural and economic deprivation, and that these forms of deprivation may have been addressed or given expression in the films themselves, leads Hansen to call for a reconsideration of those genres Altenloh found most popular with women, the romance and the social drama, genres that constitute a large part of what we now consider the classic German cinema. In analyzing these genres from the perspective of what they may have meant for women, Hansen further suggests that we speculate on the function of the cinema for spectators previously excluded from cultural reception—in other words, for spectators who were only just beginning to be addressed as an audience in the proper sense of the German word *Publikum*.

The illustrated press in Weimar provides a crucial point of reference for considering the address to female spectators in film, particularly given the artistic and institutional relationships between press and film and the extreme popularity of women's magazines in the 1920s. During their parallel years of development in Germany,

[33] Ibid., 178.
[34] Ibid., 178–79.

the cinema and the illustrated press came to recognize the economic potential of female consumers, as the film industry's attention to particular genres and stars and the press industry's attention
to a female reading public reveal. The Weimar years, for example,
witnessed a rapid growth in the number of illustrated women's
magazines. Although *Die Dame*, a quality women's fashion magazine, existed prior to the 1920s, such journals as *Frauen Welt*, *Die
Genossin*, and *Der Weg der Frau* were created specifically during
the Weimar Republic for a female reading audience. Furthermore,
even established illustrated journals, such as the *Berliner Illustrirte Zeitung* (BIZ), included features of interest to women. In
1932, for instance, the BIZ ran a "photoessay" (replete with long
shots, close-ups, and carefully composed interior compositions not
unlike films from the period) entitled "Die Frauen in der Krise,"
an essay in photographs and prose which attempted to detail the
crisis facing women amidst the effects of inflation, unemployment,
and the multiple responsibilities of being wife, mother, and industrial worker (figure 1). This is not to imply that either the illustrated
press or the cinema in Weimar addressed a female audience exclusively. There is plenty of textual evidence to suggest the contrary,
as the majority of histories of the Weimar cinema make only too
clear. Yet we can clearly discern an appeal to female audiences,
particularly when we turn to the representation of the "everyday"
world in press and film. Those spaces on the boundary between
public and private experience—the back street, the back stairs, the
Hinterhöfe—were spaces commonly associated with women's activities in the Weimar years. And when these spaces, and the figures which inhabited them, were given hyperbolic or stylized representation, we can also discern how representational instability
often relates to gender identity, documenting what theorists have
referred to as a pervasive sexual ambiguity or androgyny in the
Weimar period.

Although few film theorists have mentioned it, this sexual ambiguity or androgyny was often associated with a female figure.[35] In

[35] For a discussion of female androgyny in the cinema, see Karola Gramann and Heide
Schlüpmann, "Unnatürliche Akte: Die Inszenierung des lesbischen im Film," in *Lust
und Elend: Das erotische Kino* (Munich: Bücher, 1981). And for a specific textual analysis of lesbianism in the Weimar cinema, see B. Ruby Rich, "From Repressive Tolerance to Erotic Liberation: *Maedchen in Uniform*," in *Re-Vision: Essays in Feminist Crit-*

Figure 1. Women in the crisis
(*Berliner Illustrirte Zeitung*, 1932)

the fashion pages of illustrated magazines, for example, the visual representation of the "modern woman" who dressed in unisex clothing and wore her hair cropped short (in the fashionable *Bubi-kopf*) commonly led to extended debates in editorial pages over the alleged—and often much deplored—"*Vermännlichung der Frau*" (masculinization of woman). In the films of the period, female gender roles also verged on the androgynous or bisexual, as, for instance, in Asta Nielsen's performance as Hamlet in the 1920 screen version of the Shakespeare play, or in Elisabeth's Bergner's temporary appropriation of men's clothes and male identity in *Der Geiger von Florenz* (1926). The experimentation with traditional gender roles in Weimar, however, was not limited to the female figure alone. Indeed, as has often been noted, the passive male figure who adopts a "feminine" posture seems to dominate not only the cinema of the 1920s, but also the fashion pages of a magazine like *Die Dame*.

Given the contemporary interest in questions of sexual ambiguity and androgyny in the Weimar years, it becomes important to stress, however, that the feminized male figure serves different functions in different textual systems and in relation to specific audiences. A brief comparison will make this clear. In Murnau's 1924 film, *Der Letzte Mann* (literally, "The Last Man," but retitled "The Last Laugh" for U.S. release), the dishonored hotel doorman (Emil Jannings) might be said to adopt a visual posture and a narrative function that could be termed "feminine." As the narrative begins, the doorman is too old and weak to lift heavy luggage and must therefore exchange his ostentatious hotel uniform for the simple white jacket of a lavatory attendant. Taken from his position at the revolving door, from the space which allowed access to city and hotel traffic, the doorman is relegated to the empty and confining space of the hotel's basement lavatory. His posture becomes slumped, his movements laborious, his loss of power complete. In perhaps the most visually disorienting sequence of the film, the doorman's drunken dream state is given hyperbolic representation. A collage of women's faces laughing and sneering (including an image of Jannings himself wearing a woman's headscarf) suggests the

icism, ed. Mary Ann Doane, Patricia Mellencamp, and Linda Williams, The American Film Institute Monograph Series, vol. 3 (Frederick, Md.: University Publications of America, 1983), 100–130.

doorman's projection of an aggressive and threatening character onto those with whom he has come to identify most. In other words, the doorman is "feminized" because he has lost power, because he must occupy the position otherwise reserved for women in the film.

If *Der Letzte Mann* represents the passive male figure as an object of pity in a narrative which traces the tragedy of male economic and symbolic defeat, Carl Froelich's *Zuflucht* (1927) uses the passive male figure for an entirely different purpose. In the film's opening sequence, Martin (Franz Lederer) returns from Russia to his native Germany, exhausted after years of revolutionary activity. He is soon taken in by Hanne (Henny Porten), a woman who works in a local open market and who shares a flat with a family in the workers' section of Berlin. For the duration of the narrative, Martin is either sleeping or immobilized, shot with a soft-focus filter and arranged as a figure for both the characters and the spectator to see. In contrast to the other male characters in the fiction, particularly the male family members with whom Hanne shares living space, Martin is not virile, aggressive or demanding. Indeed, as the film's only male figure with feminine attributes, Martin allows both Hanne and the film's spectator to seek "refuge" (the literal meaning of the film's title) from the forces of confinement, repression, and control. *Zuflucht*, in other words, represents the passive male figure in order to refer to something other than male symbolic defeat. We might even say, in light of Tania Modleski's analysis of unstable male identity and film melodrama, that *Zuflucht* refers to female desire and makes its appeal to a female audience.[36]

Although Modleski's essay "Time and Desire in the Woman's Film" (1985) deals specifically with American melodrama, her approach is pertinent to an analysis of the film melodrama in Weimar. Drawing on theories of melodrama as a genre which works to overcome repression and achieve expressivity, she also speculates on the appeal of melodrama for female audiences:

> If women are hysterics in patriarchal culture because, according to the feminist argument, their voice has been silenced or repressed, and if melodrama deals with the return of the re-

---

[36] Tania Modleski, "Time and Desire in the Woman's Film," *Cinema Journal* 23, no. 3 (Spring 1984): 19–30.

pressed through a kind of conversion hysteria, perhaps women have been attracted to the genre because it provides an outlet for the repressed feminine voice.[37]

The melodramatic convention of a complicated or destablized male identity, Modleski further suggests, may allow us to discern the different appeal of melodrama for male and female viewers. The male spectator, she argues, may in fact be attached to the genre because "these films provide [him] with a vicarious, hysterical experience of femininity which can be more definitively laid to rest for having been 'worked through.' "[38] This formulation, it seems to me, goes a long way toward explaining the appeal of a film like *Der Letzte Mann* to male audiences in the 1920s, audiences who were experiencing changes in the definition of male cultural and economic authority in the wake of the lost war, inflation, and developments in the industrial division of labor. And yet, as I have already suggested in relation to *Zuflucht*, the feminized male figure may serve an entirely different function for female viewers, since "the man with feminine attributes frequently functions as a figure upon whom feminine desires for freedom from patriarchal authority may be projected."[39] Indeed, it is not difficult to imagine how the representation of a passive male figure may have addressed a historical audience, whose experience of cultural and industrial change was *not* accompanied by fundamental changes in a culturally defined gender identity; in other words, how it came to address a historical female audience, whose experience of a feminine gender identity could not be so easily laid to rest or worked through.

MELODRAMA AND EXPRESSIONISM: THE CONVENTIONS OF PATHOS

It is part of my task to suggest how the representation of sexual difference in photojournalism and film came to address female audiences in the 1920s. Yet by establishing a link between unstable

[37] Ibid., 21.
[38] Ibid., 25.
[39] Ibid., 26.

male identity and film melodrama in Weimar, I have already raised the need for a more careful analysis of those conventions in film and the press that may be called melodramatic.

If melodrama was an important representational mode in Weimar, one might well wonder why no historian or theorist of the Weimar period has adequately discussed it. There are precedents for analyzing the film melodrama in the work of Siegfried Kracauer. In contrast to the almost exclusive attention to male subjectivity in *From Caligari to Hitler*, for example, Kracauer's early writings on the cinema in Weimar often focus on female spectators and the destabilizing effects of melodramatic representation. In a series of sketches which he wrote for the *Frankfurter Zeitung* in 1927, collected under the title "The Little Shopgirls Go to the Movies," Kracauer in fact offers an extended discussion of melodramatic conventions in the Weimar cinema, including excessive visual and narrative repetition, sexual ambiguity or androgyny, and a heightened emotional appeal that he associates with an address to female audiences.[40]

Kracauer was certainly not the first to note the pervasive appeal of melodrama in Weimar, nor was he alone in associating melodrama with an emotional expression that could be termed "feminine." In *The Haunted Screen*, for instance, Lotte Eisner describes an aesthetic that is remarkably close to melodramatic forms and effects. Yet when Eisner mentions melodrama explicitly, she tends to trace it to a single influence: that of scriptwriter Thea von Harbou, better known in film historiography as Fritz Lang's wife, who chose not to accompany her husband to Hollywood, but to remain in Germany where she later assisted with Nazi film production.[41]

[40] Siegfried Kracauer, "Die kleinen Ladenmädchen gehen ins Kino," in *Das Ornament der Masse* (Frankfurt am Main: Suhrkamp, 1977), 279–94.

[41] Harbou was extremely active in campaigns for the repeal of paragraph 218 in Germany, which made abortion a criminal act. In 1931, she articulated her position at a mass rally: "Our main goal is to find a new form of preventing pregnancy and therefore to make the entire 218 unnecessary. Immediately, however, the Paragraph must fall because it is no longer morally recognized by women. It is no longer a law. We need a new sexual code because the old was created by men and no man is in a position to understand the agony of a woman who is carrying a child she knows she cannot feed. This law derived from male psychology, which forces a woman into having a child, creates, even if not deliberately, constitutional inferiority of women in relation to men which serves as a bulwark against women's activity in economic and political life."

26

For Eisner, von Harbou's influence is of dubious aesthetic and political value. Of *Spione* (*Spies*, 1928), for example, Eisner remarks, "After a film like *Mabuse*, a film like *Spione* is disappointing. . . . The fault may be Lang's for having tried to introduce too many small traits of character. More plausibly, it may be attributed to Thea von Harbou and her taste for pompous melodrama. Thea von Harbou always dwells on the feelings and reactions of her characters."[42] In her discussion of *Metropolis* (1926), moreover, Eisner attributes political meaning to von Harbou's aesthetic preoccupations when she claims that von Harbou's "sentimentalism and false grandeur were to make her lapse into the darkness of Nazi ideology."[43]

While the association of melodrama with Nazi ideology is by no means atypical, the association of melodrama with the "feminine," with an irrational and overly indulgent emotionalism, is even more common. When critics refer to melodramatic expression, for example, they commonly indict the triviality and banality of genres that make their appeal to women (for example, the soap opera or the "woman's weepie").[44] In literary history, moreover, melodrama has long been considered a mixed and even derivative mode, hardly deserving of the status or critical attention accorded to tragedy, comedy, or the epic.[45] It is not surprising, then, that melodramatic representation in Weimar has inspired so little serious atten-

---

Quoted in Atina Grossmann, "Abortion and Economic Crisis: The 1931 Campaign Against Paragraph 218 in Germany," *New German Critique*, no. 14 (Spring 1978): 131.

[42] Lotte Eisner, *The Haunted Screen* (Berkeley and Los Angeles: University of California Press, 1969), 246.

[43] Ibid., 232–33.

[44] Several feminist theorists have remarked on the association of melodrama with the feminine. For an interesting discussion of this association, see Mary Ann Doane, "Film and the Masquerade: Theorizing the Female Spectator," *Screen* 23, nos. 3–4 (September–October 1982): 74–87; and Tania Modleski, "Time and Desire in the Woman's Film."

[45] Virtually every critic who writes on melodrama refers to its "bad reputation" in literary history. James Rosenberg, for example, begins his defense of melodrama in the following way: "I would like to defend a dirty word. Like a lot of dirty words, it is dirty, I feel, only through association—and mistaken association, at that. The word is 'melodrama.' It qualifies, I should say, as just about the dirtiest word in the lexicon of the modern critic of the drama—second only, perhaps, to 'sentimental.' " Excerpted from "Melodrama," in *The Context and Craft of Drama*, ed. Robert W. Corrigan and James L. Rosenberg (San Francisco: Chandler Publishing Co., 1964), 168. The association of melodrama in its affect/effect with illicit sexuality (particularly with an illicit female sexuality) is also a recurrent theme in theater and literary criticism.

---

tion in German film histories. Indeed, because Weimar cinema has been theorized as either documenting male anxieties in mass culture or destabilizing male identity in modernist artistic forms, the melodramatic address to female spectators in the 1920s has largely been ignored by contemporary film scholars.

Recently, however, there has been an attempt to reevaluate the conventional assessment of melodrama as a low or banal form.[46] Nowhere has this attempt been more ambitious and, for the purpose of a reconsideration of the film melodrama in Weimar, more potentially useful, than in Peter Brooks's *The Melodramatic Imagination*.[47] In contrast to Eisner and, indeed, to a great many other critics and historians, who employ the word melodrama only as a pejorative term, Brooks argues for an understanding of melodrama as "the modern expressive mode." To reread Brooks from the perspective of what Eisner calls the *Kammerspiel*, or the street film, however, is nothing less than to rethink the Weimar cinema beyond the debates over mass cultural realism and modernist abstraction. It is, in fact, to reread much of what constituted Weimar's "haunted screen" in terms of a "melodramatic imagination."

In her introduction to *The Haunted Screen*, Eisner announces: "I have not set out to write a history of the German cinema. Rather, I have attempted to throw light on some of the intellectual, artistic, and technical developments which the German cinema underwent during these momentous years, the last decade of the silent period."[48] If not a comprehensive survey of film production, *The Haunted Screen* does advance a series of hypotheses about film aesthetics in Weimar. Of particular interest to an understanding of the film melodrama in Weimar is Eisner's analysis of an aesthetic which combined abstraction and stylization with an attention to the everyday. Neither modernist nor realist, this aesthetic represents for Eisner an uneasy (and short-lived) synthesis of expressionism in the fine arts and the popular theater of Max Reinhardt. Although Eisner analyzes this synthesis in a variety of genres, her discussion

---

[46] See, for example, Elsaesser, "Tales of Sound and Fury: Observations on the Family Melodrama"; Geoffrey Nowell-Smith, "Minnelli and Melodrama," *Screen* 18 (Summer 1977): 113–18; and the collection of essays *Home Is Where the Heart Is*, ed. Christine Gledhill (London: British Film Institute, 1987).

[47] Peter Brooks, *The Melodramatic Imagination: Balzac, Henry James, Melodrama and the Mode of Excess* (New Haven: Yale University Press, 1976).

[48] Eisner, *The Haunted Screen*, 8.

of the *Kammerspiel* and street film seem most representative of the synthesis of which she speaks. Both genres, for example, are described as "intimate dramas" or narratives with a limited number of characters set in an everyday milieu. Furthermore, and perhaps even more crucially, both genres are said to evidence most strikingly what Eisner calls *Stimmung*, or "an intensity of expression that comes close to pantomime."[49]

In detailing what she means by this "intensity of expression," Eisner refers to an aesthetic marked by a slow and deliberate narrative pace, an excessive or overly emphatic visual style, and a propensity for violent contrast in both tone and style. Of the *Kammerspielfilm*, for example, she writes: "The insinuating manner of the *Kammerspiele* intensifies the weight of the action and increases its ponderous slowness. . . . [The characters] stop moving their lips: those silent dialogues, whose purport had been conveyed, however inadequately, by the titles, were now quite pointless. On those rare occasions, at which, in their despair, the characters in the *Kammerspielfilm* appear to moan and let incoherent sounds escape their lips, the spectator's emotion is at its height."[50] It is here, in the kind of "mute voicing" that Eisner describes (in the wonderfully transposed sense of *Stimme* in "*Stimmung*"), that *The Haunted Screen* most clearly anticipates Brooks's analysis of melodrama as a "fundamentally expressionist drama."[51]

By referring to melodrama as an "expressionist drama," Brooks does not have in mind the endless father-son conflicts analyzed by theorists of expressionism in German literature, theater, and film. Instead, he analyzes melodrama as "expressionist" in its desire to say all, to stage and utter the unspeakable. In this regard, Brooks also suggests that melodrama is both related to and distinct from traditions in realism and modernism. He maintains, for example, that melodrama is related to realism in its attention to the drama of the everyday. Like realism, melodrama addresses the real, the ordinary, and the private life, what Diderot referred to as "the picture of the misfortunes that surround us."[52] Yet, in contrast to realism, melodrama seeks excessively to expose and draw out the im-

---

[49] Ibid., 194.
[50] Ibid., 194.
[51] Brooks, *The Melodramatic Imagination*, 55.
[52] Ibid., 13.

plications of everyday existence, to "exploit the dramatics and excitement discoverable within the real, to heighten in dramatic gesture the moral crises and peripeties of life."[53] Like traditions in modernism, melodrama originates from a conviction that realist representation itself may be inadequate, that it may no longer possess truth and epistemological value. Rather than attempt to destroy the binding or absolute status of any representation (as in some forms of modernism and postmodernism), however, melodrama aims to put pressure on the representation of the real so as to allow the unrepresented or repressed to achieve material presence. Melodrama thus represents "an intensified, primary and exemplary version of what the most ambitious art since the beginnings of romanticism has been about";[54] namely, the dual engagement with social existence and with the difficulty and importance of breaking through its repressions.

The melodramatic concern with expression nevertheless serves to highlight an apparent paradox, where the expressivity of melodrama is also related to the ineffability of what is to be expressed. Referring to melodrama as "text of muteness," Brooks analyzes such melodramatic conventions as character types, gesture, and the tableau in an effort to show how the melodramatic message is often formulated through "other registers of the sign," through recourse to expression that is nonverbal or gestural. This discussion of melodrama and muteness has obvious implications for an analysis of the silent German cinema. Of course, to say that the Weimar cinema organizes a text of muteness is to assert, on one level, the merely commonplace or banal, if one understands muteness to refer only to an absence of dialogue. But if we understand muteness as Brooks does, as pointing to fundamentally different conventions of narrative and visual expression, then we may refine Eisner's notion of *Stimmung* in Weimar intimate dramas by referring to conventions of melodrama in the Weimar cinema.

The frequent use of character types to suggest primary psychic and social roles, for example, has commonly been cited by historians and theorists as an important convention of the Weimar cin-

[53] Ibid., 13.
[54] Ibid., 21–22.

ema.[55] When Eisner remarks that primary psychic functions are often attached to characters who are not psychologized, she also explains that "the Germans do not use exaggeration to create a type, they use stylization to create a stereotype."[56] Brooks similarly explains that it is a melodramatic convention to use characters as types so as to stage a drama of ethical conflict and violent contrast, where characters are denied any illusion of depth, interiority or psychological complexity. The very unambiguous social and psychic function assigned to characters in melodrama thus allows them to be instantly recognizable to spectators and deployed in such a way as "to reveal the essential conflicts at work—moments of symbolic conflict which fully articulate the terms of the drama."[57]

It has become a commonplace in film theory to say that symbolic conflicts in melodrama usually concern the problem of identity within a family or class structure.[58] In the Weimar cinema, however, and particularly in the case of the *Kammerspiel* and street film, the instability of social and sexual identity has repeatedly been discussed in terms of male spectator identity, where depicted Oedipal conflicts are read as psychological conflicts that bear the weight of represented meanings. For this reason, it is important to comment on the melodramatic convention of hyperbolic gestures and exaggerated acting styles, where characters represent and undergo extremes. As several theorists have explained, the striking of dramatic postures and exaggeration of facial expressions in Weimar films are conventions derived from expressionist theater. But where most theorists merely describe these conventions as non-naturalistic and as serving to impede narrative flow, it is important to stress the melodramatic function of gesture and expression in dispensing with the illusion of psychological depth and pointing to a transference of meaning. Indeed, characters in the *Kammerspiel* and street film are often so typological that their exaggerated gestures and expressions must be read for how they charge the narrative with an intensified significance, with meaning in excess of what the narrative depicts.

[55] For a lucid analysis of these conventions, see Janet Bergstrom, "Sexuality at a Loss: The Films of F. W. Murnau," *Poetics Today* 6, nos. 1–2 (1985): 185–203.

[56] Eisner, *The Haunted Screen*, 229.

[57] Brooks, *The Melodramatic Imagination*, 53.

[58] See, for example, Geoffrey Nowell-Smith, "Minnelli and Melodrama."

The intensities or excesses of many Weimar films are not, of course, solely the result of hyperbolic gestures or acting styles. Visual and narrative repetition, the use of temporal and spatial ellipses, and the recourse to studied compositions at moments of narrative crisis also give the impression of a displacement of meaning. Quoting from Ernst Angel, editor of *Sylvester*, Eisner explains how the *Kammerspielfilm* typically breaks with narrative suspense in favor of an attention to composition and atmosphere:

> The *Umwelt* [atmosphere] is interpolated not as accessory action or reaction, but as accessory rhythm, in or out of tempo, as a symbol reinforcing or amplifying the given facts of the drama: it is reinforced in such a manner, that in places, at certain decisive moments, the action is apparently halted and can only continue passively, almost secretly, by means of an intensification of the *Umwelt*.[59]

As this quote from Angel suggests, the generally static impression conveyed by the *Kammerspielfilm* derives from an intensification of the mise-en-scène, from the introduction of studied compositions which serve to reinforce or to amplify the "given facts of the drama." In this regard, the function of the cinematic tableau becomes especially important, since it also serves to arrest narrative development so as to offer a fixed representation, "where characters' attitudes and gestures, compositionally arranged and frozen for a moment, give, like an illustrative painting, a visual summary of the emotional situation."[60] The preference for composition over action in the *Kammerspiel* and street films, and the generally static impression the films convey, is also reinforced by the use of intertitles. Indeed, when intertitles do appear in these films, they often describe the action to follow. In other words, they do not function to create or to anticipate action, but rather to break with action and suspense altogether in order to allow the spectator to concentrate on the manner in which conflicts are acted out, in all their ponderous slowness and meticulousness.

A final convention of the *Kammerspiel* and street film in Weimar is one on which I have already remarked: the destabilization of gen-

[59] Eisner, *The Haunted Screen*, 188.
[60] Brooks, *The Melodramatic Imagination*, 48.

der identity, which is often accompanied by a displacement of eroticism from the woman's body onto a feminized male figure or a
generalized mise-en-scène of objects and scenery. In keeping with
a less action-oriented narrative, this displacement of eroticism
might be said to encourage a less goal-oriented way of looking, one
which requires a degree of concentration, attention, and involvement on the part of the spectator.[61]

Obviously, not all films in Weimar were melodramatic. Experimental films, comedies, mountain films, and historical epics—to
name but a few common genres of the period—clearly reveal different narrative emphases and visual preoccupations. Perhaps clos-
est to the film melodrama in Weimar, yet nonetheless distinct from
it, is the "fantastic film." Films like *Schatten* (*Warning Shadows*,
1923) or *Das Kabinett des Dr. Caligari* (*The Cabinet of Dr. Caligari*, 1919), for example, share the melodramatic vocabulary of
nightmare states, claustrophobic atmospheres, and unstable identities. But where fantastic films typically focus on problems of vision and the supernatural, melodramatic films remain concerned
with problems of expression, and focus on everyday life. The difference is significant. In fantastic films, for example, the theme of
the double or split self is commonly employed to explore the crisis
of self in terms of a crisis of vision.[62] Inscribing historical anxiety in
myth—specifically, in the myth of Oedipus—fantastic films might
be said to destabilize or complicate identification by rendering vision and selfhood ambiguous. In melodramatic films, by contrast,
the theme of the double opens onto an exploration of multiple
identities, where the recourse to abstraction or ambiguity is only
temporary. Less concerned with problems of vision than with
problems of expression, the film melodrama in Weimar refers not
to myth but to the material or everyday world, employing visual
conventions to force representation to yield meanings that are legible and unambiguous. In an effort to reinvest the representation
of the everyday with renewed significance, the film melodrama also
frequently addressed women's experiences in Weimar. And, pre-

---

[61] Janet Bergstrom makes this argument in her essay "Sexuality at a Loss."

[62] For an interesting analysis of an early fantastic film, see Heide Schlüpmann, "The
First German Art Film: Rye's *The Student of Prague* (1913)," in *German Film and Literature: Adaptations and Transformations*, ed. Eric Rentschler (New York: Methuen,
1986), 9–24.

cisely to the extent that these experiences had no previous or certain status in German culture, their representation was often highly unstable, but hardly ever entirely ambiguous.

From a strictly chronological perspective, melodramatic conventions in the Weimar cinema were initially adapted from the popular theater, yet they were also indebted to later developments in photography and the visual arts. Photojournalism, in particular, became a privileged site for the synthesis of the sensational and the everyday. The photoessays which appear in the pages of the *Berliner Illustrirte Zeitung* (BIZ), *Die Dame,* and the left-wing *Arbeiter Illustrierte Zeitung* (AIZ), for example, typically heighten the representation of the real through dramatic or, more precisely, cinematic juxtaposition and stylized expression in excess of what the prose captions provide. That melodramatic conventions should mark photojournalism as well as film in the 1920s is hardly surprising, given the degree of institutional concentration and artistic collaboration between press and film. (Alfred Hugenberg, for example, controlled both the Scherl Publishing House and, in 1927, the UFA studios; Stefan Lorant, editor of the *Münchner Illustrierte Press* (MIP) in 1930, was formerly the editor of *Film Kurier* and the originator of film press bills.) Furthermore, while melodramatic representation clearly predates the 1920s, it takes on a specific character during the Weimar years, particularly within the context of a perceived tension between mass cultural and modernist modes of production and reception. Photojournalism and film, in other words, mark the space of a negotiation between mass culture and modernism, where dramatists, filmmakers, and photographers frequently contributed to a textual practice that was neither realist nor modernist, but which reinterpreted both in melodrama; that is, in a heightened and expressive representation of the implications of everyday life.

Where Weimar films tend to focus on a destabilized male identity, rendering it passive or "feminine," the illustrated magazines of the period focus on a destabilized female identity, rendering it aggressive, "masculine," even threatening. To a certain extent, the representation of the modern woman was a projection of male anxieties and fears—anxieties and fears emanating from various phenomena of modernity that were recast and reconstructed in terms of an uncontrollable and destructive female sexuality (figure 2).

Rr. 51   Berliner Illuſtrirte Zeitung   1913

Figure 2. Modernity and male anxiety
(*Berliner Illustrirte Zeitung*, 1923)

(This is also true, of course, of several discourses issuing from turn-of-the-century European culture: the tragic dramas of Strindberg and Wedekind, the literary philosophies of Weininger and Spengler, the journalistic satire of Karl Kraus.) But when we turn to the magazines and films that made their appeal explicitly to women, it is indisputable that the representation of the modern woman did address women's experiences of modernity—their dissatisfactions with traditionally defined gender roles and their desire for a transformation of those roles (figures 3 and 4).

Significantly, the approach to questions of gender in illustrated magazines was far more polemical and, indeed, far more topical than it was in films; where the films generally displace the historical dimension of issues of gender by bringing it into line with formal and narrative conventions, the magazines tend to seize on this historical dimension—especially in the editorial pages—in order to situate perceived changes in gender definition and orientation as social concerns of the highest order. Weimar photojournalism sheds considerable light on discussions of Weimar film, since it allows us to understand issues of sexual ambiguity and androgyny within a specific cultural and historical context, and not merely within formal and narrative conventions.

That traditional definitions of gender were in crisis during the Weimar years can hardly be disputed. That the multiple effects of this crisis were necessarily different for women than for men will be a guiding assumption of the analysis to follow. Such an analysis takes on a particular urgency given the contemporary fascination with notions of sexual ambiguity in the silent German cinema, for what is now seen as sexually ambiguous has actually been filtered through a perspective which purports objectivity and universality, only to render women's experience invisible. To replace this perspective with one that is truly historical, we must move beyond generalized claims for ambiguity in the Weimar cinema to explore the distinctive, clearly utopian dimension of sexual and social mobility for Weimar women, and the ways in which this dimension was fraught from the very beginning with a disquieting sense of uncertainty and doubt.

Figure 3. The modern woman
(*Die Dame*, 1927)

Figure 4. The masquerade
(*Die Dame*, 1927)

PERCEPTIONS OF
DIFFERENCE

.

[T]he remarkable juxtapositioning of women and
cities . . . is probably rooted in the historical fact
that the entire ancient world built its great cities
on rivers and coastlines, because water transport
was superior then. The freer forms of commerce
among cities released a certain proportion of
women from the most stringent patriarchal relationships and monitoring. As early as the gospel of
St. John, we find Babylon described as "the whore
sitting beside the waters."
　　　　　　—Klaus Theweleit
　　　　　　Männerphantasien (1977)[1]

For those who experienced the rapid technological and industrial
expansion of Germany, Berlin became the symbol of an almost in-
describable dynamic. As one historian explains, if the old Berlin
had been impressive, the new Berlin was irresistible, and the mere
mention of the city inspired powerful reactions from everyone: "It
delighted most, terrified some, but left no one indifferent, and it
induced, by its vitality, a certain inclination to exaggerate what one
saw."[2] The connection suggested here between *vision* and an *inflated view* of the city acquires a special significance when we con-

---

[1] Klaus Theweleit, *Männerphantasien: Frauen, Fluten, Körper, Geschichte*, vol. 1
(Frankfurt: Verlag Roter Stern, 1977), 586, fn. 88. This book is also available in English
translation. See Theweleit, *Male Fantasies: Women, Floods, Bodies, History*, vol. 1,
trans. Stephen Conway (Minneapolis, Mn.: University of Minnesota Press, 1987).

[2] Peter Gay, *Weimar Culture: The Outsider as Insider* (New York: Harper and Row,
1970), 129.

sider some of the most influential theories of perception and subjectivity written during the Weimar period. Indeed, for intellectuals, artists, and journalists in Germany in the 1920s, the evocation of Berlin served not only as a convenient shorthand for a
number of technological innovations thought profoundly to alter
perception and experience (trains, automobiles, and telephones as
well as photography, photojournalism, and film); Berlin also served
as the decisive metaphor for modernity. Modernity, in turn, was
almost always represented as a woman (figure 5).

There are, of course, immediate historical reasons for associating
Berlin in the 1920s with modernity: as the capital of the Reich and
the most populous and industrialized of all German cities, Berlin
was the center for mass cultural entertainment; hardly remarkable,
given that large scale urbanization was the precondition for the expansion and differentiation of the mass cultural audience.[3] What is
remarkable, however, is that contemporary observers repeatedly
imagined the city taking a female form. For example, in a 1929
issue of *Der Querschnitt*, an Ullstein magazine for intellectuals,
journalist Harold Nicolson describes the particular charm of Berlin
by invoking the figure of woman as metaphor for the enigmatic
and, hence, desirable "otherness" of the city:

> What on earth gives this city its charm! Movement in the first
> place. There is no city in the world so restless as Berlin.
> Everything moves. The traffic lights change restlessly from
> red to gold and then to green. The lighted advertisements
> flash with the pathetic iteration of coastal lighthouses. . . .
> Second to movement comes frankness. London is an old lady
> in black lace and diamonds who guards her secrets with dig-
> nity and to whom one would not tell those secrets of which
> one was ashamed. Paris is a woman in the prime of life to
> whom one would only tell those secrets which one desires to
> be repeated. But Berlin is a girl in a pull-over, not much pow-
> der on her face, Hölderlin in her pocket, thighs like those of

[3] For an extremely illuminating discussion of modernity and film culture in Weimar,
see Anton Kaes, "Introduction," *Kino-Debatte: Texte zum Verhältnis von Literatur und
Film, 1909–1929*, ed. Anton Kaes, (Tübingen: Max Niemeyer Verlag, 1978). A slightly
modified version of this introduction is available in English translation as "The Debate
About Cinema: Charting a Controversy (1909–1929)," trans. David J. Levin, *New German Critique*, no. 40 (Winter 1987): 7–33.

Figure 5. The woman and the city
(*Die Dame*, 1930)

Atalanta, an undigested education, a heart which is almost too ready to sympathize, and a breadth of view which charms one's repressions. . . . The maximum irritant for the nerves corrected by the maximum sedative. Berlin stimulates like arsenic, and then when one's nerves are all ajingle, she comes with her hot milk of human kindness; and in the end, for an hour and a half, one is able, gratefully, to go to sleep.[4]

Where Nicolson calls upon the image of the female adolescent (the "girl in a pull-over, not much powder on her face") to describe the curious mixture of old and new in the city, playwright Carl Zuckmayer invokes a far more sexualized and, indeed, far more demonic female figure to describe what he sees as Berlin's peculiar mixture of seduction and cruelty:

This city devoured talents and human energies with a ravenous appetite, grinding them small, digesting them, or rapidly spitting them out again. It sucked into itself with hurricane force all the ambitions in Germany, the true and the false . . . and, after it had swallowed them, ignored them. People discussed Berlin . . . as if Berlin were a highly desirable woman, whose coldness and capriciousness were widely known: the less chance anyone had to win her, the more they decried her. We called her proud, snobbish, *nouveau riche*, uncultured, crude. But secretly everyone looked upon her as the goal of their desires. Some saw her as hefty, full-breasted, in lace underwear, others as a mere wisp of a thing, with boyish legs in black silk stockings. The daring saw both aspects, and her very capacity for cruelty made them the more aggressive. All wanted to have her, she enticed all. . . . To conquer Berlin was to conquer the world. The only thing was—and this was the everlasting spur—that you had to take all the hurdles again and again, had to break through the goal again and again in order to maintain your position.[5]

---

[4] Harold Nicolson, "The Charm of Berlin," *Der Querschnitt* (May 1929) (originally in English), reprinted in *Der Querschnitt: Das Magazin der aktuellen Ewigkeitswerte, 1924–1933* (Berlin: Ullstein Verlag, 1980), 261–63.

[5] Carl Zuckmayer, *Als Wär's ein Stück von mir* (1966), 311–14, reprinted in translation as *A Part of Myself*, trans. Richard and Clara Winston (New York: Harcourt Brace Jovanovich, 1970), 217.

Berlin, it is obvious, inspired powerful reactions from everyone and induced a tendency to exaggerate what one saw. It is equally obvious, however, that this tendency to exaggerate in representing Berlin as a woman reveals less about *women* in Weimar than it does about a *male* desire that simultaneously elevates and represses woman as object of allure and as harbinger of danger. While it would seem that Zuckmayer's claim that "to conquer Berlin was to conquer the world" defines the particular contours of this male desire, it is, rather, his admission that "you had to take all the hurdles again and again . . . to maintain your position" which reveals its fundamental paradox: the paradox of a male fascination with femininity which threatens to subvert masculine identity, and which therefore requires constant vigilance to keep the fears and anxieties provoked by woman at a safe and measured distance.

The passages I have cited from Nicolson and Zuckmayer are far from anomalous. One need only look at the images of the city made famous in the paintings of Georg Grosz and Otto Dix, or read the city poems of Bertolt Brecht, Erich Kästner, and Walter Mehring, to realize how numerous artists and writers responded to modernity by imaginatively reconstructing Berlin as demonic, as alienating, and as female. Even an abstract film like Walter Ruttmann's *Berlin. Symfonie einer Grossstadt* (*Berlin, Symphony of a Great City*, 1927) builds its investigation of the city's spatial and visual fragmentation around the spectacle of woman—a spectacle barely hidden at the center of the film. Yet if there exists a wealth of evidence to read responses to modernity in Weimar as constructed on male subjectivity and desire—where woman is absent as subject and yet overpresent as object—I raise the following questions: What kind of historical response to modernity is concealed in the textual and artistic inscription of woman in Weimar? And can we discern in this historical response a different discourse on subjectivity, perception, and sexual difference in Germany of the 1920s? In other words, is there a way to reread early discussions of modernity in Weimar so as to situate woman as an inhabitant of the city she so frequently serves to represent?

To begin to answer these questions, we should recall that the Weimar years were not only marked by political, economic, and social crises, but also that these crises were often perceived as contributing to the loss of (male) cultural authority. That responses to the loss of this authority should invariably involve woman hardly comes as a surprise, especially when we consider the fact that it was only in the early twentieth century that the women's movement gained a contending voice in German political and cultural life.[6] In this regard, it is all the more significant that artists and intellectuals typically construed modernity as feminine, and as effecting an almost complete transformation of the cultural and perceptual field. While mass culture in general was frequently associated with modernity (and hence, as several theorists have pointed out, with woman),[7] the cinema in particular seemed to crystallize the relationships among modern life, modes of perception, and male responses to gender difference.

Cultural historian Egon Friedell, for example, expressed the widely held belief that perception and representation had been transformed under the impact of modernity when he remarked in 1912, "[The film] is short, quick, at the same time coded, and it does not stop for anything. There is something concise, precise, military about it. This is quite fitting for our time, which is a time of extracts. In fact, these days there is nothing which we have less of a sense for than that idyllic relaxation and epic repose with objects which earlier stood precisely for the poetic."[8] While the loss of a poetic repose with objects disturbed a thinker like Friedell, other critics, particularly those on the political left, celebrated the loss of this repose since it signaled the demise of outmoded aesthetic values

[6] On the feminist movement in turn-of-the-century Germany, see Richard J. Evans, *Comrades and Sisters: Feminism, Socialism and Pacifism in Europe 1870–1945* (New York: St. Martin's Press, 1987); Richard J. Evans, *The Feminist Movement in Germany 1894–1933*, vol. 6 (London: Sage Studies in Twentieth Century History, 1976); Jean Quataert, *Reluctant Feminists in German Social Democracy, 1885–1917* (Princeton, N.J.: Princeton University Press, 1979); Werner Thönnessen, *The Emancipation of Women: The Rise and Fall of the Women's Movement in German Social Democracy 1863–1933*, trans. Joris de Bres (London: Pluto, 1976).

[7] See, for example, Miriam Hansen, "Early Silent Cinema: Whose Public Sphere?" *New German Critique*, no. 29 (Spring–Summer 1983): 147–84; Tania Modleski, "The Terror of Pleasure: The Contemporary Horror Film and Postmodern Theory," in *Studies in Entertainment: Critical Approaches to Mass Culture*, ed. Tania Modleski, Theories of Contemporary Culture, vol. 7 (Bloomington, In.: Indiana University Press, 1986), 155–66; Andreas Huyssen, "Mass Culture as Woman: Modernism's Other," also in *Studies in Entertainment*, 188–207; and my "Mass Culture and the Feminine: The 'Place' of Television in Film Studies," *Cinema Journal* 25, no. 3 (Spring 1986): 5–21.

[8] Egon Friedell, "Prolog vor dem Film," in *Blätter des deutschen Theaters* 2 (1912); reprinted in Kaes, ed., *Kino-Debatte*, 43.

and inaugurated an address to an emerging mass cultural audience. Significantly, however, even critics on the left warned against the tendency of the cinematic image to capture and immobilize the spectator, to induce a passive response characteristic of technological modes of production more generally. As Spartacist poet Bruno Schönlank describes in his poem "Kino":

Factory workers, tired
from the drudgery of the day.
Salesgirls, seamstresses, spinning
golden fairy tales of luck and the wages of true love
Beautiful girls follow the pictures
and swallow in the lies.
They gladly let themselves be led astray
by that which enchants their souls.
Drunk with the glitter they return home
and in the dark room see yet another light,
which breaks through their dreams as bright as the sun
till grey everyday life puts it out again.[9]

This evocation of cinematic spectatorship further indicates how discussions about representation and perception in Weimar were often divided along sexual lines. In Schönlank's view, the appeal of the cinema derives from its illusory plenitude ("golden fairy tales of luck and the wages of true love") which draws one closer; it is the female spectator—not her male counterpart (as represented, for instance, by the poet himself)—who proves most susceptible to the cinematic illusion, unable to achieve a critical distance from it. Far from being a spectator who assumes an "epic repose" considered poetic in the past, the female viewer is understood as that spectator who is not only willingly duped by the image, but also most easily deceived by its lies.

While early assessments of perception and spectatorship in Germany hardly promote a neutral understanding of spectatorship and sexual difference in the cinema, it would be a mistake to assume that our current discussions of these issues have somehow moved beyond the implicit premises of the early debates. Indeed, notions

[9] Bruno Schönlank, "Kino," in *Deutsche Arbeiterdichtung 1910–1933*, ed. Günter Heintz (Stuttgart, 1974), 293–94.

about modernity that circulated in turn-of-the-century Germany—with woman equated with the image and, at the same time, situated as that spectator unable to separate from it—continue to inform some of the most sophisticated analyses of perception and spectatorship in current film theory. Most strikingly, contemporary film theorists retain the assumption that film technology so profoundly alters perception and experience that it completely reorganizes the spectator's relationship to space, vision, and structures of desire.

In his essays on psychoanalysis and the cinema, for instance, Christian Metz invokes the metaphor of the cinema as an "apparatus"—a technological, institutional, and psychical "machine" for stabilizing subjectivity—to suggest how the film spectator internalizes certain historically constituted and socially regulated modes of psychical functioning.[10] According to Metz, the cinema is more richly perceptual than other arts because it mobilizes a larger number of axes of perception: analogical image, graphic image, sound, speech, dialogue. But, as Metz explains, if the film is thus more perceptually present, that which it depicts is manifestly absent. He concludes that the cinema involves the spectator more profoundly than the other arts in the imaginary, since it is the spectator's identification with his own look—with himself as pure act of perception—which serves as the very condition for perceiving in film.

Metz goes on to argue that while the spectator's look lends coherence and meaning to the cinematic image, the coherence of the viewing subject can only be secured through processes of voyeurism and fetishism; in other words, through those psychic mechanisms which enable the viewer to assume a distance from the image. "It is no accident," Metz remarks, "that the main socially acceptable arts are based on the senses at a distance, and that those which depend on the senses of contact are often regarded as 'minor' arts (e.g., the culinary arts, the art of perfumes, etc.)." Continuing this thought, he writes:

> Nor is it an accident that the visual or auditory imaginaries have played a much more important part in the histories of

---

[10] Christian Metz, *The Imaginary Signifier: Psychoanalysis and Cinema*, trans. Celia Britton, Annwyl Williams, Ben Brewster, and Alfred Guzzetti (London: The MacMillan Press, 1982).

societies than the tactile or olfactory imaginaries. The voyeur is very careful to maintain a gulf, an empty space, between the object and the eye, the object and his own body; his look fastens the object at the right distance, as with those cinema spectators who take care to avoid being too close to or too far from the screen. . . . [For] to fill in this distance would threaten to overwhelm the subject, to lead him to consume the object (the object which is so close that he cannot see it any more), to . . . [mobilize] the sense of contact and [put] an end to the scopic arrangement.[11]

Although Metz does not concern himself with the historical reasons for the implicit (gender) hierarchizing of the visual and auditory imaginaries, his description of perceptual differences nevertheless raises fundamental questions about the function of gender in perceptual response. Are we to assume that the woman's relationship to the image is the same as the man's, and that she, too, partakes of a voyeuristic or fetishistic pleasure in looking?

In an attempt to respond to this question, Mary Ann Doane has proposed that "both the theory of the image and its apparatus, the cinema, produce a position for the female spectator which is ultimately untenable because it lacks the attributes of distance so necessary for an adequate reading of the image."[12] Doane goes on to explain that the female spectator's inability to distance herself from the image—her tendency to "over-identify" with events on the screen—suggests that the woman is constituted differently than the man in relation to forms of perception and structures of looking. "For the female spectator," Doane writes, "there is a certain over-presence of the image—she *is* the image. Given the closeness of this relationship, the female spectator's desire can be described only in terms of narcissism—the female look demands a becoming. It thus appears to negate the very distance or gap specified by Metz . . . as the essential precondition of voyeurism."[13]

Although Doane takes pains to modify the Metzian model by theorizing a kind of fetishism available to the female viewer in what

[11] Metz, "The Passion for Perceiving," in Metz, *The Imaginary Signifier*, 56–60.
[12] Mary Ann Doane, "Film and the Masquerade: Theorizing the Female Spectator," *Screen* 23, nos. 3–4 (September–October 1982): 87.
[13] Ibid., 78.

she calls the "masquerade" (which I will consider at greater length in the next chapter), her discussion of female spectatorship significantly rests on notions of perception and sexual difference that tend to corroborate—rather than challenge—certain time-honored assumptions about seeing and knowing in the cinema. In line with Metz, for example, Doane attributes both knowledge and pleasure in the cinema to a necessary distance from the image. As she proposes, the mode of looking developed by the classical narrative cinema depends on an image of woman which is fixed and held for the pleasure and reassurance of the male viewer. While this image automatically produces voyeuristic or fetishistic separation in the male spectator, she explains, it also threatens to overwhelm and consume the female spectator for whom that image is too close, too present, too recognizable. Doane surmises that when the female spectator fails to distance herself from the image of woman, she necessarily merges with that image and, consequently, loses herself. Equating the cinematic apparatus with a theory of the male imaginary, Doane winds up affirming the model of spectatorship she initially sets out to expose: conflating vision with intellection, Doane maintains that the female spectator can only "see" (and thus assume a position of knowledge) in the classical narrative cinema by manufacturing a distance from the image of woman and taking up the position of fetishist. In a formulation of the problem that is in some respects similar to Metz's own, she writes, "A machine for the production of images and sounds, the cinema generates and guarantees pleasure by a corroboration of the spectator's identity. Because that identity is bound up with that of the voyeur and the fetishist . . . it is not accessible to the female spectator, who, in buying her ticket, must deny her sex."[14]

Unlike early German film theorists, Metz and Doane ground their analyses of perception and spectatorship in a systematic application of psychoanalytic concepts. Yet behind these psychoanalytic concepts lies a historical argument about modernity and perceptual response that locates gendered spectatorship within the terms of a phallocentric discourse; indeed, Freud himself pointed out that the transition from a matriarchal to a patriarchal society

[14] Mary Ann Doane, "Woman's Stake: Filming the Female Body," *October* 17 (Summer 1981): 23.

involved the simultaneous promotion of senses at a distance (i.e., sight and hearing) and devaluation of senses of contact (i.e., touch, taste, and smell).[15] The perceptual distance thought to provide a privileged means of access to knowledge and pleasure in psychoanalytic accounts of film spectatorship thus derives its force from a historical argument which gives sense perception a quite specific meaning; to borrow from Doane, it is not sight in general, but the sight of the female body as the sign of castration, which provokes the defensive, and thus more mediated, visual response of the film voyeur and fetishist.[16]

I believe there is sufficient cause to challenge psychoanalytic accounts of perception and subjectivity in the cinema, and to distinguish the perceptual possibilities of filmviewing from the theory of a male imaginary so often employed to describe them. To pose such a challenge adequately, however, we need first to identify the historical argument underpinning discussions of perception and visual response in psychoanalytic film theory, and then to work back through the clichés about gendered spectatorship to recognize how they conceal a fairly complex history rooted in responses to modernity and male perceptions of sexual difference. My concern in the following pages is to offer such a challenge, and to trace concepts relating to perception and spectatorship back to philosophical and theoretical debates over mass culture and modernity as they were waged in Germany in the 1920s.

I focus on the writings of Martin Heidegger, Walter Benjamin, and Siegfried Kracauer, since each of these theorists aims to underline the historical nature of subjectivity and identity, and thus to situate perceptual changes within a fundamentally historical understanding of modernity. There are, of course, several other important theorists who wrote about spectatorship and perception during the Weimar years; notably, Béla Balázs, Rudolf Arnheim, and Bertolt Brecht. For several reasons, however, I see the work of Heidegger, Benjamin, and Kracauer as most useful for reconsidering the relationships among mass culture, perception, and modern experience, and for discerning the contours of a discourse on sexual-

---

[15] Sigmund Freud, *Civilization and Its Discontents*, trans. James Strachey (New York: Norton, 1962), 46–47.

[16] Mary Ann Doane, " '. . . when the direction of the force acting on the body is changed.': The Moving Image," *Wide Angle* 7, nos. 1–2 (1985): 42–58.

ity that continues to shape our understanding of cinematic representation and spectatorship.

All three theorists exert considerable influence on the way in which contemporary scholars approach questions of representation and subjectivity as they relate to the problem of modernity.[17] A reexamination of their writings from a feminist perspective, however, should allow us to pursue issues of gendered spectatorship in a manner far more precise than has hitherto been the case. Rather than appeal to the operative dualities familiar to contemporary film theory (active/passive, absence/presence, distance/proximity), Heidegger, Benjamin, and Kracauer define the impact of technology on perception in a more differentiated and subtle manner. The concepts of "contemplation" and "distraction," for instance, enable these theorists to describe the difference between artistic and mass cultural reception, and yet to conceptualize the simultaneous response of passivity and activity, proximity and distance in the spectator's relation to the image. This is not to say that they completely agree on the historical meaning of changes in representation or perceptual response. Indeed, not only do all three theorists take different approaches to questions of modernity; they also exhibit distinct attitudes toward the social and political functions of mass cultural spectatorship—attitudes ranging from contempt to ambivalence to celebration.

Most important, however, their writings disclose a historical dimension in modernity which allows us to take up questions of gender and spectatorship as they exist between the lines of the debate over mass culture. For all three theorists, male spectatorship remains the (unspoken) topic of theoretical exploration. Nevertheless, because they align the cinema with a crisis of perception (in which the subject experiences becoming an object), their writings unwittingly reveal how the crisis of male vision is inseparable from the emergence of a mass cultural audience, and from the growing

[17] The impact of Heidegger's and Benjamin's writings on theories of postmodernism is a case in point, but even Kracauer's early writings have recently gained the attention of scholars interested in defining a resolutely historical approach to questions of mass culture, modernity, and perceptual response. The renewed interest in Kracauer's early work will certainly be facilitated by the English translation of *Das Ornament der Masse*, which is forthcoming as *The Mass Ornament* from Harvard University Press, translated and edited by Thomas Y. Levin.

demands of women for an equal share in German cultural life. The writings of Heidegger, Benjamin, and Kracauer thus provide us with a philosophical framework for contesting traditional notions of perceptual response and gendered spectatorship, allowing us, in turn, to recognize in the metaphors of modernity both the city and the cinema in Weimar which were, undeniably, also inhabited by women.

PERCEPTION, MASS CULTURE, AND DISTRACTION: MARTIN HEIDEGGER

Everything is going on as if reading Heidegger had nothing to do with sexual difference, and nothing to do with man himself, or, said in another way, as if it had nothing to do with woman, nothing to interrogate or suspect. . . . Perhaps one could even speak of [Heidegger's] silence as uppity, precisely, arrogant, provocative, in a century where sexuality is common to all the small talk and also a currency of philosophical and scientific knowledge, the inevitable *Kampfplatz* of ethics and politics. . . . And yet, the matter seems to be understood so little or so badly that Heidegger had immediately to account for it. He had to do it in the margins of *Being and Time*.[18]

There are a number of reasons for the continual appeal to Heideggerian phenomenology in contemporary theories of culture and representation. Most obviously, contemporary theorists are drawn to Heidegger's attempt to think more primordially about modern existence—his effort to transcend the division between subject and object by subordinating epistemology to ontology so that critical understanding ceases to be a simple "knowing" in order to become a way of "being." Part of the appeal of this primordial thinking, however, undoubtedly derives from Heidegger's effort to get beyond questions of sexual difference and thus to transcend that inevitable *Kampfplatz* where the sexual is political and vice versa.

And yet, as Derrida himself insists, Heidegger only appears to

---

[18] Jacques Derrida, "Geschlecht: différence sexuelle, différence ontologique," *L'Herne* (September 1983): 419–30. I am indebted to Nataša Ďurovičová for her astute translation of this essay. All translations of this essay that follow are hers.

be silent on questions of sexuality and sexual difference, for in his early writings on experience and in his later writings on language, Heidegger has quite specific things to say about gender (even if he does relegate these remarks to the margins of his philosophy). To understand Heidegger's views on gender, it is necessary to outline his position on modernity; indeed, as we shall see, Heidegger's approach to the question of sexual duality in experience is fundamentally linked to his exploration of modernity and mass culture.

In his *magnum opus* on temporality and experience, *Being and Time* (*Sein und Zeit*, 1927), Heidegger identifies his thought in opposition to the technological thinking of the modern age, and thus communicates something of the sense of discontent and disillusionment with modernity that pervaded German culture in the wake of World War I. As one historian explains, "Heidegger's life—his isolation, his peasant-like appearance, his deliberate provincialism, his hatred of the city—seemed to confirm his philosophy, which was a disdainful rejection of modern urban rationalist civilization."[19] Or, in the words of Hans Georg Gadamer, who refers less to the man himself than to the reception of his writing, "The contemporary reader of Heidegger's first systematic work was seized by the vehemence of its passionate protest against . . . the levelling effects of all individual forms of life by industrial society, with its ever stronger uniformities and its techniques of communication and public relations that manipulated everything."[20]

Heidegger's critique of modernity and technological forms of communication cannot be separated from his critique of epistemology for holding vision to be a superior means of access to certainty and truth. In *Being and Time*, for example, he refers to a modern obsession with the visual over other sensory faculties and describes this as a privileging of seeing (*sehen*) over understanding (*verstehen*) which contributes to the impoverishment of the senses and a fundamental "distraction" (*Zerstreuung*). In contrast to "concern," or a mode of perception guided by circumspection and contemplation, "distraction" lends itself to what Heidegger calls a "restless" and "curious" gaze:

[19] Gay, *Weimar Culture*, 82.

[20] Hans Georg Gadamer, "Heidegger's Later Philosophy," in *Essays in Philosophical Hermeneutics*, trans. David E. Linge (Berkeley and Los Angeles: University of California Press, 1976), 214–15.

When curiosity has become free . . . it concerns itself with seeing, not in order to understand what is seen . . . but just in order to see. Consequently, it does not seek the leisure of tarrying observantly, but rather seeks restlessness and the excitement of continual novelty and changing encounters. In not tarrying, curiosity is concerned with the constant possibility of distraction. . . . Both this not tarrying in the environment and this distraction by new possibilities are constitutive items for curiosity; and, upon these is founded the third essential characteristic of this phenomenon, which we will call the character of never-dwelling-anywhere [Aufenthaltslosigkeit].[21]

As Heidegger suggests, the character of "never-dwelling-anywhere" points to the relationship between the "curious" and the "distracted" gaze, for both succumb to the restlessness and banality of the merely novel ("what one 'must' have read or seen"). In his later writings on poetry and language in the 1930s and 1940s, Heidegger specifically links the most "distracted" cultural activities to the "everyday" phenomena of mass culture—the cinema, the illustrated press, and television.[22] Rehearsing a mode of perception which Heidegger calls "amazed to the point of not understanding," these mass cultural practices produce the world as image, as picture, as purely subjective experience. As he explains in his 1938 essay "The Age of the World Picture,"

The fundamental event of the modern age is the conquest of the world as picture. The word "picture" [Bild] now means the structured image [Gebild] that is the creature of man's producing which represents and sets before. In such producing, man contends for the position in which he can be that particular being who gives the measure and draws up the guidelines for everything that is.[23]

[21] Martin Heidegger, *Being and Time*, trans. John Macquarrie and Edward Robinson (New York: Harper and Row, 1962), 216–17.

[22] See, for example, Heidegger's series of essays collected in *Poetry, Language, Thought*, trans. Alfred Hofstader (New York: Harper and Row, 1972). Heidegger was perhaps most explicit in his condemnation of mass culture in his 1955 lecture entitled "Memorial Address." This address is available in English in *Discourse on Thinking*, trans. John M. Anderson and E. Hans Freund (New York: Harper and Row, 1966), 43–47.

[23] Martin Heidegger, "The Age of the World Picture," in *The Question Concerning*

Heidegger's assessment of mass culture would seem to anticipate the feminist critique of representation for securing the male viewer in a position of mastery over the visual field. But where the feminist critique insists on the manner in which the *woman* is made into an object for the pleasure of the male gaze, Heidegger's analysis suggests how it is *man* himself who experiences becoming and then being an image, who is made to yield his existence for another's use.[24] In an early section of *Being and Time*, for example, Heidegger writes:

> *Dasein's* everyday possibilities of Being are for the Others to dispose of as they please. These Others, moreover, are not *definite* Others. On the contrary, any Other can represent them. . . . In this inconspicuousness and unascertainability, the real dictatorship of the "they" is unfolded. We take pleasure and enjoy ourselves as *they* take pleasure; we read, see, and judge about literature and art as *they* see and judge; likewise, we shrink back from the 'great mass' as *they* shrink back; we find 'shocking' what *they* find shocking. . . . Overnight, everything that is primordial gets glossed over as something that has long been well known. Everything gained by a struggle becomes just something to be manipulated. Every secret loses its force.[25]

According to Heidegger, the subject ought to distance himself from the tyranny of the "they"—from that seductive force of "distraction" which remains the preserve of others. In his view, only painting and poetry afford such distancing, since both artistic forms demand a leisurely "contemplation" that not only provokes reflection but also allows for a repossession of self (*Eigentlichkeit*). If Heidegger clearly refuses the kind of mastery he associates with a mass-produced visual culture, he also resists its effects of depersonalization and loss; in other words, contemplation becomes a means of compensating for powerlessness, a way of overcoming the radical

Technology, trans. William Lovitt (New York: Harper and Row, 1974), 134. "Die Zeit des Weltbildes" was first given as a lecture at Freiburg University in June 1938.

[24] Alice Jardine also makes this point in relation to Heidegger, Benjamin, and Barthes. See her interesting and important discussion of these three theorists in *Gynesis: Configurations of Woman and Modernity* (Ithaca, N.Y.: Cornell University Press, 1985), 73–75.

[25] Heidegger, *Being and Time*, 164–65.

otherness of the self in a more detached and, hence, more intellectually mediated aesthetic experience.

This brief analysis suggests how Heidegger retains the familiar distinctions between art and mass culture and the structures of contemplation and distraction associated with each. Significantly, however, "distraction" comes to figure in Heidegger's writings both as a perceptual response to mass culture and as the originary structure of experience—the splitting and division of the subject in language. In view of this apparently paradoxical "double meaning" of distraction, it is crucial to raise the following questions: What is the relationship between the "alienation" of mass culture and the "dissociation" of the subject in language? And does this alienation or dissociation have something to do with sexual difference?

As Derrida has suggested, Heidegger employs the concept of "distraction" in order to address the role of sexual duality in the constitution of modern experience.[26] This is not to say that Heidegger recognizes sexual duality as constitutive of different experiences in the modern world; on the contrary, he sees duality as concealing a neutrality and even a certain asexuality in our experience of being-in-the-world (our experience of being-there as marked by the term *Da-sein*). In a close reading of a series of lectures Heidegger delivered at the University of Marburg in 1928, Derrida details and defends Heidegger's attempt to "neutralize" the issue of sexual duality since, in Derrida's view, it is only by neutralizing questions of sexuality and experience that Heidegger avoids the binary logic inherent in anthropology, biology, and psychology.

Derrida points out that in his Marburg lectures, Heidegger is quite careful to pass from the masculine to the neutral term when defining the theme of his analysis: "For the being which constitutes the theme of this analysis," Heidegger writes, "we have not chosen the heading 'man' (*der Mensch*) but the neutral heading '*das Dasein*.' "[27] Heidegger's neutralization of the question of being, Derrida further remarks, also carries over to his postulation of a certain neutrality or asexuality of experience (*das Dasein*). Again, as Heidegger writes, "the neutrality signifies also that the *Dasein* is neither one of the two sexes."[28] For both Heidegger and Derrida, the

---

[26] Derrida, "Geschlecht."
[27] Quoted in Derrida, "Geschlecht," 421.
[28] Quoted in Derrida, "Geschlecht," 422.

neutrality of *Dasein* or our experience of being-in-the-world does not mark a negativity, but instead marks a positivity or powerfulness (*Mächtigkeit*). As Derrida puts it, "neutrality does not de-sexualize, rather to the contrary: it does not use ontological negativity with regard to sexuality itself (which it would instead liberate), but with regard to the mark of difference and, more strictly, to sexual duality."[29]

For Derrida, as for Heidegger, sexual difference is not a property of biology or something that originally exists in human beings. Nevertheless, because the question of "sexuality itself" comes to displace the concept of experience in the writings of both theorists, the historical and social construction of gender is effectively elided. Heidegger, for example, denies sexual difference a determining role in his analysis of experience because sexual duality marks a fundamental negativity (woman as non-man). At the same time, however, sexuality itself is said to retain a "neutral" signification (woman as the same as man) since it allows sexuality to emerge as multiplication, dissemination, even liberation. The subject whose sexuality is, in fact, liberated in the passage from the masculine (*der Mensch*) to the neutral (*das Dasein*) is suggested by the interpretive gesture which must repress the feminine term in order to achieve "neutrality." If, in this way, Heidegger's ontology avoids binary logic, it also effaces the feminine as a term within language and as a social position for women that is symbolically constructed and historically lived.

This is not to imply, however, that femininity as it relates to *male* identity is completely effaced in Heidegger's ontology. Heidegger's description of mass cultural dissociation (where the "I" is forced to yield his existence to the "they") leads him to argue for a repossession of self in contemplation—a repossession that will alone restore mastery under the conditions of pervasive powerlessness. If Heidegger's ontology represents a response to modernity and to the loss of cultural mastery, it would seem that something quite specific precipitated this loss: namely, the emergence of a mass cultural audience and the presence of others previously excluded from mass cultural reception. In this regard, it is symptomatic that Heidegger sees division both as constitutive of subjectivity and as de-

---

[29] Derrida, "Geschlecht," 423.

basing to cultural experience. Indeed, his plea for a "neutralization" of sexuality and experience would seem to be a plea to get beyond the difficulties of gender more generally: to dissolve the other which inhabits the self and, equally, to repress the other which contends for access to culture in the modern age.

PERCEPTION, MASS CULTURE, AND DISTRACTION: WALTER BENJAMIN AND SIEGFRIED KRACAUER

Benjamin recalled his sexual awakening when, en route to the synagogue on the Jewish New Year's Day, he became lost on the city streets. . . . [He writes:] "While I was wandering thus, I was suddenly and simultaneously overcome, on the one hand, by the thought 'Too late, time was up long ago, you'll never get there'—and, on the other, by a sense of the insignificance of all this, of the benefits of letting things take what course they would; and these two streams of consciousness converged irresistibly in an immense pleasure that filled me with blasphemous indifference toward the service, but exalted the street in which I stood as if it had already intimated to me the services of procurement it was later to render to my awakened drive."[30]

Few theorists have addressed Benjamin's fascination with the city and the street as it reveals assumptions about sexuality and sexual difference.[31] Indeed, it is not sexual politics but politics in general which remains the central topic of debate in Benjamin criticism. As one commentator puts it, "The Left has been . . . concerned to defend [Benjamin's] legacy from mystical appropriations of it, the Right to establish its distance from any orthodox canon of historical materialism."[32]

[30] Susan Buck-Morss, "Benjamin's Passagen-Werk: Redeeming Mass Culture for the Revolution," *New German Critique*, no. 29 (Spring–Summer 1983): 223, fn. 27.

[31] Notable exceptions, however, would include Heide Schlüpmann's discussion of early German film theory in her essay "Kinosucht," *Frauen und Film* 33 (October 1982): 45–52; and Christine Buci-Gluckmann's essay on Benjamin and allegory, "Catastrophic Utopia: The Feminine as Allegory of the Modern," *Representations* 14 (Spring 1986): 220–29.

[32] Ronald Taylor, *Aesthetics and Politics: Debates Between Ernst Bloch, Georg Lukács, Bertolt Brecht, Walter Benjamin, Theodor Adorno,* ed. Ronald Taylor (London: New Left Books, 1977), 200.

If we are to believe those theorists who claim to position themselves on neither the Left nor the Right of this debate, Benjamin's
writings owe less to Marxism and to mysticism than they do to ontological phenomenology. In his introductory essay in *Reflections*,
for example, Peter Demetz argues that Benjamin's "hermeneutical
urge" to read cities and social institutions as if they were sacred
texts reveals his allegiance to Heideggerian philosophy or the "turn
to language which alone communicates what we can philosophically
know."[33] In much the same manner, Hannah Arendt maintains that
Benjamin was as keenly aware as Heidegger of "the break in tradition and loss of authority which occurred in his lifetime," and that
both theorists discovered strikingly similar ways of responding to
the past and the present. Benjamin's remarkable feeling for language and for history, she continues, confirms that he had more in
common with ontological thought than "he did with the dialectical
subtleties of his Marxist friends."[34]

Benjamin's reflection on language and history reveals the profoundly phenomenological dimension to his thinking (and it is to
Arendt's and Demetz's credit to have pointed this out). Nevertheless, this phenomenological dimension should not be confused with
Heideggerian philosophy, for it is Benjamin's attempt to combine
phenomenology with social theory that establishes his strongest intellectual affinities: not with Heidegger or ontological phenomenology, but with Siegfried Kracauer and critical theory.

As colleagues and collaborators, Benjamin and Kracauer are
among the first Weimar intellectuals to think seriously about the
perceptual as well as the political effects of mass-produced art on
subjectivity and experience. In contrast to Heidegger, who tends
to dismiss mass culture as thoroughly vacuous and degraded, Benjamin and Kracauer insist on the perceptual possibilities of photography and film and go so far as to claim that mass culture alone
responds to the changed reality of technological and industrial society. Drawing on the phenomenology of Georg Simmel,[35] Benja-

[33] Peter Demetz, "Introduction" to Benjamin's *Reflections: Essays, Aphorisms, Autobiographical Writings*, trans. Edmund Jephcott (New York and London: Harcourt
Brace Jovanovich, 1978), xxi.

[34] Hannah Arendt, "Introduction" to Benjamin's *Illuminations*, trans. Harry Zohn
(New York: Schocken Books, 1969), 46.

[35] A founding text of critical theory is indeed Georg Simmel's "Die Grossstadt und
das Geistesleben," in *Die Grossstadt: Jahrbuch der Gehe-Stiftung* (Dresden, 1903),

min and Kracauer consider the entire urban panorama—moving from photography to film to the city and the street—in an effort to discern how all aspects of modernity register the historical process in which an absorbed or concentrated gaze has been replaced by a more distracted mode of looking. While claiming to describe psychic and economic changes as these reveal structural changes of a general historical nature, Benjamin and Kracauer at the same time elaborate a theory of subjectivity which builds on a very specific theory of sexuality and sexual difference.

In his essay "Some Motifs in Baudelaire," for example, Benjamin argues that "the experience of shock" has transformed the spatio-temporal register of sense perception. As he explains, modern modes of production and technology have submitted the human sensorium to a "complex kind of training." In order to cope with the rapid succession of ever-increasing stimuli, tactile senses have been trained in abruptness and optic senses have been trained to deal with distraction:

> The invention of the match around the middle of the nineteenth century brought forth a number of innovations which have one thing in common: one abrupt movement of the hand triggers a process of many steps. . . . One case in point is the telephone, where the lifting of a receiver has taken the place of a steady movement that used to be required to crank the older models. . . . Tactile experiences of this kind were joined by optic ones, such as are supplied by advertising pages of a newspaper or the traffic of a big city. Moving through this traffic involves the individual in a series of shocks and collisions. . . . Whereas Poe's passers-by cast glances in all directions which still appeared to be aimless, today's pedestrians are obliged to do so in order to orient themselves to traffic signals.[36]

187–206, reprinted in translation as "The Metropolis and Mental Life," in *The Sociology of Georg Simmel*, ed. Kurt H. Wolff (New York: The Free Press, 1950), 409–24. Although far less central to the development of critical theory, Simmel's writings on sexuality and the Woman's Question are of great interest. See the essays collected under the title *Georg Simmel: On Women, Sexuality, and Love*, trans. Guy Oakes (New Haven: Yale University Press, 1984).

[36] Walter Benjamin, "Über einige Motive bei Baudelaire," *Gesammelte Schriften* (hereafter cited as *GS*), vol. 1, part 2, ed. Rolf Tiedemann and Hermann Schweppen-

It is well known that Benjamin's response to these changing perceptual relations remains fundamentally ambivalent. In some instances, he argues that the modern experience of distraction and shock revealed in techniques of photography and film provide for a deepening of perception, extending the range of the "optical unconscious."[37] In other instances, however, he maintains that shock experience reduces the play of the imagination, inducing a fragmented perception that drains memory of its content.[38] Benjamin's ambivalence toward mass cultural distraction is perhaps most strikingly articulated in his essays on Baudelaire. Furthermore, the manner in which he expresses his ambivalence reveals how he often projected his own fear of and fascination with mass culture onto the figure of woman (in particular, the prostitute), and onto Baudelaire's description of the big-city crowd.

"As regards Baudelaire," Benjamin writes, "the masses were anything but external to him; indeed, it is easy to trace in his work a defensive reaction to their attraction and allure."[39] Benjamin defends his preference for Baudelaire's poetry by stressing that, in contrast to such conservative philosophers as Bergson, Baudelaire did not consider the poet to have privileged access to structures of experience and memory. Instead, like Benjamin himself, Baudelaire understood the need to direct attention to the metropolitan masses, for they alone came to experience modernity in the form of shock perception. As Benjamin acknowledges, if the metropolitan masses had a privileged relationship to modern experience, the

---

häuser (Frankfurt am Main: Suhrkamp, 1974), 630. This essay is available in English translation. See "Some Motifs in Baudelaire," in *Charles Baudelaire: A Lyric Poet in the Era of High Capitalism*, trans. Harry Zohn (London: New Left Books, 1973), 105–54.

[37] As Benjamin suggests through Baudelaire's example, "In his 'Salon de 1895,' Baudelaire lets the landscape pass in review, concluding with this admission: 'I long for the return of the dioramas whose enormous, crude magic subjects me to the spell of a useful illusion. I prefer looking at the backdrop paintings of the stage where I find my favorite dreams treated with consummate skill and tragic concision. Those things, so completely false, are for that reason much closer to the truth, whereas the majority of our landscape painters are liars precisely because they fail to lie.' " Benjamin, "Über einige Motive bei Baudelaire," 650; English translation, 151. See also "Das Kunstwerk im Zeitalter seiner technischen Reproduzierbarkeit," GS, vol. 1, part 2, first version, 431–69; second version, 471–508. The second version of this essay is available in English translation in Benjamin's *Illuminations*, 217–51.

[38] Benjamin, "Über einige Motive bei Baudelaire," 644; English translation, 146.

[39] Ibid., 620–21; English translation, 122.

spectacle of the masses also inspired fear and dread among the most sympathetic of observers. Poe and Engels, as Benjamin documents, found the big-city crowds "barbaric," a vortex of confusion inspiring fear, revulsion, even horror. And when Benjamin explains that it was precisely this image of the big-city crowd that became decisive for Baudelaire, he reveals how his own reaction to the spectacle of mass culture involves elements of attraction and dread, fascination and horror.

In Baudelaire's sonnet "A une passante," for example, Benjamin detects Baudelaire's attraction to a "figure that fascinates," an unknown woman mysteriously carried along by the crowd who comes to represent "the object of love which only a city dweller experiences."[40] That this figure becomes an object, however, anticipates the crowd's equally menacing aspect. The "distracted" gaze that has lost the ability to look in return—a crucial aspect of what Benjamin calls the "aura"—serves to describe a kind of looking which inspires as much fear as fascination in the poet:

> The deeper the remoteness which a glance has to overcome, the stronger will be the spell that is apt to emanate from the gaze. In eyes that look at us with mirrorlike blankness, the remoteness remains complete. . . . When such eyes come alive, it is with self-protective wariness of a wild animal hunting for prey. (Thus the eye of the whore scrutinizing passers-by is at the same time on its guard against the police. Baudelaire found the physiognomic type bred by this kind of life delineated in Constantin Guy's numerous drawings of prostitutes. "Her eyes, like those of a wild animal, are fixed on the distant horizon; they have the restlessness of a wild animal . . . but also the animal's sudden tense vigilance.")[41]

To cope with this experience of shock, Benjamin explains, Baudelaire adopted one of two strategies: either he would assume an "attitude of combat" and battle the crowd, or he would adopt the posture of the old women he describes in the cycle "Les Petites vieilles," who stand apart from the crowd, "unable to keep its pace, no longer participating with their thoughts in the present."[42] Ben-

[40] Ibid., 623; English translation, 125.
[41] Ibid., 649; English translation, 150–51.
[42] Ibid., 622; English translation, 123.

jamin thus assigns to the figure of woman in Baudelaire's poetry both the threatening character of distraction and the contained repose of distance. Nevertheless, at the conclusion of his essay, Benjamin recalls how Baudelaire imagined himself betrayed by the old women and suggests how this left him with only one option:

> To impress the crowd's meanness upon himself, [Baudelaire] envisaged the day on which even the lost women, the outcasts, would be ready to advocate a well-ordered life, condemn libertinism, and reject everything except money. Having been betrayed by these last allies of his, Baudelaire battled the crowd—with the impotent rage of someone fighting the rain or wind. This is the nature of something lived through (*Erlebnis*) to which Baudelaire has given the weight of an experience (*Erfahrung*). He indicated the price for which the sensation of the modern age might be had: the destruction of aura in the experience of shock.[43]

When read from the perspective of Benjamin's own critical ambivalence towards mass culture, these remarks concerning the "price" Baudelaire paid for his battle with the crowd acquire a special meaning. Benjamin, too, could not stand apart from the spectacle of mass culture but was determined to struggle with its contradictory meanings and effects. However compelling Benjamin's ambivalent relation to mass culture remains, it is important to recognize how this ambivalence came to be expressed through reference to the metaphorical figure of woman (a figure that stands as much for modernity as it does for the continually renewed search for a lost plenitude). Benjamin's essay on Baudelaire certainly provides us with enough clues to discern an ambivalence towards woman and mass culture, but it is only in his aphoristic and more speculative writing that these clues acquire the status of an explanation.

In his essay entitled "Central Park," Benjamin poses the following question: "When did the commodity come to the fore in the image of the city?" His response is composed of a remarkable series of metaphors and mythological correspondences which link the les-

---

[43] Ibid., 652–53; English translation, 154.

bian to the prostitute and the "masculinized woman," and all three female figures to commodity production and mass culture:

> The figure of the lesbian woman belongs in the most precise sense among the heroic models of Baudelaire. He expresses himself in the language of his Satanism. It can be just as easily expressed in unmetaphysical, critical language which grasps his avowal of "the modern" in its purely political meaning. The 19th century began to incorporate women wholesale into the process of commodity production. All theoreticians agreed that their specific femininity was thus threatened; masculine traits would in the course of time also appear in women. Baudelaire affirmed these traits; but at the same time he wished to deny their economic necessity. Thus it is that he came to give a purely sexual accent to this evolving tendency in women. . . . For Baudelaire, prostitution is the yeast which allows the metropolitan masses to rise in his fantasy.[44]

Although Benjamin insists that commodity production threatens *woman's* femininity, his remarks here imply that *man's* masculinity is also at stake in the modern age. Indeed, it is not a matter of a shared identity between the man of letters and the prostitute or lesbian woman; instead, it is a particular identification on the part of the man of letters with an erotic, aggressive, and therefore profoundly "masculinized" female figure which inspires his ambivalence, and hence his overriding sense of anxiety in the modern age. It is perhaps for this reason that Benjamin's analyses of modernity differ from other theorists' of the period by being self-consciously historical and at the same time highly personal, less the product of a preconceived idea about mass culture and, to use Benjamin's own words, "more a convergence in memory of accumulated and frequently unconscious data."[45]

In essays on the cinema and mass culture which he wrote in the 1920s, Kracauer not only anticipated Benjamin's analysis of modernity by several years, but elaborated a similar theory of historical changes in structures of perception and experience. In his 1927

---

[44] Walter Benjamin, "Zentralpark," *GS*, vol. 1, part 2, 655–90; my citation is taken from Lloyd Spenser's translation of this essay in *New German Critique*, no. 34 (Winter 1985): 39–40.

[45] Benjamin, "Über einige Motive bei Baudelaire," 608; English translation, 110.

essay "Cult of Distraction" (*Kult der Zerstreuung*), for example, Kracauer maintains that distraction in the cinema models itself on the rationalization of labor more generally, and thus reveals how processes of abstraction have come to permeate forms of perception, representation, and experience. Kracauer therefore argues against those artists and intellectuals who condemn the cinema as a vacuous or superficial "distraction," explaining that such condemnation fails to understand that distraction involves a complete restructuring and a different logic in social reality:

> One says the Berliners are addicted to distraction [*zerstreuungssüchtig*]; this accusation is petit-bourgeois. Certainly the addiction is stronger here than in the provinces, but stronger and more apparent here is also the tension of the working masses—a basically formal tension that fills their day without making it fulfilling. . . . This emphasis on the external has the advantage of being *sincere*. Through it, truth is not threatened. Truth is threatened only by the naive affirmation of cultural values that have become unreal and by the careless misuse of concepts such as personality, inwardness, tragedy and so on, terms which themselves refer to lofty ideas but which have lost most of their scope along with their supporting foundations due to social changes.[46]

Kracauer's insistence on the "sincerity" of the commitment to distraction is not a simple endorsement of alienation in cinematic reception or industrial modes of labor. In fact, even though Kracauer criticizes artists and intellectuals for attempting to preserve outmoded aesthetic values, he explains that distraction in the cinema carries with it a contradictory "double meaning." On the one hand, Kracauer argues that cinematic distraction has potentially progressive effects, since it translates modes of industrial labor into a sensory, perceptual discourse which allows spectators to recognize the need for collective action under the changed conditions of modern social reality: "In the pure externality of the cinema, the audience meets itself, and the discontinuous sequence of splendid

---

[46] Siegfried Kracauer, "Kult der Zerstreuung," in *Das Ornament der Masse* (Frankfurt am Main: Suhrkamp, 1977), 313–14. This essay has recently been made available in English translation. See "Cult of Distraction: On Berlin's Picture Palaces," trans. Thomas Y. Levin, *New German Critique*, no. 40 (Winter 1987): 91–96.

sense impressions reveals to them their own daily reality. Were this reality to remain hidden from them, they could neither attack or change it."[47] On the other hand, Kracauer insists that cinematic distraction contains reactionary tendencies, since it rationalizes perception to such an extent that spectators fail to recognize forms of exploitation and therefore lose the ability to act: "The production and mindless consumption of abstract, ornamental patterns distract from the necessity to change the present order. Reason is impeded when the masses into which it should penetrate yield to emotions provided by the godless, mythological cult."[48]

Significantly, however, when Kracauer discerns the most reactionary tendencies of mass cultural reception, he refers less to an emotional involvement that impedes reason and more to a rationalized response that impedes involvement. In his 1931 essay "Girls and Crisis," for example, Kracauer suggests how mass culture has adopted the capitalist goals of streamlining and administration in order to mask contradiction and promote uncritical consumption. Choosing the American dance troupe The Tiller Girls to represent this trend, he writes:

> In that postwar era, in which prosperity appeared limitless and which could scarcely conceive of unemployment, the Girls were artificially manufactured in the USA and exported to Europe by the dozens. Not only were they American products; at the same time they demonstrated the greatness of American production. . . . When they formed an undulating snake, they radiantly illustrated the virtues of the conveyor belt; when they tapped their feet in fast tempo, it sounded like *business, business*; when they kicked their legs with mathematic precision, they joyously affirmed the progress of rationalization; and when they kept repeating the same movements without ever interrupting their routine, one envisioned an uninterrupted chain of autos gliding from the factories into the world, and believed that the blessings of prosperity had no end.[49]

[47] Ibid., 315.

[48] Siegfried Kracauer, "Das Ornament der Masse," in *Das Ornament der Masse*. This essay has also been reprinted in English translation as "The Mass Ornament," trans. Jack Zipes and Barbara Correll, *New German Critique*, no. 5 (Spring 1975): 67–76.

[49] Siegfried Kracauer, "Girls und Krise," *Frankfurter Zeitung* 27 (May 1931); quoted

Kracauer's description of the abstraction and fragmentation of the female body in the service of capitalist expansion attests to his awareness of the construction of woman in mass culture as spectacle, as object of desire and endless exchange. Yet it is clear that he is less interested in the cultural construction of woman than he is in the effects of rationalization on the mass cultural spectator. Kracauer suggests, for example, that the structures of seeing which the mass ornament develops in order to ensure its readability depend on images of artificially manufactured women. And while these images serve to reassure the mass cultural spectator, they also function to "distract" or divert attention away from the irrationality at the basis of a capitalist social order. Kracauer thus implies a correspondence between the untrustworthiness of the image and the vulnerability of the mass cultural spectator, since both run the risks he associates with femininity—the risks of passivity, uniformity, and uncritical consumption.

A somewhat different reading of mass culture and spectatorship emerges from Kracauer's series of sketches "The Little Shopgirls Go to the Movies" (1927).[50] Although he continues to associate the most dubious aspects of mass culture with passivity and femininity (for example, when he refers to the vacuity of the *Tippmamsells* or the "stupid little hearts" of the shopgirls), his analysis also reveals that modes of spectatorship and representation in Weimar were not always based on rationalized models. In the eighth sketch in the series, for example, Kracauer begins his analysis of film melodrama by describing a symptomatic narrative: A young woman, left in poverty by her father's suicide, is subsequently abandoned by her fiancé, who is concerned with promoting his career as a lieutenant and avoiding any hint of poverty or indecency. In order to support herself, the young woman takes a job under an assumed name as a dancer on the stage. After many years, the lieutenant and the woman meet again, only now the lieutenant wants to put things right and suggests marriage. But, as Kracauer explains, "the unselfish dancer poisons herself in order to force her lover, through her

in Karsten Witte, "Introduction to Siegfried Kracauer's 'The Mass Ornament,' " *New German Critique*, no. 5 (Spring 1975): 63–64.

[50] Siegfried Kracauer, "Die kleinen Ladenmädchen gehen ins Kino," in *Das Ornament der Masse*, 279–94.

death, to think only of his career."[51] Following this narrative description, Kracauer offers a critique of the sentimentality in film melodrama in which he implies a correspondence between the figure of woman in melodrama and the female spectator: "There are many people who sacrifice themselves nobly, because they are too lazy to rebel. Many tears are shed because to cry is sometimes easier than to think. The stronger the position of power in society, the more tragically act the weak and stupid."[52] At the conclusion of this critique, Kracauer adds a somewhat enigmatic remark: "Clandestinely the little shopgirls wipe their eyes and powder their noses before the lights come up."[53]

Despite its patronizing tone, Kracauer's analysis clearly contests the view that all cinematic practices require a rationalized or distracted attention; the little shopgirls may be momentarily distracted from everyday life, but they are clearly in a state of concentration at the movies. Indeed, it is Kracauer himself who is distracted by the presence of women in the cinema; shifting his gaze restlessly from audience to image, he looks at women in the act of looking rather than focusing his attention exclusively on the screen. It should be recalled that Kracauer holds distraction in the cinema to be reactionary only when spectators passively consume abstract, ornamental patterns and fail to recognize the loss of individual mastery under the changed conditions of modern social reality. While the emotional response of the little shopgirls may reveal an acknowledgment of a loss of social mastery, their concentrated gaze involves a perceptual activity that is neither passive nor entirely distracted. In an effort to resolve this apparent paradox, Kracauer concludes that when spectators acknowledge their loss of mastery, they often lose the ability to act.

Although Kracauer fails to consider his earlier argument about the recognition of powerlessness as positively enabling social action, his discussion of female spectatorship provides us with a starting point from which to challenge the view of the cinema and perceptual response in Weimar as thoroughly streamlined, rationalized, and distracted. In other words, even though Kracauer refers to the little shopgirls and film melodrama in a disparaging man-

---

[51] Ibid., 291–92.
[52] Ibid., 292.
[53] Ibid., 292–93.

ner, his analysis nonetheless suggests the existence of a mode of spectatorship and form of representation that failed to keep pace with rationalized models in the realm of leisure. Following from Kracauer's observations, we may suspect that women's relationship to modernity was entirely different from what was commonly projected onto the figure of woman during the Weimar period. Indeed, it would seem that women's relationship to modernity and mass culture has all too frequently been confused with male desire, and with male perceptions of gender difference.

MEN'S MODERNISM VERSUS WOMEN'S MODERNITY: WEIMAR WOMEN AT WORK AND AT THE MOVIES

It is one thing to claim that modernity has transformed the structure of experience, but it is quite another to conclude that various phenomena of modernity, such as film, photography, and mass culture, have transformed experience so profoundly that they admit only one form of perception or one kind of experience: the form constitutive of the male spectator or subject.

However, it would be difficult to deny the similarities between early assessments of perception and representation in Weimar and contemporary theories of the cinema and spectatorship. The writings of Heidegger, Benjamin, and Kracauer serve in many ways to corroborate what Christian Metz has described as the inherently masculine economy of film technology and spectatorship, where the cinema exists as a male prerogative and vision remains a masculine privilege. More precisely, the implicit reliance on male identity in early theories of perception would seem to confirm Mary Ann Doane's argument about the nonidentity of woman in theories of representation and spectatorship: the overpresence of woman as object or metaphor and her nonexistence as subject within a phallocentric discourse.

But unless we want to dispense with the possibility of understanding female spectatorship altogether, it is crucial to challenge the assumption that cinematic vision is inherently masculine or that the cinema and mass culture are synonymous with the further repression and exclusion of women. As I have suggested, the almost obsessive attempt to preserve male authority in Weimar reveals a parallel effort to distance a mass cultural audience perceived as threatening, as other, and as female. The presence of women in the modern city—on the streets, in industry, in the arts, and in the cinema—obviously distracted the attention of male intellectuals, who aimed to efface or at least to contain the power of the female gaze.[54] And while this strategy of containment certainly testifies to the tenacity of male desire, it also points to a threat that was neither purely imaginary nor metaphorical. In other words, mass culture and the cinema in Weimar cannot be aligned simply with the further exclusion of women, since both domains, given their economic interests, were in many ways responsive to women's demands for a greater share in German cultural life.

The growing visibility of *women* in Weimar in fact helps explain the defensive reaction toward *woman* in the discourses of artists and intellectuals: their attempt to distance and thereby master the threat perceived as too close, too present, too overwhelming. While this defensive reaction can be explained in psychic terms (the threat of castration, the trauma inspired by the female body), it can be explained in historical and economic terms as well. For example, German law prohibited women from attending public meetings or joining political organizations until 1908.[55] Even after women were granted the right to assemble, the very act of a woman attending a public gathering was considered scandalous,

[54] A number of theorists have recently attempted to retrieve the concept of "distraction" for a theory of the female spectator. See, for example, the special issue on Weimar film theory in *New German Critique*, no. 40 (Winter 1987), edited by David Bathrick, Thomas Elsaesser, and Miriam Hansen. However, I have endeavored to show that although distraction was often associated with a female figure or the female gaze, it was the male critic who was in fact most distracted in the cinema, particularly by the presence of women in the audience. The intensity of the female gaze, as registered in the writings of male critics, has also led me to theorize female spectatorship in relation to the concept of "contemplation," which I discuss more fully in chapter 4. In associating a contemplative aesthetic with female spectatorship, I aim to challenge the assumption that contemplating distraction was the sole prerogative of male intellectual audiences in Weimar. Meaghan Morris makes a similar point in her book *Upward Mobility*, and poses what I believe to be a crucial question about women and modernity. "In this project," she writes, "I prefer to study . . . the everyday, the so-called banal, the supposedly un- or non-experimental, asking not, 'why does it fall short of modernism?' but:—'how do classical theories of modernism fall short of women's modernity?' " See Meaghan Morris, *Upward Mobility* (Bloomington, In.: Indiana University Press, forthcoming 1989).

[55] For a discussion of the legal status of women in turn-of-the-century Germany, see Quataert, *Reluctant Feminists in German Social Democracy.*

even immoral. Nevertheless, the cultural sanction against women's right to assemble was not heeded by the promoters of mass cultural entertainment, who sought to capitalize on changes in women's legal status and thus to profit from the economic potential of female audiences. The cinema, in particular, became one of the few places in German cultural life that afforded women a prominent position and privileged access, and the growing visibility of women at the movies did not go unnoticed by those who held mass culture responsible for exacerbating the decay of standards brought about by technology and industrial rationalization.

Of course, it was not only the presence of women at the movies but also their visibility in traditionally male spheres of labor that provoked resentment and contributed to the perception that women had made enormous strides toward reaching economic parity with men during the Weimar years. (This latter perception may indeed account for the attempt by media institutions to cater to female audiences, since women were now considered to have disposable incomes of their own.) The intensive rationalization of industry after 1925, for instance, made the hiring of cheap, unskilled labor possible—and women were a readily available source. While women never came close to replacing men in industry (and never achieved anything like economic parity in the workplace), the very fact of an industrial female labor force was nevertheless considered a powerful challenge to traditional divisions of male and female labor (figure 6). As historian Renate Bridenthal explains, "the picture of women streaming into assembly-line jobs while men were pounding the pavement looking for work [gives] a superficially persuasive but fundamentally misleading impression. Contrary to the commonly held assumption, loudly voiced during the Depression, women were not displacing men. Rather, they were themselves displaced, moving out of agriculture and home industry into factories where they were more visible as a workforce and thus more likely to provoke resentment."[56]

[56] Renate Bridenthal, "Beyond *Kinder, Küche, Kirche*: Weimar Women at Work," *Central European History* 6, no. 2 (June 1973): 158. This essay has also been reprinted, with additions from another author. See Renate Bridenthal and Claudia Koonz, "Beyond *Kinder, Küche, Kirche*: Weimar Women in Politics and Work," in *Liberating Women's History: Theoretical and Critical Essays*, ed. Berenice A. Carroll (Champaign, Il.: University of Illinois Press, 1976), 301–29.

The presence of women in places they had never been before (notably, in industry and in the cinema) explains the perceived threat of woman registered in various discourses during the Weimar years. And while it would be a mistake to assume that either the workplace or the cinema was entirely liberating for women, it would also be wrong to confuse male perceptions of woman with women's perception, for to do so would be to mistake male desire for female subjectivity.

To theorize female subjectivity in Weimar requires that we revise notions about perception and spectatorship in the cinema and explore the ways in which modernity was experienced differently by women during the 1920s. The female spectator's rapt attention in the cinema, for example, suggests that women were indeed situated differently from men with respect to the image and to structures of looking. In psychic terms alone, we may say that women did not share the male fear of the female body, and thus did not retain the same investment in aesthetic distance and detachment. Although the female spectator's particular passion for perceiving was commonly disparaged and set against the male spectator's more objective, detached, and hence more mediated gaze, it is obvious that women's closeness to the image can only be conceived as a "deficiency" within a masculine epistemology. In other words, women's absorption in the image can only be considered regressive or dangerous if representation itself is assumed to be so thoroughly masculine that it admits only one kind of vision or perceptual response. The threat of losing oneself in mass culture, it should be recalled, was central to Heidegger's claim that the loss of self is inseparable from the specter of losing oneself to others. Since it would be difficult to equate this sense of self with female subjectivity, it becomes crucial to discern the psychic and historical determinants of women's experience in Weimar—their experience of mass culture and of everyday life as well.

Here the writings of Benjamin, Kracauer, and Heidegger prove useful in revising notions about spectatorship and perception in Weimar. In spite of their almost exclusive attention to male spectatorship and identity, all three theorists aim to account for the ways in which sense perception is neither natural nor biological but the result of a long process of differentiation within human history.

Figure 6. Women and rationalization
(*Berliner Illustrirte Zeitung*, 1930)

Die Abbildung zeigt den großen klimatisch regulierten Mischungssaal für die

REEMTSMA-CIGARETTEN

OVA

5 Pf.

Each theorist succeeds to a certain degree, even as each only partially manages to account historically for his own experience of this process. Benjamin's analysis of changes in perception, for example, clearly underscores the ways in which technology and capitalism have transformed vision and experience. Furthermore, Benjamin focuses his attention on the metropolitan masses since, in his view, the masses alone have a privileged relation to industrial modes of labor and thus to changes in perception and experience. While Benjamin insists on the historical nature of subjectivity and experience, his apparently gender-neutral concept of "the masses" nevertheless elides any discussion of female subjectivity, proposing that all forms of perception are modeled on industrial modes of labor and reveal the extent to which an absorbed or concentrated gaze has been replaced by a distracted and defensive way of looking. However, Benjamin's approach to questions of perception and experience can still be appropriated for an analysis of female subjectivity in Weimar, since his strategy of tracing possibilities for engagement in the cinema reveals as much about the parameters of perceptual responses to modernity as it does about different social experiences: that is to say, about experiences of cultural and economic change that were not accompanied by fundamental changes in the cultural definition of labor.

The years between 1916 and 1929, for example, are commonly described as years of intensive and rapid transition in the employment patterns of German women. Historian Tim Mason explains that "older types of work, many of them of a pre-industrial kind, persisted alongside a proliferation of new opportunities in commerce, administration and industry, and in the 1920s, women had a remarkably wide range of roles in the economy."[57] But, as Mason goes on to point out, this apparently remarkable range of roles served merely to reflect in an accentuated form the unequal development of German capitalism as a whole: the tensions within a social and economic structure in which technically advanced industrial monopolies existed side-by-side with peasant farms and economically precarious corner shops. For women seeking employ-

---

[57] Tim Mason, "Women in Germany, 1925–1940: Family, Welfare and Work," *History Workshop: A Journal of Socialist Historians* 1 (Spring 1976): 78.

ment outside the home, this usually meant that job possibilities were limited to the least modern sectors of the economy: shops, bars, cafes, or the workshops of husbands, fathers, or other male relatives. The vast majority of women in Weimar, moreover, lived on unearned income, or pensions, or the earnings of children or husbands: the vast majority of women, in other words, did not work outside the home at all.[58]

The economic crises in Germany in the 1920s merely exacerbated the already precarious definition of women's work in the industrial and domestic spheres. Women who kept their jobs in industry, for instance, typically suffered cutbacks in unemployment insurance, received lower compensation due to an original wage differential, and in many cases were more likely to find employment in uninsured home industry or temporary jobs.[59] After 1925, when the demand for unskilled, underpaid female labor actually increased, women's household tasks similarly increased. Historian Atina Grossmann points out that inflation and depression particularly affected lower-middle- and working-class women, who not only fell victim to unemployment but also endured physical and emotional stress, since most of them had two additional jobs: housework and childcare. "On a material level," Grossmann explains, "social reproduction such as health care and food production was reprivatized into individual households" as a result of governmental cutbacks in social welfare. Furthermore, on an emotional level, "women were called upon to stabilize the family in a turbulent time, to soothe the tensions of unemployment, and to mediate the conflicts supposedly caused by increased competition for jobs between men and women."[60] Given the multiple demands placed on female labor during the 1920s, it is hardly surprising that women often experienced modernity as merely intensifying traditionally defined gender roles and responsibilities.

The positioning of women's work between modernity and tradi-

[58] Ibid., 77–79.

[59] Atina Grossmann, "Abortion and Economic Crisis: The 1931 Campaign Against Paragraph 218 in Germany," *New German Critique*, no. 14 (Spring 1978): 119–38.

[60] Atina Grossmann, "The New Woman and the Rationalization of Sexuality in Weimar Germany," in *Powers of Desire: The Politics of Sexuality*, ed. Ann Snitow, Christine Stansell, and Sharon Thompson (New York: Monthly Review Press, 1983), 157.

tion may also account for what Kracauer recognized as the female spectator's very different mode of attention in the cinema. The sensory deprivation of household labor, where women were called on to manage an ever more precarious family existence, may indeed explain women's particular passion for the cinema: their desire to escape the monotony of routine in the heightened experience of filmviewing. Kracauer's analysis certainly suggests that female viewers were capable of maintaining a high degree of perceptual activity (managing turns in narrative development as well as shifts in point of view), even while they were intensely involved with the images on the screen. And although Kracauer implies that the absorbed attention of the little shopgirls in the cinema has nothing to do with contemplation (given his view that they are merely "swept away" by the image and lack the capacity to reflect on its meaning), a contemplative aesthetic may actually account for women's emotional and highly concentrated gaze, precisely because it afforded the kind of heightened sensory experience which simultaneously responded to and compensated for women's experiences of everyday life.

To associate the film melodrama with a contemplative aesthetic does not necessarily entail sustaining the kind of distinction between art and mass culture that Heidegger makes in his use of contemplation as a perceptual category. Indeed, although Heidegger believes mass culture to be thoroughly rationalized and degraded, it is obvious that mass culture in Weimar actually adapted older artistic conventions within the context of popular forms. Furthermore, although Heidegger links contemplation to perceptual distance and intellectual detachment, it is reasonable to assume that a contemplative aesthetic may also account for the female viewer's intensely concentrated gaze. For male intellectuals, who experienced the demise of poetic forms with the advent of cinema, the film melodrama may have in fact entailed disinterestedness and detachment, but for female audiences, who were only just beginning to be addressed as spectators, the film melodrama almost certainly provoked an intensely interested and emotional involvement, particularly since melodramatic representation often gave heightened expression to women's experiences of modernity.[61]

[61] On this point, see Wolfgang Schivelbusch's analysis of changes in the perceptual

Once we understand the appeal of contemplation in this way, it becomes possible to appropriate certain tenets of Heideggerian phenomenology for a more precise conceptualization of female spectatorship. Heidegger's critique of epistemology for holding vision alone to confirm knowledge and subjectivity, for example, is especially useful for revising clichés about gendered spectatorship. The female spectator's concentrated attention in the cinema cannot be understood in terms of vision alone, since modes of looking— even contemplative modes of looking—only become meaningful when we attend to the historical determinants of subjectivity and experience. Male or female spectatorship, in other words, cannot be theorized apart from questions of gender and experience, for perceptual response is constructed as much in history as it is by positioning and address within individual films.

To insist on gendered spectatorship and perceptual difference is thus to insist on differentiations within mass cultural production. Although theorists in the 1920s tended to universalize mass culture by appealing to concepts of distraction, rationality, and technological domination, it is clear that a number of textual practices in Weimar actually adapted conventions associated with more archaic representational forms. For example, Ruttmann's *Berlin. Symfonie einer Grossstadt* (*Berlin, Symphony of a Great City*) and Pabst's *Die freudlose Gasse* (*The Joyless Street*) take up similar issues of modernity and city life. But where Ruttmann's film directs our attention to the movement of objects in a fragmented urban space, Pabst's film involves an intensive relationship with images observed in a static urban space. Film and photojournalism in Weimar play out various scenarios of looking and respond to different versions of modernity so as to outline the terms of their own un-

---

apparatus in the nineteenth century in *The Railway Journey: Trains and Travel in the 19th Century*, trans. Anselm Hollo (Oxford: Basil Blackwell, 1980). Schivelbusch's assessment of the tension between older and newer modes of perception has informed my analysis of subjectivity and perception in the silent German film. Schivelbusch writes, for example, of the coexistence of different perceptual responses to train travel: "The lower classes, who really join the rank of travelers only after the advent of the railroad, are unencumbered by memories of previous forms of travel: thus the new forms are not as strange to them as they are to those classes that have to abandon their private coaches for the train" (70). If we substitute "cinema" for "railroad," and "women" for "lower classes," the implications of Schivelbusch's analysis for an understanding of the Weimar cinema become apparent.

derstanding. To discern the contours of gendered spectatorship in Weimar, it is therefore necessary to account for the differences between textual practices and their anticipated audiences, exploring photojournalism and film in relation to the image of the city, and in relation to the figure of the modern woman who invariably appears there.

WEIMAR PHOTOJOURNALISM AND THE FEMALE READER

·

What is the modern woman?
A charming *Bubikopf*—says the hairdresser
A model of depravity—says Aunt Klotilde
A complex of sexual problems—says the psychoanalyst
Comrade and soul friend—says the youth
Miserable housewife—says the reactionary
Expensive—says the bachelor
The best customer—says the stocking dealer
An unhappiness for my son—says the mother-in-law
The center of the sanitorium—says the doctor
The same, since the dawn of history—says the wise man.
—*Die Dame* (1925)[1]

G. W. Pabst's *Die Büchse der Pandora* (*Pandora's Box*, 1928) offers a particularly effective image of Weimar's modern woman. Following a trial sequence in which Lulu (Louise Brooks) is named a modern-day Pandora and then convicted of manslaughter, there is a fade to the apartment of Dr. Schoen (Fritz Kortner), Lulu's alleged victim and the now-deceased newspaper mogul. We next see Lulu, who has managed to elude the police by returning to Schoen's apartment. Momentarily free from the disapproving gaze of the judge and jury—from the authority which seeks to convict her both for the crime of murder and for the "crime" of female sexuality—Lulu unexpectedly stretches out and relaxes with an issue of *Die*

---

[1] *Die Dame*, Heft 4 (erstes Novemberheft 1925): 3.

Dame, an illustrated woman's magazine (figure 7). In this brief scene, which gives us remarkably little narrative information, Lulu is seen to derive a pleasure in looking which is not dependent on the gaze of a male who either fears or desires her. Indeed, in one of the rare moments in the film where Lulu is seen to have desires of her own, her desire in looking is simultaneous with her role as a female reader who is given something specific with which to identify.

I take Lulu in this scene to be exemplary of both the modern woman and the female reader in Weimar, particularly because this scene emphasizes a woman's pleasure in looking and because it marks an unambiguous instance of intertextual play. It is, in fact, highly significant that Pabst chooses to identify Lulu as a reader of *Die Dame*, a woman's magazine noted in the 1920s for its experimentation with gender roles and female sexual identity. As critics have pointed out, *Pandora's Box* is itself fundamentally concerned with issues of female sexuality (hence the presence of Countess Geschwitz, one of the first screen lesbians, and the film's very title which plays on the multiple meanings of "Büchse/Box.")[2] Although most critics have failed to consider issues of androgyny and lesbianism in Pabst's film as they relate to a female spectator, preferring instead to treat the representation of female desire as the mirror image of male desire or male homosocial relations, I would like to suggest that *Pandora's Box* provides us with the clues to discern the historical process by which the popular arts in Weimar attempted to address a female viewing audience. Pabst's self-conscious reference to *Die Dame*, and the film's more general appeal to conventions associated with the illustrated press, in fact invite us to take up questions of female subjectivity and desire as they were constructed within an expanded representational field.

There are, of course, important precedents for considering the intertextual nature of representation and spectatorship in the Weimar cinema. Lotte Eisner's *The Haunted Screen*, for instance, provides a detailed analysis of theatrical influences on the German silent film: the impact of expressionist drama on cinematic acting styles, and the influence of various innovations in stage direction

---

[2] Thomas Elsaesser makes this point in his essay "Lulu and the Meter Man: Louise Brooks, Pabst, and *Pandora's Box*," *Screen* 24, nos. 4–5 (July–October 1983): 33.

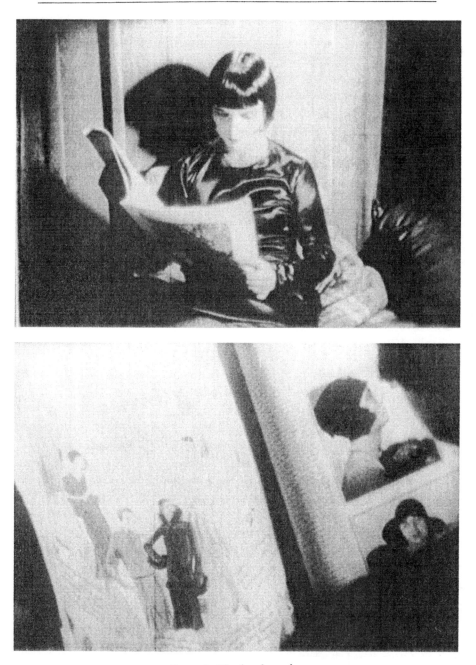

Figure 7. The female reader
(*Pandora's Box*, 1928)

(notably, those associated with Max Reinhardt, Leopold Jessner, and Erwin Piscator) on film space and mise-en-scène.[3] More recently, Janet Bergstrom has drawn attention to particular genres and styles in painting (especially those associated with the Symbolists and Pre-Raphaelites) in an effort to demonstrate how modes of looking in the Weimar cinema were frequently adapted from traditions in the fine arts.[4] For Eisner, as for Bergstrom, questions of representation in the Weimar cinema are best understood once the boundaries of the cinematic text are expanded to include other dramatic and artistic forms. In other words, both insist on filmic textuality as an intertextuality, where the individual film remains a manifestation of wider historical processes in the arts.

While I share Eisner's and Bergstrom's interest in questions of intertextuality, I believe that the illustrated press constitutes one of the most relevant intertexts for understanding gender and spectatorship in the Weimar cinema. I do not mean to underestimate the significance or importance of other entertainment forms in Weimar; the theatricality of the film melodrama, for instance, clearly owes much to conventions adapted from the popular stage and, as Eisner's study convincingly suggests, the theater became for the Weimar cinema what vaudeville had been for the American: an entertainment form representative of the period before the advent of filmmaking, upon which the cinema subsequently modeled itself. It is nevertheless symptomatic that most analyses of intertextuality in Weimar have been confined to traditions in the established arts. In her analysis of conventions relating to gender and looking in the Weimar cinema, for example, Bergstrom focuses on the representation of the male body in film and the fine arts, linking the destabilization of male identity in Murnau's films to a broadly defined historical audience—to "an audience willing to look at film with the pace and attention required in looking at paintings."[5] Her assessment of sexual ambiguity in the Weimar cinema therefore implies an intertextual as well as a social mode of address: unstable sexual identity, she suggests, refers primarily to

---

[3] Lotte Eisner, *The Haunted Screen* (Berkeley and Los Angeles: University of California Press, 1969).

[4] Janet Bergstrom, "Sexuality at a Loss: The Films of F. W. Murnau," *Poetics Today* 6, nos. 1–2 (1985): 185–203.

[5] Ibid., 202.

the representation of male identity and serves to highlight the homoerotic component of spectator identification among intellectual audiences. Close analysis of Weimar photojournalism, however, reveals that the androgynous or feminized male figure was a staple feature in women's fashion magazines, and that androgyny was not confined to male identity alone. The androgyny of the New Woman—the female figure who appropriated masculine styles and gestures—was a common element in photojournalism and film and also the topic of extended and heated debate in the illustrated press. Given the institutional connection between press and film in Weimar, this shared concern with female gender identity is hardly surprising, not only because the illustrated press often assumed a gender-specific readership, but also because issues of sexuality loomed large in the press where they often took on an explicitly political and ideological dimension.[6]

It would not be entirely accurate, however, to imply that film scholars have somehow purposely ignored the illustrated press in their analyses of the Weimar cinema. Indeed, research into twenties photojournalism remains extremely problematic, not least of all given the situation of press archives in post–World War II Germany.[7] While the difficulties presented by research into Weimar

[6] As this book goes to press, I have learned of Maud Lavin's interesting work on "Hannah Höch, Photomontage, and the Representation of the New Woman in Weimar Germany" (dissertation in progress at the C.U.N.Y. Graduate Center). Lavin's study intersects at several points with my own, although she focuses on photojournalism in relation to the work of a female avant-garde artist, rather than on photojournalism in its specific relationship to film.

[7] Press archives in Berlin, for example, register the historical effects of foreign occupation and political division: while most newspapers and magazines were confiscated by the Allies and preserved in West Berlin, the indexes to these journals were retained in East Berlin. In 1984, various indexes were finally put on microfilm and made available to Western scholars; prior to this, any serious research into the press necessitated constant travel between East and West. In addition to the difficulties stemming from occupation and division, there are also a number of problems traceable to the pre–World War II period. To begin with, much of the left-wing press was destroyed by the Nazi regime, and those leftist publications that survived the fascist era did so only in private collections. The press archive in Leipzig has recently done a great deal of work in retrieving left-wing magazines, but it still remains difficult for Western scholars to get access to these documents. Finally, and perhaps most importantly, a vast number of early illustrated magazines were never preserved, since their mass cultural status marked them as trivial and immediately disposable—in other words, as undeserving of a place in state or federal archives.

Although I learned much about press archives from firsthand experience, I am in-

photojournalism should therefore not be underestimated, problems of research do not suffice to explain the pervasive blindness
toward issues of sexuality and gender in existing studies of the illustrated press. Scholars who have successfully tackled the obsta-
cles to archival research, for example, almost invariably highlight
the political function of the press during the Weimar Republic. In
a sense, this focus on politics is entirely justified, since the topical-
ity of the illustrated press virtually demands a political and ideological assessment. But even the most sophisticated analyses of Weimar photojournalism build on a rather dubious notion about the
"politics" of representation in Germany of the 1920s; politics are
either inherently institutional or fundamentally textual, but there
is absolutely no attempt to link the politics of representation to the
sexual politics of the day.

In the following pages, I explore the relationships among institutions, texts, and the politics of sexuality in Weimar so as to situate the address to female audiences in a more extensive historical
context. Since both press and film were engaged in a concerted
effort to address a highly profitable female audience, discussion of
their common strategies of representation should reveal the extent
to which the politics of media institutions are linked to the politics
of sexual difference, and thus how the gendered subject remains a
crucial category for understanding representation in the Weimar
period.

INSTITUTIONAL AND TEXTUAL POLITICS: PHOTOJOURNALISM AND FILM IN WEIMAR

The symbolic construction of gender does not seem to have concerned historians of the illustrated press, who focus their attention
almost exclusively on the political organization of various media institutions. Indeed, for those who have surveyed the development
of Weimar photojournalism, the political effects of media institutions and textual practices are determined solely by the political
affiliations of various "media empires": Alfred Hugenberg's conservative Scherl Publishing Company, the liberal House of Ullstein,

debted to numerous conversations with Professor Diethart Kerbs, who generously
shared with me his ideas and research on photojournalism and photography in Weimar.

and Willi Münzenberg's communist International Workers Aid (*Internationale Arbeiterhilfe*, or IAH).[8]

In his monograph *Weimar Culture*, for example, Peter Gay reiterates the commonplace view of media institutions in the 1920s when he explains that the political ideology of individual "press lords" had a direct impact on film and press production. Alfred Hugenberg, he argues, "was a hopelessly reactionary and politically ambitious magnate [who] built up an empire in the communications industry and became the strident, enormously influential voice of counterrevolution."[9] Gay goes on to explain how Hugenberg's political interests were advanced through his acquisition of several local newspapers and, especially, through his takeover of the UFA studios in 1927. He writes: "Not all of Hugenberg's propagandistic efforts were so direct and blatant as the editorials in his newspapers; his UFA ground out films that helped his cause more indirectly—cheerful musicals which diverted attention away from politics and unemployment, historical films about German heroes with pointed allusions to the Versailles *Diktat*, and equally pointed celebrations of qualities that the men of Weimar conspicuously lacked."[10]

Gay's description of UFA's film production under Hugenberg serves to support his thesis that Weimar culture merely played out the father-son conflicts it inherited from expressionist literature and drama. Not surprisingly, his description of conservative and liberal media institutions implies a similar competition between "revengeful fathers" and "rebellious sons" (to paraphrase two of his chapter titles), where Hugenberg's reactionary designs on press and film faced serious competition from the liberal House of Ullstein. The Ullstein press, Gay explains, nearly dominated the popular magazine market: "Its weekly picture magazine, the *Berliner Illustrirte*, claimed to be the most widely read magazine of its kind in Europe. In the profitable field of women's magazines, Ullstein's

[8] The assumption of a direct relationship between textual politics and the political affiliations of various media empires in Weimar is pervasive in cultural and economic histories of the period. For a representative example of this approach, see the essays collected in *Germany in the Twenties: The Artist as Social Critic*, ed. Frank D. Hirschbach et al. (New York: Holmes and Meier, 1980).

[9] Peter Gay, *Weimar Culture: The Outsider as Insider* (New York: Harper and Row, 1970), 133.

[10] Ibid., 134.

Die Dame was a leading journal. For middle-brow tastes, mixing well-tailored essays . . . and photographs of naked girls, there was the pocket-sized *Uhu*. Housewives had the well-edited *Blatt der Hausfrau*, children the *Heitere Fridolin*, and intellectuals . . . the *Querschnitt.*"[11] Gay concludes that Ullstein's monopoly on publishing was "remarkable, even frightening." But in keeping with his thesis, he maintains that Ullstein was nevertheless a liberal institution, and hence that its doors were open to a wide variety of opinions and positions.

It is significant that Gay's analysis of Oedipal rivalries between conservative and liberal media institutions fails to mention Münzenberg's IAH. In Gay's estimation, political affiliation translates into a direct political influence on media production: Hugenberg was conservative, hence UFA was conservative; Ullstein was liberal, hence its publications were liberal. Since the IAH was neither conservative nor liberal, Gay simply ignores it. It is equally significant that Gay uses the term "empire" to suggest a kind of political control and industrial management of culture that focuses attention on individual personalities rather than on the types of entrepreneurial capitalism which formed the organizational basis of media institutions in the 1920s. The Scherl Publishing Company, for example, was an expansive cartel which linked a number of firms, subsidiaries, and branches in loose corporate relationships. When Hugenberg's Scherl acquired the UFA studios in 1927, it also acquired a company which divided film production among various autonomous branches (i.e., publicity and film marketing, documentary film production, weekly newsreels, and feature film production).[12] Undoubtedly, one of the reasons for Scherl's acquisition of UFA was to displace Ullstein's interests in the company—interests which Ullstein had acquired early in 1921.[13] Yet even though nominal institutional authority for UFA could be traced to Hugenberg's Scherl

[11] Ibid., 134.

[12] For an analysis of film production at UFA, see Paul Monaco, *Cinema and Society: France and Germany During the Twenties* (New York, Oxford, and Amsterdam: Elsevier, 1976), 29–31.

[13] A brief discussion of the attempt by Hugenberg to outbid and discredit Ullstein's interests in UFA is provided by Klaus Jaeger, Horst-Diether Kalbfleisch, and Helmut Regel in *Der Weg ins Dritte Reich: Deutscher Film und Weimars Ende* (Oberhausen: Verlag Karl Maria Laufen, 1974), 116.

after 1927, UFA continued to carry out feature film production much in the way it had before.

This is not to say that Hugenberg exercised no political influence over newspapers or newsreel film production. It is merely to emphasize that neither Scherl nor Ullstein—nor the IAH for that matter—was organized around the kind of individual control that Gay describes, or on the model of industrial rationalization suggested by contemporary descriptions of a "culture industry."[14] Münzenberg's IAH, for example, was affiliated with and supported by the Comintern but retained considerable independence from it. The official program of the IAH was to create a flexible framework to attract sympathizers and uncommitted groups to the cause of international communism. At its height in 1931, the IAH comprised over nine hundred local groups and provided a host of social services: bureaus offering information about federal welfare benefits, children's homes, and nurseries, as well as campaigns for the repeal of paragraph 218 of the Penal Code which classified abortion as a felony.[15] The IAH also sponsored a variety of cultural activities: poetry and cabaret evenings, dance recitals and art exhibitions, film screenings and production, left-wing book clubs and the illustrated weekly newspaper, the *Arbeiter Illustrierte Zeitung* (AIZ).

The flexible institutional framework of the IAH also allowed for collaboration between artists and intellectuals, some of whom were communist supporters and some of whom were not. Furthermore,

[14] I am referring here to Kracauer's assessment of film production in Germany in his early essays collected in *Das Ornament der Masse* (Frankfurt am Main: Suhrkamp, 1977). As Karsten Witte has explained, Kracauer's use of the concept "distraction factory" (*Zerstreuungsfabrik*) as a metaphor for the places where the middle-class spends its leisure time "is what Horkheimer and Adorno later diagnosed as the trend of the 'culture industry.' " Witte continues: "In his pioneering study, *Die Angestellten* [*The White Collar Workers*, 1929], Kracauer employed a revealing metaphor to illustrate how quasi-militaristic regimentation became coupled with the Taylorization of the leisure-time industry: he described the amusement sports of the 'white collared ranks' as 'pleasure barracks.' " Witte, "Introduction to Siegfried Kracauer's 'The Mass Ornament,' " *New German Critique*, no. 5 (Spring 1975): 64.

[15] Helmut Gruber provides a detailed account of the IAH's social and artistic activities in his essay, "Willi Münzenberg's German Communist Propaganda Empire, 1921–1933," *Journal of Modern History* 38, no. 3 (September 1966): 278–97. Atina Grossmann also provides an excellent analysis of the IAH's involvement in campaigns for the repeal of paragraph 218 in her essay, "Abortion and Economic Crisis: The 1931 Campaign Against Paragraph 218 in Germany," *New German Critique*, no. 14 (Spring 1978), 119–38.

a number of contributors to the AIZ were also contributors to the
Ullstein press: Ernst Barlach, Bertolt Brecht, Käthe Kollwitz, Walter Hansenclever, Emil Nolde, Kurt Tucholsky, to name only a
few. Even the editor of the AIZ, Lilly Becher, began her journalistic career at Ullstein.[16] As these examples suggest, the relationship
between media institutions and textual practices in Weimar cannot
adequately be explained by referring to the political ideology of
individual personalities, or to the conflicts between conservative
and liberal institutions. Instead, recognizing the historically specific function of media institutions in Weimar in negotiating the
transition from early industrial to highly technological and commercial modes of production makes it possible to account for the
collaboration and intertextuality often in evidence between photojournalism and film.

Feature film production at UFA under Erich Pommer brought
together writers, scenarists, and actors from the established arts
and provided them with the institutional support to experiment
and collaborate in a highly technological medium.[17] The existence
of picture press agencies (*Pressbildagenturen*) similarly brought together freelance photographers and newspaper editors and allowed
for collaboration in the work of composing, editing, and placing
photoessays and montages.[18] The pages of the illustrated press typically incorporated serialized novels, poetry, lithographic prints,
high quality color reproductions of paintings, photomontages, and
photographs—in short, established literary and artistic practices as
well as newer, technological ones. It is not surprising that Weimar
film and photojournalism are often praised for their craftsmanship,

[16] Cited in Hanno Hardt and Karin Becker, "The Eyes of the Proletariat: The Worker
Photography Movement in Weimar Germany," *Studies in Visual Communication* 7, no.
4 (Fall 1981): 75.

[17] Feature film production at UFA under Pommer is briefly discussed by Thomas Elsaesser in his essay "Film History and Visual Pleasure: Weimar Cinema," *Cinema His-
tories/Cinema Practices*, ed. Patricia Mellencamp and Philip Rosen, The American Film
Institute Monograph Series, vol. 4 (Frederick, Md.: University Publications of America,
1984), 75–78. The institutional support for collaboration at UFA among scenarists, actors,
and writers from the established arts has been researched by Ursula Hardt, who is currently completing a dissertation at the University of Iowa entitled "Erich Pommer, Producer: Leaving a Mark on the History of the German Cinema."

[18] For an excellent analysis of picture-press agencies in Weimar, see Diethart Kerbs,
"Die Epoche der Bildagenturen," in *Die Gleichschaltung der Bilder: Pressefotografie
1930–1936* (Berlin: Frölich und Kaufmann, 1983), 32–73.

for their artistic qualities and level of technological sophistication. Neither avant-garde nor fully rationalized, film and photojournalism in Weimar negotiated traditional artistic practices and modes of production within the boundaries of commercial, mass cultural institutions.

The kinds of projects undertaken at UFA, Ullstein, and the IAH also suggest that textual experimentation was often accompanied by an address to female audiences. The UFA studios, for example, aimed to capture an international audience, whose importance was crucial to maintaining the economic viability of the German cinema, as well as a domestic audience, whose importance was equally crucial to establishing the cinema as a legitimate entertainment form in Germany.[19] Although UFA's aim to capture a domestic market has been seen as an attempt to address a minority intellectual audience alone,[20] there was a considerable degree of overlap in the production of films at UFA that catered to intellectuals and female audiences alike, most notably in the production of literary adaptations and film melodramas which featured such stars as Asta Nielsen and Henny Porten, who were extremely popular with female audiences. (That female audiences and, indeed, female intellectuals should have interests in common is a point to which I will return shortly.) The Ullstein press, for example, recognized the economic potential of female audiences by devoting its energies to women's magazines and by developing the scope and quality of its already popular *Die Dame*. The IAH was also well aware that it needed to attract German women to the cause of international communism, since the woman's vote was crucial to the success of the Communist Party in Germany. The IAH's attention to social services, its involvement in campaigns for the legalization of abortion, and its creation of a special woman's page in the AIZ were

[19] Janet Staiger and Douglas Gomery provide a useful analysis of UFA's attempt to compete in the international film market in their essay, "The History of World Cinema: Models for Economic Analysis," *Film Reader* 4 (1979): 35–44. For a discussion of UFA's attempt to capture a domestic market, see Siegfried Kracauer's *From Caligari to Hitler: A Psychological History of the German Film* (Princeton, N.J.: Princeton University Press, 1947); George Huaco, *The Sociology of Film Art* (New York: Basic Books, 1965); Andrew Tudor, *Image and Influence* (New York: St. Martin's Press, 1974); Monaco, *Cinema and Society*.

[20] See, for example, Elsaesser, "Film History and Visual Pleasure."

some of the ways in which it attempted to address the concerns of women voters and appeal to the interests of female audiences.

While media institutions clearly recognized the importance of female audiences, they also understood the need to channel and direct those audiences for commercial or political purposes. Not surprisingly, illustrated magazines and films in Weimar returned to remarkably similar issues when addressing female audiences—issues concerning sexuality, gender identity, and heterosexual relationships. In the bourgeois cinema and press, these issues were fundamentally bound to economics and consumerism—to the need to address women's experiences and bind them to pleasurable forms of consumption. In the left-wing cinema and press, these issues were highly controversial and potentially explosive, tied as they were to the long-standing ambivalence on the left toward the autonomy of women's interests. For example, while the AIZ did address women's experiences, it was also careful to link female oppression to capitalist oppression and to frame women's issues in such a way as not to alienate its male constituencies. The politics of representation in Weimar were therefore not simply those of conservative, liberal, and left-wing institutions; the politics of representation in Weimar were also indisputably the politics of gender.

MODES OF REPRESENTATION IN THE ILLUSTRATED PRESS

The German illustrated press developed two related representational strategies in order to gain audiences in an increasingly competitive magazine market: the cover photograph, which was designed to attract street sales, and the serialized novel (*Illustriertenroman*), which aimed to capture and keep readers' interest over a period of weeks, even months. The appeal to a new vision of women's modernity, however, was clearly responsible for the most significant gains in magazine circulation. As Hanno Hardt and Karin Becker point out in a recent study of the illustrated press, novels like Vicki Baum's *Stud. chem. Helene Willfüer* (1928), which tells the story of an unmarried working mother, added over

200,000 readers to the circulation of the *Berliner Illustrirte Zeitung* (BIZ).[21]

While such an address to female readers obviously affected magazine sales and promotional techniques, it also had an impact on cinematic representation and reception because the widespread circulation of images established conventions of representation re lating to female sexuality and gender identity, and new ways of perceiving modern life. The development of German photojournalism might in fact be described as a gradual turn to the visual and the cinematic, since the Weimar years mark the first time in the history of the German press that photographs began to take precedence over prose as the primary mode of journalistic communication. As Hardt and Becker suggest in an essay on Weimar worker photography:

> Old magazines from well-established houses such as Ullstein's *Berliner Illustrirte Zeitung* . . . were gradually redesigned to take advantage of this trend toward journalistic photography. New independent magazines, such as the *Münchner Illustrierte Press* and the *Kölnische Illustrierte Zeitung* . . . overcame their provincialism in part by using photography to establish cosmopolitan content and appeal. Nor was there any question that photographs could be directed toward political goals, for picture magazines covered the range of the political spectrum: from the National Socialist *Der Illustrierte Beobachter* to the communist party's principal organ, *Die Arbeiter Illustrierte Zeitung*.[22]

Not only did the "cosmopolitan content and appeal" of illustrated magazines establish a link between press and film; the composition and organization of photographs in the illustrated press also established this connection. By the late 1920s, a staple of the illustrated

[21] Karin Becker and Hanno Hardt, *Picture Story: The Birth of the Photo-Essay, 1928–1940*, unpublished manuscript. The successful marketing of Vicki Baum's novel with female readers is symptomatic of promotional strategies which were not limited to the Ullstein press alone. The *Arbeiter Illustrierte Zeitung* (AIZ), for example, followed up on the success and controversy of the Prometheus film *Cyankali* (1929) by serializing in its pages Franz Krey's novel *Maria und die Paragraph*, a story in which a young stenotypist survives a botched abortion. The success of this serialization is briefly discussed by Atina Grossmann in her essay, "Abortion and Economic Crisis."

[22] Hardt and Becker, "The Eyes of the Proletariat," 73.

press was the "photoessay": a series of photographs on a single topic edited as narrative in a single- or multiple-page format. The cinematic quality of the photoessay is perhaps most striking in the function of composition, camera angle, camera distance, and point of view in constructing the reading of the photoessay as narrative. Although in some photoessays the photographs were actually numbered in the order in which they were to be read, the majority of photoessays relied upon a degree of visual literacy or, perhaps more precisely, upon conventions already established by filmviewing. In 1930, for example, the BIZ published a photoessay which reported on the dangers of night driving in Berlin (figure 8). Five photographs, varying in shape and size, recount the staging of an accident on Potsdamer Platz: from the crowded and congested city streets (in long shot) to the auto accident and the arrival of the authorities (in one medium-long shot and two medium shots) to the condition of the victim pinned beneath the wheel of the car (in dramatic close-up and an extremely large half-page image). That this photoessay recounts a "staged event" or a narrative fiction is revealed by the captions beneath the photographs. That the composition and organization of images also elicit a reading of this photoessay as narrative becomes apparent when we consider how press photography adapted conventions from the cinema.

Of course, cinematic conventions were themselves adapted from traditions in the visual arts, and the turn to the visual or the cinematic was not limited to press photography alone. Publications of literature and poetry, for instance, employed lithographic and photographic illustration with increasing frequency during the Weimar period.[23] Poster art and advertising, moreover, made use of photographic and print techniques and were said to have transformed Berlin "into one large art gallery, a gallery turned outward to the city streets."[24] As suggested in chapter 2, the pervasive influence of the cinema in German cultural life became the topic of extended speculation and theoretical discussion in the 1920s. For theorists like Benjamin and Kracauer, the popularity of the cinema underscored the transformation of subjectivity under the impact of in-

[23] For a brief discussion of the "turn to the visual" in book publishing, see Anton Kaes, "Introduction," *Kino-Debatte: Texte zum Verhältnis von Literatur und Film, 1909–1929*, ed. Anton Kaes (Tübingen: Max Niemeyer Verlag, 1978), 18.
[24] Ibid., 18.

Figure 8. From film to photojournalism: narration in pictures
(*Berliner Illustrirte Zeitung*, 1930)

dustrialization and modernity. Borrowing from Simmel's analysis of urbanization and structures of perception, they maintained that the cinema had restructured subjectivity and vision according to principles of rationalization, abstraction, and shock. In contrast to Benjamin and Kracauer, however, some intellectuals suggested that the cinema and the visual arts provided a refuge from the abstraction and fragmentation of modern life. As Béla Balázs proposed, the unmediated experience of the sensuous world may have indeed been terminated with the industrial revolution, but the desire for immediacy resurfaced in the new technology of cinema, with its intense appreciation of landscapes and emphasis on faces revealed in close-up. For Balázs, the appeal of the cinema did not so much suggest that rationalization and distraction had restructured vision as it served to reveal the "painful longing in an intellectualized and abstract culture for the experience of a concrete and immediate reality."[25]

While these two assessments of the cinema offer different readings of a shared cultural and perceptual field, they also suggest the reasons behind the coexistence of distinct modes of representation in the visual arts. In the illustrated press, for example, the photomontages of John Heartfield and the lithography and poster art of Käthe Kollwitz constitute very different approaches to documentary photography. Where Heartfield's work may be said to structure vision and representation according to principles of shock, fragmentation, and abstraction, Kollwitz's work may be said to structure vision and representation according to an intensified documentary realism—what we might usefully call conventions of melodrama in the representation of everyday life in the illustrated press.

Heartfield's and Kollwitz's work appeared regularly in the pages of the AIZ, and both artists were widely recognized in the 1920s for their political approach to documentary representation. Heartfield's and Kollwitz's documentary practices nevertheless differ in fundamental respects. For Heartfield, documentary realism was inadequate for the purposes of radical photography. In a photomontage which appeared in a 1929 issue of the AIZ, he graphically dem-

---

[25] Béla Balázs, *Der sichtbare Mensch* (Halle, 1924); quoted in Kaes, *Kino-Debatte*, 19.

onstrates the need to reject documentary realism so as to "Use Photography as a Weapon" (Benütze Foto als Waffe) (figure 9). The arrangement combines two images within a single representation: an image of Heartfield, who looks at us directly, is combined with a cutout image of the police president of Berlin. Heartfield holds the image of the president's head in one hand and, with the pair of scissors he holds in the other, is poised to cut the image at the president's throat. In this photomontage, the rejection of conventional documentary and the call for an analytical approach to photography are unmistakable: the photographer, Heartfield demonstrates, must expose reality as constructed and dynamically produced, whether through recourse to scissors, darkroom chemistry, or both.[26]

In contrast to this view of documentary photography, Kollwitz's lithography and poster art experiment with the very conventions of documentary realism that Heartfield rejects. As Heartfield does, Kollwitz appropriates documentary for political purposes. But unlike Heartfield, she does not reconstruct images analytically; instead, she conscripts conventional documentary realism and traditions in expressionism in order to complicate certain expectations of them. In her numerous depictions of proletarian mothers and their starving children, Kollwitz dispenses with expressionism's father-son conflicts and gives documentary realism an exaggerated, expressive quality (figure 10). Neither realist nor modernist, Kollwitz's work is perhaps best described as melodramatic, as an attempt to put pressure on the representation of the real so as to heighten its meaning and give the unrepresented and repressed a material presence.

As several historians have suggested, melodramatic representation has frequently been appropriated by and for society's outgroups—the working class and women.[27] It is therefore not surprising that Kollwitz's approach to documentary was taken up by the AIZ in its photographic representation of women and working-class

---

[26] This reading of Heartfield's documentary practice is indebted to Abigail Solomon-Godeau's essay "Reconstructing Documentary: Connie Hatch's Representational Resistance," *Camera Obscura*, nos. 13–14 (1985): 113–48.

[27] Peter Brooks makes this point in *The Melodramatic Imagination: Balzac, Henry James, Melodrama and the Mode of Excess* (New Haven: Yale University Press, 1976), as does Martha Vicinus in her essay, "Helpless and Unfriended: Nineteenth Century Domestic Melodrama," *New Literary History* 13, no. 1 (Autumn 1981): 127–43.

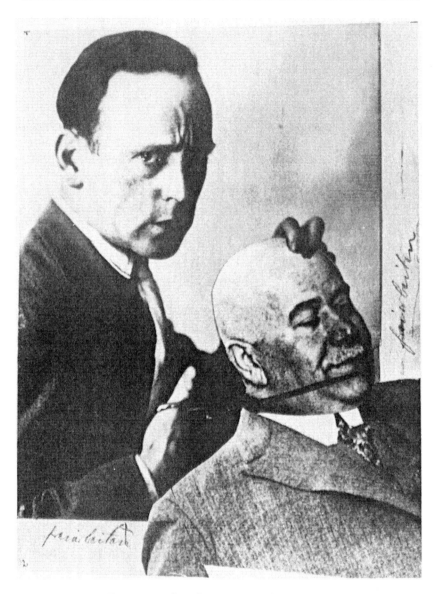

Figure 9. Analytic documentary: John Heartfield
(*Arbeiter Illustrierte Zeitung*, 1929)

Nr. 12   Berliner Illustrirte Zeitung   263

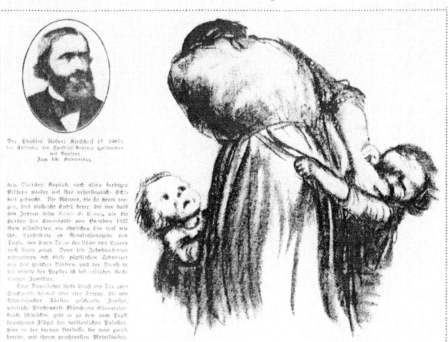

Figure 10. Expressionist documentary: Käthe Kollwitz
(*Berliner Illustrirte Zeitung*, 1923)

life (figure 11). In an issue of the AIZ from the early 1930s, for example, a photograph that accompanies Erich Weinert's poem "Eine deutsche Mutter" depicts an image made familiar by Kollwitz's work: a proletarian woman, crouched on a doorstep, holds her head in her hands in a gesture of despair (figure 12). In keeping with conventions of melodrama, the proletarian woman is rendered without any illusion of depth or psychological complexity: we cannot see the woman's face; instead, our attention is directed to the drama of suffering, to the emphatic gesture of despair. Indeed, this image aims to forge identification less with the individual woman than with the plight of proletarian women—a plight rendered unambiguous through conventions of melodramatic representation. Former editor of the AIZ Lilly Becher explains that the workers' press quite consciously aimed to render the invisible visible and to address the "social reverse side" of reality. She writes, "If one looks through the pages of the AIZ, one will find photographs which grasped a non-visible social reverse side. . . . Visible becomes a world and a people consistently overlooked by professional photographers and bourgeois reporters, who were only interested in the glittering facade of our planet and who thus failed to discover the enigmatic shadows . . . which were waiting in factories and tenement buildings."[28]

While the AIZ was undeniably more attuned to the "enigmatic shadows" and conditions of working-class life, melodramatic conventions are also apparent in the pages of the BIZ. At the height of the inflation in 1923, for example, the BIZ published a series of lithographic prints documenting "The Cry for Bread" (Der Schrei nach Brot) and "Complaining Women" (Klagende Frauen) (figure 13). These prints are strongly reminiscent of Kollwitz's work, particularly in their expressive and exaggerated depiction of social unrest and suffering. Of particular interest in this regard is the cover image of the BIZ in August 1923 (figure 14). Here, it is a photograph rather than a lithographic print that documents the conditions of the inflation. The image depicts a crowd of women who stand outside a shop waiting to buy food. We cannot make out individual faces, since the women's attention is turned to a notice

---

[28] Lilly Becher, "Vorwart," in Heinz Willmann, *Geschichte der Arbeiter-Illustrierten Zeitung 1921–1938* (Berlin: Dietz Verlag, 1975), 8.

Figure 11. Käthe Kollwitz and the left-wing press
(*Arbeiter Illustrierte Zeitung*, 1927)

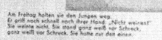

Figure 12. Melodramatic expression in the left-wing press
(*Arbeiter Illustrierte Zeitung*, 1934)

Figure 13. Melodramatic expression in the bourgeois press
(*Berliner Illustrirte Zeitung*, 1923)

Figure 14. The inflation and the illustrated press
(*Berliner Illustrirte Zeitung*, 1923)

posted on the shop door (perhaps informing them that the shop is closed or that supplies have run out; it is impossible to tell). The prominence given to the "Butter, Käse, Wurst" sign, to the lettering on the shop front, serves to put the image in the context of narrative as an instantly recognizable and everyday occurrence. Although we see no obvious signs of social unrest or despair, the contrast between the dark clothes of the women and the white lettering of the shop sign nevertheless intensifies the image as an exaggerated yet exemplary scene created by the inflation.

This photograph calls to mind several scenes from *Die freudlose Gasse* (*The Joyless Street*, 1925) as well as Pabst's response to the allegation that his representation of the inflation was overly dramatic and too romantic. Pabst asked, "What need is there for romantic treatment? Real life is too romantic, too ghastly."[29] Certainly the same could be said of the cover photograph on the BIZ. Not only is the price of the newspaper prominently displayed at 50,000 marks (and this price would reach 50 billion marks by the end of the year), but the captions which accompany the photograph also comment on violent contrasts in contemporary evaluations of the inflation. The first caption reads, "German housewives must wait long hours in every big city to buy a quarter pound of butter." Following this, there is an additional statement from French minister Poincaré: "Germany is the richest country in the world and threatens to conquer the world economically." We may surmise that violent contrast had not only become a convention in the illustrated press, but that it also was experienced in its manifestations as a real, material force during the Weimar years (figure 15).

It is nevertheless symptomatic that the recourse to contrast and extreme stylization in the illustrated press almost always involved images of women or female identity in crisis. The examples I have cited from the AIZ and the BIZ suggest that melodramatic lithography and photography drew on a female figure to represent social unrest and despair: the one-dimensional and tragically expressive proletarian woman. In addition to this figure, however, there was also a preoccupation with an allegedly "masculinized" female figure or the New Woman in the illustrated press. Although initially con-

---

[29] G. W. Pabst, "A Survey," *Close-Up* (December 1927), 60; quoted in Kracauer, *From Caligari to Hitler*, 167.

1000 Mark = 3 bis 4 Goldpfennige

Ein trauriges Kapitel in fünf banalen Bildern

Figure 15. Inflated images and everyday life
(*Berliner Illustrirte Zeitung*, 1923)

fined to the fashion pages of *Die Dame*, the New Woman who dressed in unisex clothing and wore her hair cropped short soon became the topic of heated debate and intense fascination. In 1925, for example, an editorial appeared in the BIZ entitled "Now That's Enough! Against the Masculinization of Woman" (Nun aber genug! Gegen die Vermännlichung der Frau) (figure 16). In this editorial, the masculine quality of women's fashion is denounced as "unnatural" and an affront to "the fully developed appearance of the female body." The editorial is worth quoting in some detail:

> What was at first just a whimsical play with women's fashion has now become an embarrassing aberration. At first it seemed like a capricious joke, that fragile and slender women cut their long hair and appeared in a page-boy cut [*Pagenfrisur*]; that they put on clothes that denied the voluptuousness of the female body. . . . Such a being could have once been called, with the now lost term of endearment, "My Angel," because even though the angels are sexless [*Geschlechtslos*] they have always been imagined in a female form just before that form has fully ripened. . . . But this fashion, which suits young girls so well, becomes morally embarrassing for male feelings when it is appropriated by women. . . . The masculinization of the female countenance takes away real attractiveness and gives women, if anything at all, an unnatural appearance: to look like a mawkish boy is disgusting for any real boy or man.[30]

The tone of moral outrage suggests that something more than women's fashion was at stake in disputes over the New Woman. For a number of critics, changes in women's fashion were in fact indicative of a far more disturbing trend, one in which women seemed to renounce femininity and regress to an adolescent sexuality—and thus to deviate from the path of "normal" female sexual development. Of course, not all responses to the New Woman were so explicit or impassioned. In November 1927, for example, the BIZ sponsored a contest based on its cover sketch of a masculinized woman and a feminized man, who are dressed in almost iden-

---

[30] "Nun aber Genug! Gegen die Vermännlichung der Frau," BIZ, no. 15 (29 März 1925): 389.

Figure 16. "Now that's enough! Against the masculinization of woman"
(*Berliner Illustrirte Zeitung*, 1925)

tical suits, ties, and matching monocles (figure 17). These two figures, who occupy the foreground of the image, have elicited responses from three figures framed behind them. On the left sits a bearded old man with a bewildered expression. On the right, a middle-aged man with a mischievous grin leans forward to whisper something to a young woman seated near him. She listens with interest as she scrutinizes the androgynous couple. Beneath this image, the contest question (worth 3,000 marks) addresses the reader in a highly ironic manner: "What do *you* say about Fräulein Mia?"

Clearly, the BIZ had assimilated the play with gender roles so often commented on by historians and theorists of the Weimar period. Femininity, for example, has clearly been displaced from Fräulein Mia to the male figure who accompanies her. Yet it is significant that the contest question does not ask the reader to respond to the representation of unstable male identity; instead, the question asks the reader to respond to the representation of unstable female identity and thus prescribes the meaning of the image as an interrogation—however playful or ironic—of female sexuality as that which is "other." This androgynous female figure remains the focus of intense speculation precisely because she appears so "unnatural," so masculine and unmaternal. As one critic explains, "the well-known anxiety attaching to male jokes about the 'masculine woman' in no way extenuates the strategy that it energizes: which is to render the woman who is their target external to the system of sexual difference that gets along quite well without her."[31]

Since it would be difficult to claim that the BIZ depiction of the New Woman challenges traditional representations of women, a feminist reading might argue that the reversal involved in the joke

[31] D. A. Miller, "*Cage aux folles*: Sensation and Gender in Wilkie Collins's *The Woman in White*," in *The Making of the Modern Body*, ed. Catherine Gallagher and Thomas Laqueur (Berkeley and Los Angeles: University of California Press, 1987), 127. In light of Miller's observations, it is interesting to note that the BIZ sponsored a second contest question in May 1928 (almost one year after the contest involving Fräulein Mia) which asked readers to determine the gender of young people pictured in six photographs. The bold caption which states "Bub oder Mädel?" (Guy or Gal?) suggests the extent to which the New Woman was literally rendered external to the system of sexual difference, which could only accept gender ambiguity as manifested by adolescent sexuality.

Figure 17. Imagining androgyny
(*Berliner Illustrirte Zeitung*, 1927)

on the New Woman was fundamentally a projection of male anxieties and fears. Such an argument has been advanced by Atina
Grossmann in her recent essay, "The New Woman and the Rationalization of Sexuality in Weimar Germany."[32] For Grossmann, the
celebrated sexual freedom of the Weimar years was also a symptom
of a new kind of repression which aimed to rationalize female sexuality and institutionalize certain standards of "healthy," socially
responsible sexual behavior. The Sex Reform Movement in Weimar, Grossmann explains, brought together doctors, scientists, and
social workers, many of them associated with working class political
parties, in the name of a commitment to legalized abortion, contra-
ception, and sex education. These reformers, who often contributed editorials to the illustrated press, were concerned about fall-
ing birth rates and saw female frigidity as a major problem in family
and erotic life. As Grossmann points out, a number of reformers
were worried that modernization had incorporated women into
public life and wage labor too quickly, with the result that women
had become "masculinized" or alienated from their bodies and re-
sistant to childbearing. In their desire to reform marriage and heterosexual relationships, and thus to make marriage more attractive
to women, sex reformers sought to rationalize female sexuality by
defining and controlling what seemed most dangerous about it.
The most threatening and sexually deviant type of woman, Grossmann suggests, was typically portrayed in Sex Reform literature "in
a manner suspiciously close to the malicious stereotype of the New
Woman: short, dark hair, dressed in a unisex shift, distinctly unmaternal—the image not only of the prostitute but also of the Jew-
ess and the lesbian."[33]

While Grossmann's analysis underscores the affinities among mi-
sogyny, anti-Semitism, and homophobia in representations of the
modern woman, it would be misleading to see the New Woman
simply as a projection of male anxieties and fears. As Grossmann
herself points out, "the New Woman was not merely a media myth
or a demographer's paranoid fantasy, but a social reality that can
be researched and documented: she existed in office and factory,

[32] Atina Grossmann, "The New Woman and the Rationalization of Sexuality in Weimar Germany," in *Powers of Desire: The Politics of Sexuality*, ed. Ann Snitow, Christine
Stansell, and Sharon Thompson (New York: Monthly Review Press, 1983), 153–71.
[33] Ibid., 167.

in bedroom and kitchen, just as surely as in café, cabaret, and film."[34] Without a doubt, the New Woman was depicted as suspiciously or ironically unmaternal in several editorials and images in the illustrated press. In a woman's magazine like *Die Dame*, however, the New Woman often served an entirely different function, and this function can only be understood once the New Woman is seen not as a "stereotype" but, more precisely, as a one-dimensional type. The New Woman and the proletarian woman in fact came to represent primary psychic and social roles in the illustrated press: where the New Woman was middle-class and frequently deeroticized, the proletarian woman was working-class and often tragically maternal. That these two figures developed as readily identifiable types suggests that they were related to female gender experience in the 1920s. Yet as types or textual constructs, they came to serve different functions in different textual systems, taking on meanings other than male anxiety and fear when we consider their function in the address to female audiences.

Gender, Looking, and the Address to Female Readers: *Die Dame* and the *Arbeiter Illustrierte Zeitung*

"The Weimar cinema," writes Janet Bergstrom, "allowed for modes of viewing more commonly associated with the fine arts, to cast a kind of aesthetic veil over images of feminized male figures as well as one-dimensional female characters."[35] I find this formulation particularly useful for analyzing the representation of sexual identity and the address to female readers in a woman's magazine like *Die Dame*. As suggested earlier, both *Die Dame* and the AIZ placed a high value on photography and the fine arts: reproductions of paintings, lithographic prints, photoessays, and photomontages were regular features of both illustrated magazines. More important, however, *Die Dame* and the AIZ overlaid traditions in the vi-

---

[34] Atina Grossmann, "*Girlkultur* or Thoroughly Rationalized Female: A New Woman in Weimar Germany?" in *Women in Culture and Politics: A Century of Change*, ed. Judith Freidlander, Blanche Wiesen Cook, Alice Kessler-Harris, and Caroll Smith-Rosenberg (Bloomington, In.: Indiana University Press, 1986), 63–64.

[35] Bergstrom, "Sexuality at a Loss," 188.

sual arts with conventions relating to sexual identity in quite specific ways when addressing a female audience.

In 1926, for example, *Die Dame* introduced the spring fashion season with an unmistakable manipulation of traditional gender roles: sketches of female models in smoking jackets and short mannish haircuts are accompanied by a male model who is dressed in strikingly similar fashion (figure 18). Although this representation of the New Woman was frequently condemned for reinforcing the "masculinization" of female gender identity, it seems more appropriate to consider sexual mobility or an oscillation between femininity and masculinity to be the distinguishing feature of women's fashion. The female figures depicted in this 1926 fashion layout, for instance, retain connotatively feminine styles in their ruffled shirts and ribbon bow ties but appropriate at the same time an excess of masculine styles in their dinner suits and waistcoats which deemphasize the female body. Intending, perhaps, to respond to those who denounced the New Woman as unnatural and socially deviant, Anita, a fashion editor for *Die Dame*, describes the alleged "masculinization" of women's fashion as a quintessentially feminine gesture—a self-consciously masculine masquerade (figure 19). She writes:

> The woman is once again proving her royal capriciousness. . . . She is obsessed with the outward signs of masculinity—she wants the man's stiff collar, his coat, his cane, his waistcoat. Yes, even his holiest possession, the cylinder hat. . . . The masculinization of the woman supersedes masculinity itself, and the weak/strong sex stands before this onslaught without a clue. . . . [And yet, the] masculine masquerade . . . is really the old-unanswering Eve-instinct, for nothing occurs in fashion which does not reveal the erotic sense and the erotic needs of a time. In epochs when the man is very masculine, very sure of his strength and very positive, he wears his clothing broadly: broad shoulders, broad chest, bold legs. . . . In other epochs, after wars or revolutions, when the man has lapsed into femininity and nervous exhaustion, this is reflected in fashion with sentimental curls and romantic high collars. . . . Today, however, the man is neither strong nor weak but too realistic, too neuter; he has 'no time'

Figure 18. The masculine masquerade
(*Die Dame*, 1926)

Nr. 35   Berliner Illustrirte Zeitung   897

DIE VERMÄNNLICHUNG DER FRAU

Für den Winter prophezeit man eine noch stärkere Betonung des männlichen Stils in der Frauentracht: Bubenkopf, Zylinderhut, Herrenmantel.

Die Frau gibt wieder einmal einen Beweis ihrer launischen Launenhaftigkeit. Während alle Schätze der Erde ihr zu Füßen gelegt werden, rastlose Künstler die Phantasie anspornen, um Neues, Schöneres, Zarteres für sie zu ersinnen, weist sie alles spöttisch zurück. Es gelüstet sie nach dem ernsteligen Besitz des Mannes — sie will seinen steifen Kragen, seinen Gehrock, seinen Stock, seine Weste. Ja, selbst sein herrliches Eigentum, den Zylinder, stülpt sie sich lachend auf das kurz geschnittene Haar und bringt ihn auf alle Zeiten um seine Würde, indem sie eine übermütige Hahnenfeder oder ein witziges Bändchen pietätlos daran anbringt. Die Vermännlichung der Frau verdrängt die Männlichkeit, und rätlos steht das schwache starke Geschlecht vor diesem Ueberfall. Ein kurzer Versuch, mit gleichem zu vergelten, brachte Feminismus in die Herrenmode — jetzt denken

Die Vermännlichung der Frau: Amerikanische junge Expräsidentin mit der allermodernsten Bubenfrisur, die den Frauenkopf wie den eines Jünglings erscheinen läßt.

viele Anzeichen auf einen großen Stimmungsabfall. Die Herren der Schöpfung lassen sich wieder Bärte wachsen: bis bleibe und nicht weiter!

Noch steht die männliche Mode in höchster Blüte, und doch ist sie in ihrer augenblicklichen Form dem baldigen Untergang geweiht. Der bescheidene Mann beschäftigt sich jahrzehntelang mit den ihm liebgewordenen Formen, glücklicherweise aber die Frau! Ein deutliches Zeichen für den beginnenden Uebergang ist die Tendenz zur Mode des Directoire. Jener Zeit mit dem stark femininen Einschlag in der männlichen Kleidung. Mit dem Spitzenjabot scheint das starre Regime gebrochen zu sein.

Auch auf anderem Gebiet wird die Frau der männlichen Maskerade müde. Einige Pariser Schönheitskünstler haben gefunden, daß der Rauch der unzähligen Zigaretten früher altern lasse, kleine Runzeln unter den Augen verursache und den Teint verderbe — schon gibt es unerschütterliche Nicht-Raucherinnen. Auch die vielumstrittene

Bubenkopf-Frisur aus der amerikanischen Zeitschrift Harpers Bazar.

Die Vermännlichung der Frau: Die neue Wintermode, die für die Straßenkleidung einen männlichen Charakter betont. Wintermäntel für Damen im neuen "Garçonne"-Stil.

Figure 19. The masculinization of woman
(*Berliner Illustrirte Zeitung*, 1924)

113

for his soul and for his wife. For this reason, the suffering woman responds ironically to this neutered being by parodying his masculinity; she makes fun of these men whenever she is among those who are like her.[36]

In focusing upon the "erotic needs" of a time as they are revealed in style and fashion, this editorial offers an extremely suggestive analysis of historical changes in the representation of sexual difference. The feminization of male fashion, for example, is linked to periods of political and social instability—to the aftermath of wars and revolutions—when male identity is in crisis and lapses into "femininity" and "nervous exhaustion." Significantly, however, the feminization of male identity is not said to cause a problem for the woman; instead, it is male in-difference which is said to encourage the woman to parody masculinity and engage in a "masculine masquerade."

This formulation of masquerade is particularly interesting in light of the work done by sociologists and psychoanalysts in the 1920s on questions of female sexuality, and in view of the continuing interest of this early work for contemporary feminist theory. The overriding concern with female sexual development and with woman's masculinity becomes strikingly apparent from the titles of papers written by prominent analysts during the Weimar period: Karl Abraham's "Manifestations of the Female Castration Complex" (1922), Karen Horney's "On the Genesis of the Castration Complex in Women" (1924), Helen Deutsch's "The Psychology of Woman in Relation to the Function of Reproduction" (1925), Ernst Jones's "The Early Development of Female Sexuality" (1927), and Freud's "Female Sexuality" (1931). It was Joan Riviere's essay "Womanliness as a Masquerade" (1929), however, that posed the question of female identity specifically in terms of artifice and representation, arguing that to be a woman is to dissimulate a fundamental masculinity, to put on a mask of femininity to avert anxiety and the retribution feared from men.[37] For the woman, writes Riviere,

---

[36] Anita, "Die Vermännlichung der Frau," BIZ, no. 35 (31 August 1924): 997–98.

[37] Joan Riviere, "Womanliness as a Masquerade," first published in *The International Journal of Psychoanalysis* 10 (1929), reprinted in *Formations of Fantasy*, ed. Victor Burgin, James Donald, and Cora Kaplan (London and New York: Methuen, 1986), 35–44. Stephen Heath provides an extremely perceptive analysis of Riviere's essay, sketching

"womanliness [can] be assumed and worn as a mask, both to hide the possession of masculinity and to avert the reprisals expected if she was found to possess it—much as a thief will turn out his pockets and ask to be searched to prove that he has not the stolen goods."[38]

This association of female sexuality with criminality and artfulness—with performance, representation, and acting out—had considerable cultural currency before the 1920s, but it was the spectre of masculinity in women during the Weimar years that inspired new critical insights alongside old anxieties and fears. Responding to the common charges leveled against the New Woman, for example, sexologist Max Hodann claimed that the unstable psychic makeup of the masculine woman need not necessarily lead to criminal activity, for in some women this instability "often implies extreme sensibility to impressions and inspirations, which may be gloriously active and creative in music and art."[39] In seeking to rescue women's masculinity for creative pursuits in the arts, Hodann was merely reiterating a well-known social fact of turn-of-the-century European life. As Käthe Kollwitz's biographer explains:

> Celibacy was the first commandment of the art school. The woman art students considered marriage an act of betrayal, for it meant abandoning their artistic work. What value did the sacrifice, troubles, and expenses of training have, they argued, if studying art was only a transitional stage between adolescence and marriage?[40]

It is precisely this "transitional phase" which Riviere addressed in terms of the changing cultural and psychic imperatives in women's lives. "Not long ago," she writes, "intellectual pursuits for women were associated almost exclusively with an overtly masculine type of woman who in pronounced cases made no secret of her wish or claim to be a man. This has now changed. Of all the women engaged in professional work today, it would be hard to say whether

the history of its reception in the writings of feminist and psychoanalytic critics. See his "Joan Riviere and the Masquerade," in *Formations of Fantasy*, 45–61.

[38] Riviere, "Womanliness as a Masquerade," 38.

[39] Max Hodann, *History of Modern Morals* (London: William Heinemann Medical Books Ltd., 1937); reprinted in facsimile by AMS Press, New York, 1976, 40.

[40] Martha Kearns, *Käthe Kollwitz: Woman and Artist* (Old Westbury, N.Y.: The Feminist Press, 1976), 41.

the greater number are more feminine than masculine in their mode of life and character."[41] In contrast to other critics and theorists, who associate women's transition from adolescence to adulthood with a "phallic phase" in female sexual development, Riviere maintains that woman's masculinity is neither momentary nor merely transitional. The elaborate display of femininity in the intellectual woman, she argues, actually serves to hide the possession of an unconscious masculinity—a masculinity against which the intellectual woman must continually defend herself.

Extending Riviere's concept of the feminine masquerade to a critical analysis of film, feminist scholars have recently theorized the cinema as an elaborate apparatus which attempts to stabilize a given image of female sexual identity.[42] In her essay "Film and the Masquerade," for example, Mary Ann Doane addresses the problematic status of identification in the cinema for women, describing how theories of the female spectator tend to view the woman "as the site of an oscillation between a feminine and a masculine position, invoking the metaphor of the transvestite":

> the woman who identifies with a female character [is said to] adopt a passive or masochistic position while identification with the active male hero necessarily entails an acceptance of what Laura Mulvey refers to as a certain "masculinization" of spectatorship. [Mulvey points out that] "as desire is given cultural materiality in a text, for women (from childhood onwards) trans-sex identification is a habit which very easily becomes second Nature. However, this Nature does not sit easily and shifts restlessly in its borrowed transvestite clothes."[43]

Although Doane maintains that spectatorial identification operates according to processes of fetishism and voyeurism normally present only to a male subject, she also points out that the female spectator in fact finds it difficult to fetishize—to disown or assume

---

[41] Riviere, "Womanliness as a Masquerade," 35.

[42] See, for example, Claire Johnston, "Femininity and the Masquerade: *Anne of the Indies,*" in *Jacques Tourneur,* ed. Claire Johnston and Paul Willemen (London: British Film Institute, 1975), 36–44; and Mary Ann Doane, "Film and the Masquerade: Theorizing the Female Spectator," *Screen* 23, nos. 3–4 (September–October 1982): 74–87.

[43] Doane, "Film and the Masquerade," 80.

a distance between herself and the image of the woman on the screen. Doane therefore takes pains to suggest how certain filmic practices can indeed "manufacture" a critical distance from the image of woman—either through representations of "female transvestism" or the "feminine masquerade." As Doane explains, the representation of the female transvestite or the woman who appropriates masculine styles and gestures would seem to allow the female spectator a certain identification with the image. (This much is also implied by the quote from Mulvey, which emphasizes how female transvestism reproduces the experience of the female subject who is also crossed by gender lines.) Yet for Doane, not only is such transvestism easily recuperable for male desire, but it also serves to "masculinize" the female spectator position. For this reason, Doane adapts Riviere's concept of the masquerade and argues for a "feminine" rather than a "masculine" masquerade, for a parody of femininity rather than masculinity to break with patriarchal structures of vision and desire:

> The masquerade, in flaunting femininity, holds it at a distance. Womanliness is a mask which can be worn or removed. The masquerade's resistance to patriarchal positioning would therefore lie in its denial of the production of femininity as closeness . . . as precisely imagistic. The transvestite adopts the sexuality of the other—the woman becomes a man in order to attain the necessary distance from the image. Masquerade, on the other hand, involves a realignment of femininity. . . . It effects a defamiliarization of female iconography. . . . The effectivity of masquerade lies precisely in its potential to manufacture a distance from the image, to generate a problematic within which the image is manipulable, producible, and readable by the woman.[44]

In Doane's estimation, only an excess of femininity will defamiliarize female iconography and allow the female film spectator to challenge the patriarchal positioning of women. It seems highly significant, however, that a woman's magazine like *Die Dame* did *not* engage in a feminine masquerade; in other words, that it did not succumb to the elaborate display of femininity demanded of

[44] Ibid., 81–82.

women in so much of the illustrated press. Whereas Doane theorizes female transvestism as mere role reversal ("the woman becomes a man in order to attain the necessary distance"), the New Woman represented in *Die Dame* is more usefully understood as a figure of sexual mobility, exhibiting what Teresa de Lauretis has theorized as "the simultaneous presence of two positionalities of desire."[45] Without a doubt, the New Woman's "masculine masquerade" was often described in *Die Dame*'s editorial pages in a way that verged on an uncritical celebration of femininity, where the parody of masculinity was declared a quintessentially feminine gesture—"the old unanswering Eve-instinct." Yet in its self-consciously *masculine* masquerade—its parody of masculinity as neither ontologically given nor unalterable but as sheer artifice of male power—*Die Dame* succeeded in destabilizing both male and female iconography, and thus in generating an image of gender identity that was, to quote Doane, "manipulable, producible, and readable by the woman."

In both the editorials and the images in *Die Dame*, the ongoing interrogation of masculinity was in fact inseparable from the attempt to offer female readers a different vision of gender identity and another space for identification and desire. In a 1926 editorial entitled "Men" (Männer), for example, a staff writer for *Die Dame*, Jot Jot, satirizes masculinity as it relates to male identity and provides a description of recurrent male types: the "strongly built egotistical" male, the "tyrannical and cowardly" male, the "womanizing and narcissistic" male and, finally, the truly "sensitive and attractive" male.[46] Of this last type, the author explains: "These men are never demanding, they never hurt, they know everything. Eternal beauty is inborn in them. But these men don't exist. They live only in literature." While this final type of male functions as a figure upon whom female desire may be projected, this male figure was not confined to literature but was frequently depicted in the fashion pages of *Die Dame*. The male figure represented alongside the New Woman, for instance, was not a virile, broadly-built male but a feminine male: an elegantly dressed cosmopolitan man who adopts the gestures and the body posture that could be termed

[45] Teresa de Lauretis, *Alice Doesn't: Feminism, Semiotics, Cinema* (Bloomington, In.: University of Indiana Press, 1984), 83.

[46] Jot Jot, "Männer," *Die Dame*, Heft 8 (zweites Maiheft 1926): 2–3.

feminine (figure 20). In a number of fashion layouts, the body of the male model is shaped to complement the posture of the female models: his gestures are softened, his posture is lithe and passive. In thus representing gender identity, these fashion layouts destabilize male and female iconography by displacing eroticism onto an aestheticized male figure.

The representation of gender identity in *Die Dame* may be said to encourage a vision of sexuality as shifting between masculinity and femininity, where sexuality and eroticism are not confined to the female body alone. The function of this shifting identification takes on particular significance for female readers, especially when we consider how the destabilization of male identity allowed for the expression of women's dissatisfactions with traditionally defined male *and* female gender roles. In the late 1920s, however, editorials written by sociologists and psychologists began to appear with increasing frequency in *Die Dame*, and these attempted to define the "masculinization" of female gender identity as a problem for the sexually mature woman. In a 1927 editorial entitled "The Understood Woman" (Die verstandene Frau), for example, Dr. J. Löbel acknowledges the long-standing view of female sexuality as enigmatic and indecipherable but nevertheless insists that "the days of the incomprehensible woman are numbered."[47] "Naturally," he concedes, "there will always be innumerable women who feel themselves misunderstood." But, he declares, "from science the woman no longer has a secret."[48] Löbel goes on to offer an explanation of bisexuality, especially female bisexuality, and then advances a "scientific" reason for women's need to return to a traditionally defined gender role and sexual orientation:

> When Otto Weininger maintained twenty-five years ago that "man" and "woman" do not at all exist in absolute purity, that every human being presents a union, a mixture of both masculine and feminine aspects . . . he created an incredible uproar among laymen. . . . The professional community, which was accustomed to explaining sexuality chemically or bacteriologically, also dismissed his hypothesis. . . . But today,

[47] Dr. J. Löbel, "Die verstandene Frau," *Die Dame*, Heft 8 (erstes Januarheft 1927): 12.

[48] Ibid., 12.

Figure 20. The feminized male
(*Die Dame*, 1928)

Mathes' standard work of medical science, *Biology and Pathology of Woman*, has provided a sure scientific footing for what Weininger intuitively suspected. . . . Mathes calls the clear cut sexual type of woman the "absolute female." . . . Marriage and motherhood are no problem for her—everything happens effortlessly, easily. . . . The more masculine a woman's given structure, the more she borders on the "intersexual" type. . . . Consistently, she has a problematic nature; both sexual aspects, which are united in her, fight a continuous and bitter battle. . . . [If the intersexual type marries], the marriage will be deeply unhappy. Scenes will occur in which the husband hits his wife. Naturally, the man aims to pull out what is hidden in the woman: her masculine strain is conquered and she is grateful for the liberation from masculinity. This is the scientific basis for the understanding that beatings are united with love.[49]

Like many other theorists of his day, Löbel clearly recognizes that bisexuality is a problem for the woman—a problem in that it incites male violence. And although he insists that the woman is grateful for this violence in restoring to her a "hidden" and uncomplicated sexual identity, we may certainly read this violence in another way: as an attempt to repress female bisexuality by constructing femininity as the most "natural" and appropriate identity for women.

Löbel's attempt to provide "scientific" justification for conquering women's bisexuality is nevertheless prophetic of changes in *Die Dame*'s representation of gender identity in the 1930s. The cover images of *Die Dame* in 1931, for example, dispense with the oscillation between masculinity and femininity in women's fashion in favor of an excessive femininity in fashion and a glorification of motherhood. In April 1931, the cover image combines photographs of a female model dressed in a long, classically styled gown with photographs of ancient statues of Athena (figure 21); in July 1931, the cover sketch depicts a young woman riding an old-fashioned frame bicycle although dressed in a Victorian-style bodice and bustle (figure 22); in December 1931, the cover sketch features a mother smiling contentedly as she cradles her child in her arms

---

[49] Ibid., 34, 36.

Figure 21. Return to classicism
(*Die Dame*, 1931)

Figure 22. Femininity in fashion
(*Die Dame*, 1931)

(figure 23). Where female bisexuality was replaced by an excessive femininity in fashion, the feminized male was replaced by a virile, overtly masculine male in fashion layouts. In 1932, for instance, the spring fashion season is introduced much as it had been in 1926, with sketches of female models accompanied by a male model (figure 24). In this 1932 fashion layout, however, the male model appears strikingly different from the female models who accompany him: he is visibly taller, with an extremely heavy body build and an expression of stern manliness.

One could argue that the representation of sexual difference in *Die Dame* of the 1930s merely confirms what Löbel described as women's desire for a more "effortless" sexual identity. Alternatively, one could suggest that women's return to excessively feminine styles and fashions simply lends further support to Riviere's analysis of womanliness as a masquerade, where the woman takes on the accoutrements of femininity so as to defend herself against the implications of her masculinity. Yet if such assessments partially explain the massive restoration of femininity in women's fashion, they fail adequately to account for women's conscious and persistent difficulty with traditional definitions of gender difference. In an editorial which appeared in *Die Dame* in 1931, for example, Martha von Zobeltitz describes the new femininity in women's fashion as "impractical" and an indication of a male desire for control over the woman.[50] In this same year, in another editorial in *Die Dame*, Vanna Brenner maintains that the failure to contain or direct female sexuality has always resulted in an indictment of the woman as frigid, as masculine, or as simply "too intellectual." Commenting on the overdetermined relationship between intellectuality and female identity, she writes, "Ever since men have discovered the swear word 'intellectual' for our reserve, some of us have drawn the consequences and become active. . . . Men have never acknowledged that they are simply unsympathetic to our needs . . . [that] our intellectuality is a form of self-protection against a thousand futile pains. . . . They say 'you are simply too intellectual' and express with that what they believe is unnatural or abnormal. For us, however, there remains the consciousness of our in-

---

[50] Martha von Zobeltitz, "Frauen sehen einander an," *Die Dame*, Heft 1 (erstes Oktoberheft 1931): 11–12.

Figure 23. Glorification of motherhood
(*Die Dame*, 1931)

Rings um den Hals

Wohlgeeignet ist das Material dieser Bluse, ein leises Wollstoff wie die Jacke, der in Form eines Mieders sticht sich den unteren Abschnitt in der unwesigsten Handdarstellung. Der Rock ist aus kariertem Wollstoff, das Futteres aus diesem vorfarligem Jersey.

Rechts unten: Kräftige werden viel verwendet. Jetzt weicht die blähende Linie um den Hals, die durch kernenishe Drapierung erreicht wird. — Auch hier ist die Halsumschmeichung charakteristisch. Sie hat den Charakter eines drapierten und geschlungenen Schals.

Bluse und Rock sind dem Kleide gleichwertig geworden. Das wird im Frühjahr noch deutlicher hervortreten. In vielen Fällen ist die Bluse mit dem Rock sogar schicker als das Kleid im ganzen, besonders am Vormittag zum einfachen Mantel. Durch den hohen, niederartigen Ansatz des Rockes bekommt der Anzug sogar etwas Kleidartiges, doch gewinnt er nicht immer an Kleidsamkeit. Der Miederrock ist eine gefährliche Mode. Nur bei sehr zarten Körperformen ist er vorteilhaft, sonst wirkt er gedrungen und macht plump. Sehr leichte Stoffe werden zu diesen Röcken verwendet, und Knöpfe aus glänzendem Metall oben am Gürtel oder am „Mieder" sind ein typischer Aufputz.

Jersey ist jetzt das modische Schlagwort. Was man oft für Frottee, für Serge oder irgendeinen Krepp hält, läuft unter dem Namen Jersey, denn es wird zur dem Rundwirkt

tellectuality and of [man's] great misunderstanding."[51] The alliance between women and intellectuals in Weimar—an alliance suggested as much by Kracauer's description of the little shopgirls as by Riviere's discussion of the masquerading woman—is here inflected with a particular vision of Weimar's modern woman. In Brenner's view, the modern woman is none other than the female intellectual, who found the simple equation of femininity with femaleness as difficult to accept in the 1930s as it had been in the 1920s—and this in spite of the massive attempts to stabilize and "understand" female sexuality.

Turning from *Die Dame* to the AIZ, we might expect to find an illustrated magazine that highlights class over gender identity in forging reader identification. Unlike *Die Dame*, the AIZ addressed a working-class audience and not a female audience exclusively. First established as *Sowjet-Russland im Bild* in 1921, then as *Sichel und Hammer* in 1922, and finally as the *Arbeiter Illustrierte Zeitung* in 1924, the AIZ did not create a woman's page until 1926.[52] Once established, moreover, this woman's page appeared only sporadically, offering a marked contrast to the AIZ's sports page, which appeared in virtually every issue. Furthermore, even the representation of the proletarian woman in the AIZ was intended to establish a class rather than a gender identification. Numerous cover images of the AIZ, for example, depict the proletarian woman as passive and helpless, and usually as pregnant (figures 25 and 26). These images of the proletarian woman, moreover, are clearly meant to serve as a point of identification for both male and female working-class readers: as the symbolic victim of capitalist exploitation, the helplessly maternal proletarian woman dramatizes the effects of an economic system which not only denies man's role as producer outside the home, but also threatens woman's role as reproducer inside it.

[51] Vanna Brenner, "Gnädige Frau sind zu Intellektuell," *Die Dame*, Heft 14 (erstes Aprilheft 1931): 42–44.

[52] For a historical overview of the development of the AIZ, see Heinz Willmann, *Geschichte der Arbeiter-Illustrierten Zeitung 1921–1938*. Although the AIZ established a woman's page in 1926, this page did not appear regularly until 1928. Hanno Hardt has suggested that it may have been Lilly Becher's influence that motivated the AIZ to respond to women's concerns in a special woman's page. In any case, the IAH clearly recognized the need for a left-wing woman's illustrated magazine and therefore sponsored a journal entitled *Der Weg der Frau* in 1931.

Figure 25. The proletarian mother
(*Arbeiter Illustrierte Zeitung*, 1930)

Figure 26. The working-class family
(*Arbeiter Illustrierte Zeitung*, 1924)

Perhaps most interesting, however, is the image of the proletarian woman that appeared on the woman's page of the AIZ. In addition to self-help columns offering female readers advice about food preparation and home improvement, the AIZ's woman's page devoted a great deal of attention to matters of style and fashion. The working woman depicted in these fashion pages is, in many respects, indistinguishable from the New Woman represented in *Die Dame*: one-dimensional and deeroticized, this proletarian woman also wears her hair cropped short and appropriates connotatively masculine fashions which deemphasize the female body (figure 27).

The editorials that accompanied these fashion pages rarely commented on the visual similarities between the New Woman and the proletarian woman; they stressed instead the function of class difference in separating the interests of bourgeois and working-class women. In a 1927 editorial entitled "The Fashion of 'Die Dame' " (Die Mode 'der Dame'), the AIZ explains the reasons for maintaining class distinctions in matters of fashion: "The working-class starves while bourgeois women concern themselves only with the new fashion. . . . These bourgeois women have 1000 marks to spare for a new coat whereas working-class women, who sew for weeks to make this coat, are only paid 30 to 50 pfennig per hour."[53] If the decadence of the bourgeois woman was a common theme in AIZ editorials, this assessment was much in line with the Left's position on bourgeois women generally. In 1914, for example, Rosa Luxemburg argued, "The women of the bourgeoisie have no part in social production. They are simply joint consumers on the surplus value that their men squeeze out of the proletariat. They are parasites on the parasites of the people."[54] As if to counter the apprehension of even a visual similarity between the New Woman and the working-class woman, a 1930 editorial on the AIZ's wom-

---

[53] "Die Mode 'der Dame,' " AIZ, no. 42 (1927): 7.

[54] Rosa Luxemburg, "The Proletarian Woman," in Rosa Luxemburg, *Gesammelte Werke* (Berlin: Dietz Verlag, 1974); translated by Hal Draper and Anne G. Lipow, and reprinted in "Marxist Women versus Bourgeois Feminism," *The Socialist Register 1976*, ed. Ralph Miliband and John Saville (London: The Merlin Press, 1976), 214. It is noteworthy that the article by Draper and Lipow, which precedes the Luxemburg translation, is itself marked by the same left anti-feminism as existed in the 1920s. The very title of the article—"Marxist Women *versus* Bourgeois Feminism"—makes obvious the attempt to divide women along class lines.

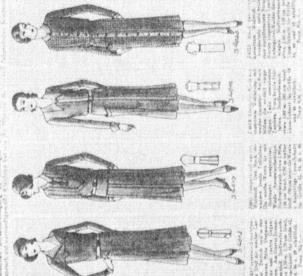

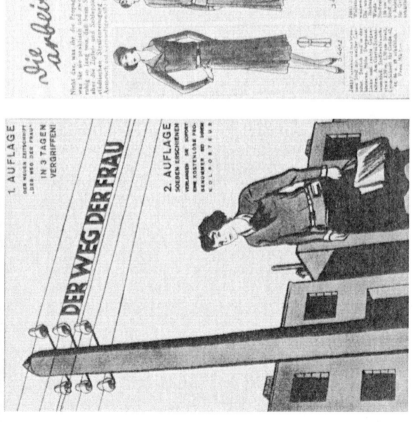

Figure 27. The working woman
(*Arbeiter Illustrierte Zeitung*, 1931)

an's page insists: "The working woman does not wear what the propagandists of the fashion industry dictate; instead, she wears what is practical and appropriate and therefore really pretty. . . . Certain new fashions are fine, but we have more to do than to be fashion plates. We demand the same practical clothing that men have had for centuries."[55]

While this demand for equality was answered by the AIZ's representation of women's activities in ways that altered the traditional iconography of the proletarian woman (figure 28), there was no attempt to destabilize male identity (indeed, there are no images of feminized or eroticized males in the AIZ). Editorials and photoessays in the AIZ, however, frequently took up issues of male insensitivity and of women's dissatisfactions with marriage. In 1929, for example, an AIZ photoessay begins with the question "What embitters the marriage?"[56] The photographs answer this question with a particular poignancy by narrating in successive images the relationship between a man and a woman who occupy the same domestic space: he waits for supper or reads the newspaper while she engages in routine domestic chores. The final images of this photoessay aim to offer a resolution to the problems of marriage by showing the man and the woman happily sharing household tasks. The caption beneath the photograph reads: "Household comrades. While the man with bourgeois prejudices considers it 'unworthy of a man' to help in the household, the good comrade does not shy away from helping his wife." Other photoessays and editorials were far less convincing. In 1927, an AIZ editorial entitled "Bourgeois Marriage" (Bürgerliche Ehe) condemns bourgeois morality and religion for contributing to the inequality of women in social, economic, and family life.[57] The Daumier drawings which accompany this editorial, however, offer an expressive illustration of violence against women within a range of social classes: physical violence in the upper and middle classes; emotional violence in the working class. Although the editorial indicts bourgeois marriage alone—and thus remains silent on the position of woman within the working-class marriage—the drawings serve to dramatize an overarching

[55] "Die bürgerliche Modeberichterstatterin spricht: Die arbeitende Frau trägt," AIZ, no. 38 (1930): 756.

[56] "Kameradschafts-Ehe?" AIZ, no. 12 (1929): 4–5.

[57] "Bürgerliche Ehe," AIZ, no. 34 (24 August 1927): 11.

Figure 28. Women of the revolution
(*Arbeiter Illustrierte Zeitung*, 1927)

violence against women which transcends distinctions between social classes.

It would seem that the editorials and photoessays in the AIZ formulated a highly contradictory message to female readers, since
visual illustration frequently worked to charge political commentary with meaning in excess of what that commentary could actually
support. The AIZ's address to female voters is particularly interesting in this regard. In February 1933, for example, the cover image
of the AIZ appeals to female voters by employing melodramatic
conventions of excess, exaggeration, and violent contrast (figure
29). Two images of readily identifiable female types are set side by
side: an image of a proletarian woman and an image of a bourgeois
woman. The image of the proletarian woman recalls Käthe Kollwitz's lithographic prints: holding one child in her arms while a
second tugs at her shirt, the proletarian mother turns her head
away in a gesture of despair. The image of the bourgeois woman,
by contrast, recalls the representation of female characters in the
commercial Hollywood cinema: posed as well as poised, expressive
but without pathos, the bourgeois woman addresses us directly.
Their class identities marked in unambiguous iconographic terms,
both female figures are denied any illusion of depth or psychological complexity. The caption which joins the two images states "For
work, bread and freedom, all working women choose list three."
While the significance of this statement appears unambiguous,
even obvious, its function with respect to the polarized images suggests another, implied meaning.

To grasp this meaning, it is necessary to consider other cover
images of the AIZ during the tense election years of the early 1930s.
The cover image of the AIZ published in March 1933—appearing
one month after the cover image addressed to female voters—appeals to male voters by depicting three male figures within a single
image: a worker, a farmer, and a white-collar worker (figure 30).
The caption superimposed on this image states "Worker, farmer
and white collar worker, all in a line for list three." Quite obviously, where the cover image addressed to female voters emphasizes visual contrast and class difference, the cover image addressed to male voters deemphasizes contrast and class difference
in a highly unified image. A third cover image of the AIZ published
in 1932 makes a general appeal to male and female voters and re-

Figure 29. The address to female voters
(*Arbeiter Illustrierte Zeitung*, 1933)

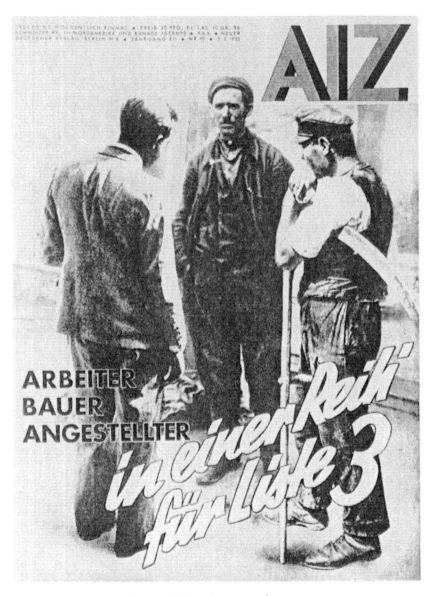

Figure 30. The address to male voters
(*Arbeiter Illustrierte Zeitung*, 1933)

tains a compositional arrangement similar to the cover image addressed to female voters alone (figure 31). It therefore seems appropriate to analyze this cover image in some detail and to comment on its use of conventions and its mode of address.

Composed by John Heartfield, this 1932 cover image situates two patently constructed and polarized images side by side: an image of a Nazi officer and an image of a crippled working-class man on crutches. The Nazi officer raises his arm in a Hitler salute; the working-class man extends his arm for a handout. Detailed commentary on these images is provided by lengthy captions set off in boxes in the corner of each image. As the captions explain, the Nazi officer is in fact Prince August Wilhelm of the wealthy and exploitative Hohenzollern family. The crippled worker, on the other hand, is identified as Paul Michel, a man who lost his leg in 1910 and who has been forced ever since to beg for alms to support his wife and family. The extremely bold title above these two images comments ironically, "Prince and worker in one party?"

When we read the AIZ's address to female voters in terms of this Heartfield montage, it would seem that the juxtaposition of instantly recognizable female figures has a transparent meaning. Just as the Heartfield montage combines two exaggerated and conventionalized images in order to comment ironically on attempts to unify princes and workers in one party, so, too, does the first 1933 cover image combine two polarized images of female figures in order to discredit attempts to join proletarian and bourgeois women in one party. Such an interpretation certainly suggests itself in light of the AIZ's persistent attempts throughout the 1920s to forge female reader identification by emphasizing issues of class over gender. Indeed, it would seem reasonable to conclude that both the Heartfield montage and the cover image addressed to female voters employ melodramatic conventions so as to induce the recognition of class privilege as the fundamental barrier to "work, bread, and freedom."

To leave it at this, however, would be to obscure the difference between modernist and melodramatic representation in the illustrated press and to undervalue the conditions of address to female readers. The Heartfield montage, for example, is both modernist and confrontational: it seeks to expose and diffuse the contradictions made explicit by the juxtaposition of polarized images. The

Figure 31. General appeal to voters
(*Arbeiter Illustrierte Zeitung*, 1932)

ironic question—"Prince and worker in one party?"—does not elicit an interpretation of the images but insists on their single, unequivocal meaning: there can be no unification of Nazis and workers. While adapting modernist conventions of representation, the 1933 cover image addressed to female voters is neither explicitly confrontational nor necessarily ironic. The caption—"All working women choose list three"—does not require that the images be read ironically (even though both the proletarian and the bourgeois woman appear to be unemployed) but instead stresses the need for interpretation.

Of course, it is significant that the address to female voters emphasizes class contradiction, whereas the address to male voters calls for class reconciliation and reunification. But given the AIZ's consistently contradictory message to female readers—where visual illustration typically generated meaning in excess of editorial commentary—we may surmise that female readers did not identify with class difference alone. On the woman's page of the AIZ, for example, it was possible for female readers to make use of a visual likeness between the proletarian and the bourgeois "New" woman. In AIZ editorials and photoessays, moreover, female readers may have recognized sexual violence and oppression as issues that transcend class politics. The dramatic, or more precisely, melodramatic juxtaposition of images in the 1933 address to female voters may have thus forged women's identification with an image of gender alliance that overrides the potentially disunifying message of economic disparity and class difference. To put this in slightly different terms, we might say that the AIZ's attempt to address the "social reverse side" of reality did not merely render the invisible visible, as Lilly Becher had hoped, but also produced—however unintentionally—the conditions of visibility for a female reader.[58]

---

[58] This formulation comes from de Lauretis, *Alice Doesn't*, 8–9. "In view of the redefinition of the notion of imaging," writes de Lauretis, "the present task of women's cinema may be not the destruction of narrative and visual pleasure but rather the construction of another frame of reference, one in which the measure of desire is no longer just the male subject. For what is finally at stake is not so much how 'to make visible the invisible' as how to produce the conditions of visibility for a different social subject."

WEIMAR CINEMA AND
THE FEMALE SPECTATOR

·

> Man sees woman . . . only in terms of surface.
> Woman looks at woman plastically, indeed, she
> even sees the dimensions which lie beyond her
> momentary field of vision.
> —*Die Dame* (1931)[1]

It would hardly seem controversial to argue that the *AIZ* and *Die Dame* addressed a female reader. Yet it may seem controversial to argue that the Weimar cinema addressed a female spectator, at least in part because Weimar films are not so explicitly labeled as the illustrated magazines produced for women. While the illustrated press provides us with an intertextual field of reference for analyzing the address to female spectators in film, it is not merely a matter of textual labels that makes the issue of female spectatorship in the Weimar cinema so controversial or such a matter for debate.

The existence in Weimar narratives of Oedipal rivalries and unsuccessful challenges to patriarchal authority, it should be recalled, leads Siegfried Kracauer to interpret Weimar film history allegorically, where a sequence of historical events (the lost war, revolution, Nazi rule) is understood in terms of a deeper, underlying, and presumably more fundamental narrative: one of male passivity and male symbolic defeat. Kracauer's allegorical interpretation of Weimar film history, moreover, lends itself to inherently circular reasoning; the Oedipal logic of Weimar narratives, he argues, reflects

---

[1] Martha von Zobeltitz, "Frauen sehen einander an," *Die Dame*, Heft 1 (erstes Oktoberheft, 1931): 11.

German social history, because it refers to the disturbed development of male subjectivity, which is in turn made evident by the Oedipal logic of Weimar narratives.

Kracauer's analysis of the mass cultural character of the Weimar cinema and its audience implies a similar circularity and inevitability. He claims, for instance, that the cinema's pretensions toward art and cultural respectability both mirrored and contributed to the "mental forlornness" among mass cultural spectators: their inability to choose between two equally limiting options, either identifying with cultural authority or lapsing into passivity, self-destruction, and despair. And although he poses authority and submission as two distinct alternatives, he ultimately insists that the choice for hierarchy and authoritarianism was inevitable:

> Irretrievably sunk into regression, the bulk of German people could not help submitting to Hitler. Since Germany had carried out what had been anticipated by her cinema from the very beginning, conspicuous screen characters came to life. . . . Homunculus walked about in the flesh. Self-appointed Caligaris hypnotized innumerable Cesares to murder. Raving Mabuses committed fantastic crimes with impunity, and mad Ivans devised unheard of tortures. . . . It was as it had been on the screen. The dark premonitions of a final doom were also fulfilled.[2]

For the most part, historians and theorists have accepted Kracauer's postulation of a male spectator as the historical subject anticipated and addressed by Weimar films. What they have taken issue with, however, is the manner in which Kracauer determines the aesthetic and political meaning of the cinema during the Weimar years. Thomas Elsaesser, for example, attributes the distortions and generalizations implicit in Kracauer's reading of Weimar film history to Kracauer's tendency to conflate the historical male spectator with a much more complex and uncertain textual system. As he rightly points out, Kracauer not only narrates German film history with terms and categories derived from the films themselves; he also tends to focus on the narrative content of individual

[2] Siegfried Kracauer, *From Caligari to Hitler: A Psychological History of the German Film* (Princeton, N.J.: Princeton University Press, 1947), 272.

films, eliding the marks of stylization, excess, and ambiguity which define the Weimar cinema as formally distinct from classical narrative traditions.

While Elsaesser thus objects to Kracauer's interpretation of the Weimar cinema for aesthetic reasons, historians also take issue with Kracauer's assessment of the conservative character of the Weimar cinema on political grounds. Calling attention to the left-wing film activities sponsored by Münzenberg's IAH (especially the film production company, Prometheus, and the distribution company, Weltfilm), these historians challenge Kracauer's thesis about the political nature of film production and reception in Weimar.[3] To be sure, historians who analyze the proletarian cinema agree with Kracauer that a male, petit bourgeois spectator was anticipated by UFA films. In their view, however, Kracauer and, perhaps more obviously, art historians like Lotte Eisner, fail to account adequately for left-wing film production in the 1920s and therefore exclude any analysis of the address to a working-class audience. Given the existence of conservative and left-wing media institutions in Weimar, they argue, it is impossible to analyze aesthetic

[3] A great deal of the research on the proletarian cinema has been done in the German Democratic Republic. See, for instance, Gerd Meier, "Materialien zur Geschichte des Prometheus Film-Verleih und Vertriebs GmbH, 1926–1933," *Deutsche Filmkunst*, nos. 1–8 (Berlin, DDR, 1962): 12–16, 57–60, 97–99, 137–40, 177–80, 221–24, 275–77, 310–12; and Gertraude Kühn, Karl Tümmler, Walter Wimmer, eds., *Film und revolutionäre Arbeiterbewegung in Deutschland 1918–1932*, 2 vols. (Berlin, DDR: Hochschule für Film und Fernsehen der DDR, 1975). There has also been critical work done on the proletarian cinema in West Germany. See, for example, the exhibition catalog, *Erobert den Film! Proletariat und Film in der Weimarer Republik: Materialien zur Filmgeschichte*, eds. Neue Gesellschaft für Bildende Kunst und Freunde der deutschen Kinemathek (West Berlin, 1977), and especially Toni Stoos's article, " 'Erobert den Film!' oder Prometheus gegen UFA & Co.," 482–525. Finally, there has been a renewed interest in the German proletarian cinema in England (particularly in association with the journal *Screen*) and in the United States. A representative survey of this literature would include: Bernard Eisenschitz, "Who Does the World Belong To? The Place of a Film," *Screen* 15, no. 2 (1974): 65–73; James Pettifer, "Against the Stream—*Kuhle Wampe*," *Screen* 15, no. 2 (1974): 49–64; Bert Hogenkamp, "Workers' Newsreels in the 1920s and 1930s," *Our History* 68 (n.d.): 1–36; David Welch, "The Proletarian Cinema and the Weimar Republic," *Historical Journal of Film, Radio, and Television* 1, no. 1 (1981): 3–18; Bruce Murray, "*Mutter Krausens Fahrt ins Glück*: An Analysis of the Film as a Critical Response to the 'Street Films' of the Commercial Film Industry," *Enclitic* 5–6, nos. 1–2 (1981–1982): 44–54; Jan Christopher Horak, "*Mother Krause's Trip to Happiness*, Kino-Culture in Weimar Germany, Part 2, 'Tenements Kill Like an Ax,' " *Jump Cut* 27 (July 1982): 55–56; and Vance Kepley, "The Workers' International Relief and the Cinema of the Left," *Cinema Journal* 23, no. 1 (Fall 1983): 7–23.

meaning apart from institutional factors or to assume that all films adhere to a conservative ideology. As one historian explains,

> [Any] film history of the Weimar Republic that concentrates on the most spectacular films, films made with the most advanced technology, or films of particular aesthetic merit, is likely to concentrate on films made with the largest production budgets. These are most frequently films by UFA . . . Germany's largest and most prolific film enterprise which had a management with strong conservative leanings. . . . [And] any film history that focuses largely on UFA is a history of conservative film production and is likely to overlook the crucial role that the interaction between companies on the political right and those on the political left played in the Weimar Republic's film history. . . . Such histories by their very nature ignore the broader context in which films are produced and hence miss issues involved in their making. Consequently, they risk misinterpreting the films themselves.[4]

These are very large claims, but they are not altogether consistent with the conditions of film production and reception during the Weimar years. As suggested in chapter 3, it is difficult to maintain absolute dividing lines between conservative, liberal, and left-wing media institutions in Weimar, and it is impossible to determine the political effects of textual practices on the basis of institutional affiliation alone. In its attempt to forge an alternative sphere for film reception, for instance, Weltfilm distributed proletarian and Soviet films, as well as commercially produced German films: notably, Gerhard Lamprecht's *Menschen untereinander* (*People Side By Side*, 1926) and G. W. Pabst's *Die freudlose Gasse* (*The Joyless Street*, 1925).[5] Furthermore, early feature film production at Prometheus not only derived themes and conventions from popular entertainment films, but also consciously addressed an audience distinguished as much by gender as by class; indeed, this much is suggested by such titles as *Das Mirakel der Liebe* (*The Miracle of Love*, 1926) and *Das Mädchen aus der Fremde* (*The Girl*

[4] Thomas Plummer, "Introduction," *Film and Politics in the Weimar Republic*, ed. Thomas Plummer et al. (New York: Holmes and Meier, 1982), 7.

[5] On this point, see Kühn, Tümmler, and Wimmer, eds., *Film und revolutionäre Arbeiterbewegung in Deutschland*, 462–67.

from Abroad, 1927). In their desire to retrieve and reestablish the working class as an agent of history, historians of the proletarian cinema typically resort to reductive interpretations of the politics of representation in Weimar. And in their near blindness to issues of sexuality and gender, they often implicitly assume the working-class spectator to be male.

It is important to recognize what arguments for textual ambiguity share with arguments for the political value of proletarian films. Just as one elides questions of female spectatorship in the name of a self-conscious (and therefore aesthetically "progressive") textual modernism, so the other elides questions of gendered spectatorship in the name of a left-wing (and therefore politically "progressive") institutional practice. Whether appealing to the text or its institutional conditions of production, claims for inherent progressivity nevertheless collapse once a notion of a viewing subject is introduced.

Of course, to speak of a viewing subject is to speak of a male as well as a female subject. And nowhere is the inscription of male subjectivity more illuminating than in Weimar films which borrow fantastic themes of split personalities and terrifying doubles, or in films which explore the crisis of male identity as primarily a crisis in vision. Although the male subject continues to be the topic of intense scrutiny and elaborate speculation (evidenced by such recent studies as Klaus Theweleit's *Männerphantasien* and Peter Sloterdijk's *Kritik der zynischen Vernunft*),[6] it is clear that much work remains to be done on contours of male subjectivity during the Weimar period. Feminist film theorists have had an obvious interest in pursuing questions of male spectatorship in the Weimar cinema, and in investigating strategies of representation with an eye to discerning what they make visible and what they leave undisclosed. Fritz Lang's *Metropolis* (1926) has served as a key film in this respect, in part because it so clearly thematizes the relationships among film technology, female sexuality, and male-centered vision.[7] While analyses of male subjectivity in the Weimar cinema

[6] Klaus Theweleit, *Männerphantasien*, 2 vols. (Frankfurt: Verlag Roter Stern, 1977, 1979); Peter Sloterdijk, *Kritik der zynischen Vernunft*, 2 vols. (Frankfurt am Main: Suhrkamp, 1983).

[7] See, for example, Patricia Mellencamp, "Oedipus and the Robot in *Metropolis*," *Enclitic* 5, no. 1 (Spring 1981): 20–42; Stephen Jenkins, "Lang: Fear and Desire," in

enable us to locate the sites of unstable identities and structures of vision, such analyses also allow us better to understand the appeal of the film melodrama to female audiences, and thus to challenge the exclusive attention to male subjectivity in Weimar film histories. As we shall see, the fantastic film and the film melodrama in Weimar played out fundamentally different scenarios of looking and desire so as to outline the terms of their understanding. Close analysis of these genres therefore serves to reveal the ways in which male and female subjectivity were not only figured differently in the Weimar cinema, but also in a patriarchal power structure.

Gender, Looking, and Identification in the Weimar Cinema: Male and Female Spectatorship

Although rarely discussed by historians or theorists, Arthur Robison's *Schatten* (*Warning Shadows*, 1923) takes up themes and visual motifs long associated with the Gothic and the fantastic: the preoccupation with nightmare states and the supernatural, the fascination with processes of desire and repression, and the dramatization of the double or split self as the symbolic representation of unconscious motives or wishes. Recounting the story of marital infidelity and sexual rivalry, *Schatten* begins by focusing on the wife of a wealthy count who divides her attention among three courtiers and a lover, much to the chagrin of her jealous husband. One evening, just when the wife's relations with her admirers threaten to provoke the husband's aggression, a shadow-player appears on the scene and offers to entertain, to amuse, and thus to contain a potentially explosive domestic situation. Hypnotizing the entire group—the count, his wife, the courtiers, and the lover—the shadow-player conjures up a strikingly cinematic illusion. The hypnotized figures are not consciously aware that their shadows have been separated from their bodies or that they have become spectators to a shadow-play—quite literally to a film-within-the-film—

Fritz Lang: The Image and the Look, ed. Stephen Jenkins (London: British Film Institute, 1981), 38–124; and Andreas Huyssen, "The Vamp and the Machine: Technology and Sexuality in Fritz Lang's *Metropolis*," *New German Critique*, nos. 24–25 (Fall–Winter 1981–1982): 221–37.

in which they are the principal players. The shadow-play condenses earlier themes of infidelity and sexual rivalry but culminates in an act of violence when the count arranges for his wife to be bound with ropes and chains, provides his four rivals with swords, and orders that they kill her. After witnessing this imaginary drama (which concludes with the count's own demise at the hands of his four rivals), the group wakes up from its hypnotic trance. The three courtiers silently take their leave, the lover departs with hesitation and regret, and the wife turns her attention to her husband, whose honor and identity have been restored.

Schatten is undeniably a self-conscious meditation on the act of representation and the desire to represent. It is also a remarkable illustration of how female desire is put into play in narrative, only to be channeled and remade for the pleasure of one man. But *Schatten* is fundamentally a film about cinematic representation and filmviewing as particular kinds of "therapy" for containing dangerous desires and impulses. Speaking of *Schatten* as a "Freudian inspiration," Lotte Eisner suggests that when "the little illusionist steals shadows" he also "opens the flood-gates of repressed desires of the other characters who start acting out their secret fantasies."[8] It is interesting that Eisner refers to the repressed desires of the *other* characters, for it is the shadow-play or the film-within-the-film which effectively dispenses with the wife's story and inaugurates a specifically male fantasy. In acting out this fantasy, the shadow-play not only constitutes the female body as the site of male violence and control, but also reveals filmmaking and filmviewing as mechanisms for subduing female desire and subjecting the image of woman to a controlling male gaze.

The fantastic film is rarely discussed in terms of female sexuality and male desire, and no suggestion has been made about why women in these films are often made into passive objects of male voyeuristic and sadistic impulses—how they exist to express the desires and anxieties of an anticipated male audience. Instead, the fantastic film in Weimar is typically celebrated for its formal virtuosity, and for its ability to render male spectatorship transparent or problematic. *Das Kabinett des Dr. Caligari (The Cabinet of Dr.*

---

[8] Lotte Eisner, *Haunted Screen* (Berkeley and Los Angeles: University of California Press, 1969), 136.

Caligari, 1919) has received the greatest amount of scholarly attention in this regard, although critics and historians continue to dis-
pute the meaning of its framing device (which precedes and follows
the narrative proper) for an understanding of spectatorship in the
fantastic film.[9]

In *From Caligari to Hitler*, Kracauer argues that the framing device transforms a revolutionary film into a premonition of authoritarianism. "While the initial story exposed the madness inherent
in authority," he writes, the framing device "glorifies authority and
convicts its antagonist of madness."[10] Thomas Elsaesser has recently challenged this reading of the framing device, claiming that
it focuses too narrowly on Caligari and Francis. In his view, *The
Cabinet of Dr. Caligari* is a multiperspectival narrative that condenses Oedipal themes and relationships in a lacunary, elliptical
text which provides "an entry point for a number of distinct and
different fantasies focused on male and female Oedipal scenarios."[11]
In support of his claim for female spectator identification, Elsaesser
points to the film's inscription of Jane in a female Oedipal fantasy.
Motivated to visit Caligari by "her father's long absence" (the intertitle explains), Jane arrives at Caligari's tent. Elsaesser describes
the scene: "[Caligari] beckons Jane inside, shows her the upright
box, flings it open with a leer to reveal the rigid figure of Cesare,
who, as she gets closer, opens his eyes, whereupon she stands
transfixed until she breaks away with a terrified, distraught expression on her face."[12] Underscoring the sexual connotations of the
scene, Elsaesser suggests that Caligari's behavior toward Jane
could be read as "the very epitome of the 'dirty old man' exposing
himself: showing Cesare is literally an exhibition." But, Elsaesser
continues, to read this scene merely in terms of male voyeurism or
perversion would be to deny the manner in which Caligari actually
serves as the double for Jane's father and Cesare as the "disavowed

---

[9] For a discussion of the framing device, see Kracauer, *From Caligari to Hitler*, 64–
66; Frieda Grafe, "Doktor Caligari gegen Dr. Kracauer," *Filmkritik* 5 (May 1970): 242–
44; Peter Wuss, "Film Concepts in the Brechtian Era," *Filmwissenschaftliche Mitteilungen* 6, no. 1 (1965): 39–48; Thomas Elsaesser, "Social Mobility and the Fantastic:
German Silent Cinema," *Wide Angle* 5, no. 2 (1982): 20–23.

[10] Kracauer, *From Caligari to Hitler*, 67.

[11] Elsaesser, "Social Mobility and the Fantastic," 23.

[12] Ibid., 22.

phallus-fetish of curiosity which the scene in Caligari's tent marks as explicitly sexual."[13]

In contrast to this assessment, I believe the scene in Caligari's tent reveals less about female Oedipal fantasies than it does about male fears of a different kind of sexuality. Rather than interpret Caligari as the double for Jane's father or Cesare as a "phallus-fetish," I would argue that Cesare's hypnotic and terrifying powers make him in many ways the double for Jane. Linda Williams's analysis of the classical horror film is especially relevant in this regard, for, as she points out, the close affinity between monster and woman in early horror films often suggests the extent to which they share a "similar status within patriarchal structures of seeing."[14]

To begin with, both Cesare and Jane are perceived as powerfully different from others: Cesare, the somnambulist, inspires the fear and dread of virtually everyone who sees him, while Jane, the only female character in the film, attracts and threatens Francis with an equally trancelike passivity. Cesare is literally the instrument of Caligari, the odd sideshow spectacle who is induced to act out his master's murderous intentions and desires. Jane, too, is constituted as a spectacle, most obviously when she visits Caligari's tent and is made to confront Cesare's hypnotic stare. Although Jane's terrified expression reveals her fear of Cesare, her paralyzed look also becomes the source of Caligari's own voyeuristic pleasure—the object of his leering gaze—which constitutes Jane simultaneously as victim and as spectacle. That Cesare seems to recognize her vulnerability and difference as similar to his own may indeed account for the strange sympathy that he later demonstrates for her. While Jane sleeps (a state that also links her to Cesare, the somnambulist), Cesare breaks into her bedroom and lifts his dagger to kill her. Curiously, he hesitates. He gazes longingly at her, puts his dagger away, and then abducts her, fleeing over rooftops and roads. When pursued by the townspeople, Cesare suddenly drops Jane, becomes weak and, as the intertitle explains, "dies of exhaustion."

If, as I have suggested, Cesare recognizes in Jane his own differ-

---

[13] Ibid., 23.

[14] Linda Williams, "When the Woman Looks," in *Re-Vision: Essays in Feminist Film Criticism*, ed. Mary Ann Doane, Patricia Mellencamp, and Linda Williams, The American Film Institute Monograph Series, vol. 3 (Frederick, Md.: University Publications of America, 1984), 85.

ence from the other male figures in the film, there nevertheless exists an important difference between Cesare and Jane. Not only is Jane Cesare's victim, but it is Jane—and not Cesare—who comes to signify the near absence of desire in the film. The framing device, for example, establishes the flashback (the narrative proper) as narrated by Francis, whose memory of past events is provoked by his sight of a white figure, whom we later know to be Jane. Moving slowly, like an apparition (or even a somnambulist), Jane passes by Francis, who turns to his companion and says, "What I have experienced with her is still stranger than what you have encountered. I will tell you." That Jane serves as the marker through which Francis's story proceeds to its conclusion is suggested by the framing device which ends the film. Having finished his narration, Francis returns with his companion to the asylum. Struggling to assert his sanity in the midst of madness, Francis turns to Jane for recognition. He pleads with her to marry him, to accede to his name and thus to confirm his identity. But Jane replies, "We queens may never choose as our hearts dictate." If the question of female desire is therefore raised and answered negatively in these final moments of the film, it is clear that woman's difference remains at issue in the film. Indeed, the question of woman in *The Cabinet of Dr. Caligari* seems not only to be a question of and for the man but also, as the framing device reveals, a question upon which a stable male identity depends.

It would seem that *Schatten* and *The Cabinet of Dr. Caligari* merely confirm Kracauer's remarks about male spectator identification in the Weimar cinema, where the spectator is offered the limited choice either to identify with authority or to allow the crisis of self-identity to follow its destructive course. More precisely, Kracauer's formulation of these alternatives would seem to confirm Laura Mulvey's analysis of the two avenues for female spectator identification in the classical narrative cinema: the option to identify either with the dominant male look or with the passive object of male desire. But to assume that all Weimar films are merely variations on classic films of the fantastic—that they are, in fact, films of and for an anticipated male spectator—would simply be to repeat the gesture of historians and theorists who exclude any consideration of female spectatorship in the Weimar cinema. Fritz Lang's *Der Müde Tod* (*Destiny*, 1921), for example, offers what may be read as an allegory of the position of women in Weimar culture and at the movies. In a highly elliptical fashion, *Der Müde Tod* tells the story of a woman's struggle with the Angel of Death to effect her lover's return from the grave. Situated as both the actor and the spectator in three separate dramas, the woman is made to bear witness to her own desperate attempts to outwit the inexorable logic of Death and narrative development, over which she is seen successively to lose control.

A less self-conscious but no less interesting example of a film that highlights the dilemma of female spectator identification in the cinema is Piel Jutzi's *Mutter Krausens Fahrt ins Glück* (*Mother Krause's Journey into Happiness*, 1929). Produced by Prometheus, *Mutter Krausens* was the company's first commercial success and first attempt to address a specifically female working-class audience. The film opens with a documentary montage of the back streets and tenements of Wedding, a working-class district in Berlin, and then the camera tracks in to a single worker's apartment. In this apartment, Mother Krause lives with her daughter, Erna, her son, Paul, and three boarders she has taken on to make ends meet: a prostitute, her daughter, and a pimp. The narrative development and resolution of *Mutter Krausens* is especially interesting for an analysis of female spectator identification, since the alternatives of authority and resignation are thematized in two separate but interrelated stories: the story of Erna's uneven but successful socialist education, and the story of Mother Krause's intense and insuperable despair.

From the very start, Erna is represented as the victim of male oppression and an underdeveloped class identity. The pimp who rents a room from Mother Krause continually watches Erna as she washes or dresses; on one occasion, he enters her bedroom while she sleeps, stares at her exposed leg, and considers raping her. Erna wakes up and pushes him away, and yet we soon learn that the pimp's attempt at rape had indeed been successful in the past. The pimp's advances toward Erna are temporarily complicated when Erna visits a fairground and meets Max, a socialist and conscientious party organizer. Later in Max's apartment, Erna becomes fascinated with Max's picture of Karl Marx and his extensive book collection. Ever the party organizer, Max admits that his apartment lacks a woman's touch and he offers Erna a copy of Be-

bel's *Woman and the Class Struggle.* Max and Erna decide to
marry, but when the pimp tells Max that Erna is no longer a virgin,
Max deserts her. In her despair, Erna comes to recognize her
mother's growing anxiety about finances and, with the encourage-
ment of the pimp, she seeks employment as a prostitute. But Erna
is unable to go through with it and flees instead to find Max. She
finally locates him at a working-class demonstration: he pulls her
into the column of marching male workers, who carry banners urg-
ing proletarian women and mothers to join the class struggle.

If Erna's story focuses on the difficulties of class and gender identity, Mother Krause's story explores remarkably similar difficulties.
Honest and hardworking, Mother Krause is represented as the typical proletarian mother, oppressed by her gender, her age, and her
family. Constantly engaged in household chores, Mother Krause
ekes out a meager living selling newspapers. One day while she is
out at work, her son steals her earnings as well as the money she
still owes the newspaper vendor. When Mother Krause finds her
son in a pub and confronts him with his crime, his sense of guilt
and shame erupts in an uncontrollable rage and he strikes her
down. From this point on, Mother Krause becomes increasingly
desperate, preoccupied with her son's behavior and worried that
she may be summoned by the court to account for the stolen
money. Erna and Max convince her to attend a workers' garden
festival to take her mind off her worries, but when Mother Krause
returns home to find her son being arrested for yet another rob-
bery, she lapses into utter despair and resignation. Taking the prostitute's young daughter from the bedroom into the kitchen, Mother
Krause laments, "What does a poor creature like you have to gain
in this world?" With that remark, she turns on the gas from the
stove and willingly accepts death as a "journey into happiness."

The narrative concludes with a series of abrupt and disorienting
images: Erna and Max arrive at Mother Krause's apartment and
discover her suicide, and a rapid montage of their shocked expressions is followed by a final image of Erna's marching feet—an image
that refers us back to the previous day's demonstration. In an effort
to make sense of these images, virtually every critic explains that
the film dramatizes the two choices open to a working-class spectator—death and resignation or life and class struggle—only to in-

sist, by the final image, on the necessity for class struggle.[15] As one critic proposes, "The closing image of the workers' feet marching brings us back to the masses, indicating that the struggle will be carried on. Erna stands above the hopeless resignation of her old mother as a positive image for working-class women. . . . The final image, then, is one for the hope of the revolution to come."[16]

This reading of the film's final images certainly corroborates the filmmakers' intention, but it fails to consider the film's inscription of a far more complicated position for the female spectator. Erna's choice of Max, of socialism and class struggle, is clearly a choice that is deliberately made for her: it is Max who forces her decision by pulling her into the ranks of male workers and, as one critic puts it, "she is literally carried away, borne away with her feet hardly touching the ground."[17] That Max represents an authority that is itself problematic is rendered most explicitly when Erna first meets him at the fairground. Joining an audience at a fairground theater, Max and Erna watch a performance which dramatizes a fat woman's manipulation of a helpless man. Erna, like the rest of the audience, is fascinated by the performance, but Max becomes visibly uneasy, and then so disgusted that he dramatically stands up and walks out. If Erna's choice of Max represents a choice of a particular kind of male working-class authority, it would be difficult to assume that the female spectator identifies solely with Erna or that Erna alone serves to represent the future for working-class women. The very poignancy of Mother Krause's suicide, and the fact that the youngest proletarian female dies with her, would suggest that the female spectator identifies equally with authority and resignation—in other words, with the very contradictions of a choice that is dramatized in the narrative and hardly contained by the film's final images.

The address to female spectators in *Mutter Krausens* recalls the address to female readers in the AIZ, where a similar construction of polarized and dramatic conflict serves to forge identification with contradiction itself. Significantly, *Mutter Krausens* is a melodrama and, as at least one theorist has pointed out, the inscription of mul-

---

[15] See, for example, Murray, "*Mutter Krausens Fahrt ins Glück*," 52–53; and Horak, "*Mother Krause's Trip to Happiness*," 55–56.

[16] Horak, "*Mother Krause's Trip to Happiness*," 55–56.

[17] Stephen Heath, "Discussion," *Screen* 16, no. 4 (Winter 1976–1977): 13.

tiple spaces for spectator identification is a convention of the melo-dramatic mode.[18] The mobility of spectator identification in the film melodrama, moreover, often carries over to the representation of sexual mobility in films that address a female audience. To understand the significance of this mobility in the representation of gender identity, it is necessary to consider how conventions in the illustrated press were often taken up in the Weimar cinema.

The image of the New Woman in *Die Dame*, for example, was frequently linked by contemporary critics to the screen persona of Asta Nielsen.[19] In her appropriation of masculine styles and gestures and, in the case of *Hamlet* (1921), male identity, Nielsen indeed represents a figure of sexual mobility—a figure who destabilizes the polarized opposition between masculine and feminine identities. Although Elisabeth Bergner was also cast in roles that highlighted sexual mobility—in *Der Geiger von Florenz* (1926), for instance, she temporarily assumes a male identity—it was Nielsen who paved the way for the popular acceptance of female androgyny in the cinema and Nielsen who, in the view of several critics, actually inspired Bergner's later screen roles.[20] What is perhaps most interesting about Nielsen's image, however, is the manner in which it evidences an extremely subtle and complicated alternation between sexual mobility and emotional pathos—as if the image of the New Woman had been overlaid with the image of the tragically expressive proletarian woman. It is this particular combination of female bisexuality and melodramatic expression, I believe, that serves to explain Nielsen's enormous popularity with female audiences in the 1920s.

It is nevertheless significant that the representation of female androgyny and bisexuality in the Weimar cinema was often accompanied by an attempt to disavow the vision of alternative kinds of desire. In Pabst's *Tagebuch einer Verlorenen* (*Diary of a Lost Girl*, 1929), for example, Thymian (Louise Brooks) moves through three

[18] I am referring here to Linda Williams' essay "Something Else Besides a Mother: Stella Dallas and the Maternal Melodrama," *Cinema Journal* 24, no. 1 (Fall 1984): 2–27.

[19] See, for example, the essays collected in *Asta Nielsen*, ed. Helga Belach, Gero Gandert, Eva Orbanz, and Peter Schulz (Berlin: Stiftung Deutsche Kinemathek, 1973).

[20] See, for example, the essays collected in *Asta Nielsen: Ihr Leben in Fotodokumenten, Selbstzeugnissen und zeitgenössischen Betrachtungen*, ed. Renate Seydel and Allan Hagedorff (Munich: Universitas Verlag, 1981).

distinct social and institutional spaces: an oppressive bourgeois home, a regimented girls' correctional facility, and a carnivalesque brothel. This last environment—where women dance with women, and where various social classes freely intermingle—appears to promise Thymian a release from the demands of bourgeois morality and institutional authority. But even this site of sexual and social mobility is ultimately seen to be monitored by a controlling, calculating gaze: following the steps of the dancers, the camera pans the space of a brothel in a relaxed, fluid movement, finally coming to rest on the gaze of the madam, who oversees and channels all forms of social and sexual activity.[21]

Renate Müller's role as Susana in *Victor und Victoria* (1933) offers yet another vision of sexual mobility, but here this mobility is explicitly linked to a female character who mimes masculinity in an act of role reversal. An aspiring young singer, Susana is "discovered" by Victor, an unemployed actor who is clearly homosexual, and Victor convinces her to take on a male identity so as to break into show business as a female impersonator. Most of the comic situations in the film result from Susana's extreme uneasiness with her "masculine masquerade": her discomfort with using male dressing rooms or with submitting to the barber's chair. The meaning of Susana's androgyny is, in one sense, absolutely clear; masculinity is a mask that hides her truly feminine identity. (This is advanced in narrative terms as well when Robert, a wealthy playboy, sees through her masquerade and unmasks it as mere pretense—much to Susana's relief.) But the formal construction of female androgyny nevertheless opens up a potential discrepancy between narrative movement and spectator identification. During one of her first performances as a female impersonator, Susana elicits the admiring gaze of a female spectator within the film. Unlike the spectator of *Victor und Victoria*, who knows full well that Susana is a woman, this female spectator assumes that Susana is a feminized male and exclaims, "What a wonderful boy!" At least momentarily, then, the image of female androgyny opens up to fe-

---

[21] Heide Schlüpmann elaborates on this reading in her essay "The Bordello as an Arcadian Site? G. W. Pabst's *Diary of a Lost Girl*," in *The Films of G. W. Pabst*, ed. Eric Rentschler (New Brunswick, N.J.: Rutgers University Press, forthcoming 1989).

male desire, where the look of the female spectator within the film may be combined with the look of the female spectator of *Victor und Victoria* and thus disrupt the narrative construction of female bisexuality as masquerade, as merely a case of mistaken identity.

Without a doubt, this look of the female spectator at what appears to her to be a feminized male serves to make narratively acceptable an otherwise unacceptable representation of desire (the female spectator's desire for the woman). The very fact that it was narratively acceptable to represent a female spectator who looks at a feminized male, however, would also suggest that there was an established precedent for this kind of looking during the Weimar period. As suggested in chapter 3, the representation of a feminized, eroticized male in the fashion pages of *Die Dame* did indeed establish a precedent for female viewers to look at a different kind of male identity. And as Janet Bergstrom has pointed out in her analysis of Murnau's films, the Weimar cinema similarly inscribed an erotic look directed at a passive male figure, where femininity and sexuality are typically displaced from the woman's body onto an aestheticized male character.[22]

Although Bergstrom does not specify any relationship between the representation of unstable male identity and a gendered spectator, I should like to do so. For instance, it is possible to identify at least three different types of male figures in the Weimar cinema that exhibit an unstable masculine identity. There is, first of all, the impotent, self-punishing, and frequently sadistic male who projects his sense of powerlessness onto a female figure with whom he comes to identify. This type of male figure is best described by Kracauer and perhaps most strikingly exemplified by Emil Jannings's role as the hotel doorman in *Der Letzte Mann* (*The Last Laugh*, 1924) and his role as Professor Unrat in *Der Blaue Engel* (*The Blue Angel*, 1930). Jannings's earlier and more masculine persona in films like *Kohlhiesers Töchter* (*Kohlhieser's Daughters*, 1920) and *Anna Boleyn* (1920) may have contributed to the sense of pathos surrounding his later screen roles. His depiction of the impotent, symbolically defeated male was nevertheless matched by

---

[22] Janet Bergstrom, "Sexuality at a Loss: The Films of F. W. Murnau," *Poetics Today* 6, nos. 1–2 (1985): 185–203.

other actors of the period, most notably by Fritz Kortner in *Hintertreppe* (*Backstairs*, 1921) and Peter Lorre in *M* (1931).

In addition to the impotent and defeated male, the Weimar cinema also represents a passive and homoerotic male. This type of male figure was most obviously depicted in films that explicitly deal with themes of male homosexuality (as, for example, *Anders als die Andern* (*Different from the Others*, 1919) or *Geschlecht in Fesseln* (*Sex in Fetters*, 1926). But this type of male also fits Bergstrom's description of Murnau's films and particularly her analysis of *Faust* (1926). For instance, Bergstrom explains that although the narrative establishes Faust's identity through his relationship to Gretchen, the spectator is able to treasure Faust's youth "as a sensuous, artistic wonder, much as the old Faust is taken with the image of the young Faust." Continuing this argument, she writes:

> Because the young man is said to represent his own youth, Faust's desire is designated by the narrative as natural, rather than as a result of a sexualized seduction. Desire for the young Faust is represented as being even more indirect by the fact that Mephisto, the mediator, is necessary to Faust's temptation. That the temptation is sexual is made clear by the first act Mephisto performs after endowing Faust with a young man's body: he presents a diaphanous vision of a woman, almost naked in transparent veils, as the pleasure Faust's youth is entitled to. . . . Thus, the woman's body is presented (very briefly) as sexuality, and in a way that directs our narrative interest away from the sight of the young Faust himself. Given all this narrative and stylistic machinery, the viewer is left to enjoy the beauty of the young Faust without thinking twice.[23]

---

[23] Ibid., 195–96. It is particularly interesting that Dreyer's *Michael* (1925), which was released in Germany a year earlier than *Faust*, also aims to make male homoerotic desire narratively acceptable by establishing a connection between Michael, an aspiring painter, and Claude Zoret, the "master painter," through the mediator of the princess. This film overdetermines the representation of male homoerotic desire, however, by frequently directing the viewer's attention to the portraits of male nudes painted by Zoret with Michael as his model. In this regard, it is interesting to note that Asta Nielsen was originally asked to play the role of the princess in *Michael*. In an interview with Marguerite Engberg, Nielsen responded to the question "Have you ever had artistic contact with Carl Th. Dreyer?" in the following way: "Yes, once. He wanted me to play the leading role in 'Michael,' but it didn't interest me. But his film 'Jeanne d'Arc' I found very interesting." See Marguerite Engberg, *Asta Nielsen*, trans. into German from the

The image of the young Faust, Bergstrom argues, invites an erotic and contemplative look on the part of the spectator who is "encouraged to relax rigid demarcations of gender identification and sexual orientation." While I would agree that both male and female spectators are invited to contemplate the young Faust's image, I believe Bergstrom's analysis makes it clear that it is a male spectator who is encouraged to relax rigid demarcations of gender and sexual orientation.[24] In contrast to *Victor und Victoria*, for example, *Faust* inscribes a male spectator who gazes at his own image (the old Faust gazes at his youthful self) and thus makes narratively acceptable an otherwise unacceptable representation of desire (the male spectator's desire for the man). If, as Laura Mulvey explains, "the male figure cannot bear the burden of sexual objectification" in the classical narrative cinema,[25] then *Faust* may be said to call upon a different sort of spectator convention than is operative in most narrative films by allowing the male spectator to enjoy male eroticism "without thinking twice." But when we consider the presence of a female spectator looking at a passive, eroticized male, it is difficult to assume that she thinks about male identity in the same way as the male spectator does; in other words, that she necessarily feels compelled to think twice or derives the same kind of pleasure in imagining an alternative male identity.

This brings me to the third type of male figure in the Weimar cinema, the passive and eroticized male who elicits the desiring

Danish by Børge Trolle and Erik Ziese (Bad Ems: Verband der deutschen Filmclubs E. V., 1967).

[24] The same thing could be said of Bergstrom's reading of *Nosferatu* (1922). Bergstrom argues that in this film, Jonathan serves as a double for the vampire, since both male figures are associated with sexuality: Jonathan, as a passive, feminized character, becomes the site of erotic attraction, just as the vampire represents "sexuality itself," a highly charged visual presence. Bergstrom further claims that the vampire and Jonathan are connected indirectly through the mediator of Nina, thus making narratively acceptable an otherwise unacceptable representation of (male, homoerotic) desire. While I think this reading is certainly plausible, it could be argued that *Nosferatu* opens up a different perspective for viewer identification, since the vampire serves in many ways as a double for Nina. Both are seen to possess "mystical" powers: the vampire cannot be controlled by rational measures, and only the woman's passion and self-sacrifice eventually subdue him. There is, moreover, an intense identification between the monster and the woman in the film, and both are seen to share a similar fate at the conclusion of the narrative. On this point, see Williams, "When the Woman Looks."

[25] Laura Mulvey, "Visual Pleasure and Narrative Cinema," *Screen* 16, no. 3 (Autumn, 1975): 6–18.

gaze of a textually inscribed female spectator. Franz Lederer's roles in *Zuflucht* and *Pandora's Box* are perhaps most representative of this type of male who functions both narratively and visually to refer to the female character's desire for a different image of male identity. Iconographically, this eroticized male fits Bergstrom's description of the image of the young Faust. Yet if it is reasonable to assume that the image of male eroticism in *Faust* appeals to a female spectator, then it seems all the more significant that *Zuflucht* takes up this image so as to refer to female desire in a melodrama that addresses a female audience.

Of course, if the image of the passive and eroticized male elicits a contemplative gaze and may be linked to film melodrama, there are a number of Weimar melodramas which show no trace of an eroticized male but which nevertheless organize a contemplative, less goal-oriented way of looking. As suggested in chapter 1, the film melodrama in Weimar adapted conventions usually associated with the *Kammerspiel* and street film, and these conventions typically function to break with narrative suspense in favor of an attention to composition and atmosphere. Hyperbolic gestures and exaggerated facial expressions, for example, are used conventionally in film melodrama to charge the narrative with an intensified significance, with meaning in excess of what the narrative depicts. The recourse to narrative repetition and studied composition, moreover, also gives the impression of a transference or a displacement of meaning which requires the spectator to concentrate on the manner in which conflicts are acted out, in all their ponderous slowness and meticulousness. Finally, and perhaps most importantly, the film melodrama in Weimar frequently dramatizes women's experiences and puts pressure on the representation of these experiences so as to force the unrepresented or the repressed into material presence. The intensity of expression so characteristic of the Weimar melodrama therefore opens up a space for female subjectivity and desire, where the contemplative gaze is inseparable from an alternative conception of female spectatorship and visual pleasure.

In order to make this argument more specific, I would like to look closely at four representative Weimar films: *Dirnentragödie* (1927), *Hintertreppe* (1921), *Zuflucht* (1927), and *Die freudlose*

Gasse (1925). Before we turn to these films directly, however, it is important to comment briefly upon their female stars. Asta Nielsen, who stars in *Dirnentragödie* and *Die freudlose Gasse*, and Henny Porten, who stars in *Hintertreppe* and *Zuflucht*, began their careers in the formative years of the German cinema and both were, from the very start, indisputable favorites with female audiences.[26] Nielsen, for example, started her film career at Paul Davidson's Union film (where she starred in a number of films dealing with the early women's movement), and has typically been associated with ambitious art films and literary adaptations which catered to an intellectual audience. Porten, by contrast, worked first with Oskar Meester and later with Ernst Lubitsch before forming her own production company, and has commonly been associated with romantic comedies which catered to a popular audience. While Nielsen's and Porten's early screen careers often serve to corroborate the split between art and mass culture that organizes so much of German film history, both actresses appeared in film melodramas where the distinction between the artistic and the popular does not hold. *Zuflucht* and *Die freudlose Gasse*, for instance, are quite obviously artistic films and yet they were highly popular with contemporary audiences. The very presence of Porten and Nielsen in leading roles, moreover, ensured that they would appeal to the female audience long established for the films of both stars.

It is symptomatic that neither Nielsen nor Porten has received the kind of attention accorded to other female stars of the Weimar period, for most critics choose to privilege Marlene Dietrich and Louise Brooks as the very embodiment of woman during the Weimar years. Without a doubt, Dietrich and Brooks remain convenient figures upon which to project a reading of male subjectivity in crisis; as figures of female eroticism, they were typically featured in films where male characters are brought to their doom as a result of their uncompromising devotion to a feminine ideal. Given that

---

[26] I was fortunate to be in Berlin for the Henny Porten film retrospective sponsored by the Berlin Film Festival in conjunction with the Stiftung Deutsche Kinemathek (Berlin) and the Bundesarchiv (Koblenz). For further information on Porten's star status, see Helga Belach's *Henny Porten: Der erste deutsche Filmstar* (Berlin: Hände und Spener, 1986), a book published on the occasion of the Porten retrospective.

Dietrich and Brooks only began their screen careers in the final years of the Weimar Republic, however, this kind of retrospective reading would seem to reveal as much about a fascination exerted by a certain type of woman in contemporary scholarship as it does about the figure of woman in the late Weimar period. The intense, dramatically focused gaze of Nielsen, for example, offers a striking contrast to the unfocused, almost mirrorlike gaze of Brooks, and it is hardly coincidental that Brooks's screen debut involved a remake of *Pandora's Box*—a film which originally featured Nielsen in the starring role. As critics have pointed out, the late Weimar cinema might be described as a transitional cinema to the extent that it was only beginning to adapt conventions relating to the representation of female sexuality later solidified by the Hollywood studio system (figure 32). In the early twenties, however, there remains a sense of both a different view of woman and an entirely different way of looking associated with the female figure: whether featured in the role of prostitute or traditional *Hausfrau*, Nielsen and Porten belong to a period of filmmaking when a focused and highly motivated female gaze was imbued with a pathos so intense that their performances become emblematic of an era, and a premonition of things to come.[27]

Dirnentragödie: SEXUAL MOBILITY, SOCIAL MOBILITY, AND MELODRAMAS OF THE STREET

People today cannot understand what that pale mask, with its immense blazing eyes, meant for the nineteen-teens and twenties. . . . It was impossible to put a label on this great actress: she was neither 'modernist' nor 'Expressionist.' Her warm humanity, full of the breadth of life and presence, refuted both abstraction and the abruptness of Expressionist art. . . . Never did she stoop to mawkishness, never did her travesty shock. For Asta Nielsen's eroticism was without equivocation, her passion was always authentic.[28]

[27] It is interesting given Nielsen's previous screen roles as a suffragette and Porten's screen persona as "the German Mary Pickford," that the two stars only appeared together on the screen on one occasion: Nielsen as Mary Magdalen and Porten as the virgin mother in Robert Wiene's little-known biblical drama, *I.N.R.I.* (1923).

[28] Eisner, *The Haunted Screen*, 261.

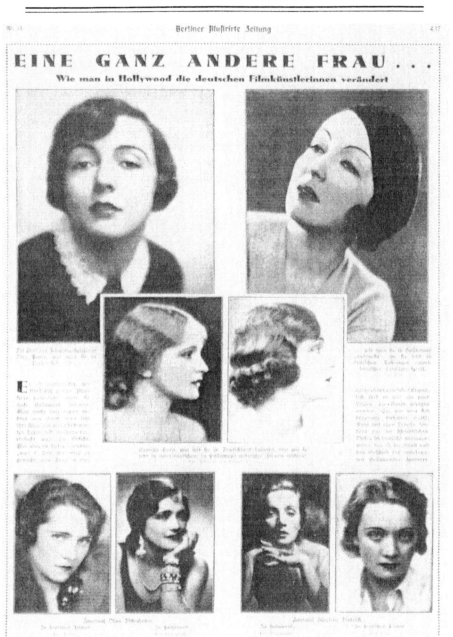

Figure 32. How Hollywood changes German actresses
(*Berliner Illustrirte Zeitung*, 1930)

Figure 33. The prostitute, the city, and the street film
(*Dirnentragödie*, 1927)

Dirnentragödie (*Tragedy of the Whore*, 1927) would seem to have all the conspicuous marks of the street film. The street itself serves as the setting for narrative transactions and interactions; dimly lit and mysterious, the image of the street is studied, arranged, and emphatic (figure 33). Furthermore, *Dirnentragödie* features a middle-class male character who follows his desire for adventure into the street, only to find himself enmeshed in dangerous intrigue, which leads him inexorably back to the arms of his mother. Finally, *Dirnentragödie* takes up the theme of social mobility associated with several Weimar film genres, including the street film (*Der Letzte Mann*, for instance), but centers the fantasy of upward mobility on an aging prostitute, whose ultimate failure to rise in society stands in direct relation to the struggle to establish an alternative sexual identity.

In their attempt to fix *Dirnentragödie* as an exemplary street film, critics and historians have not failed to mention the film's use of certain recognizable conventions. As one critic explains,

> *Dirnentragödie* (*Tragedy of the Street*) is one of the most notable examples of the 'street' film genre. These films portrayed the 'street' as a poor section of the city controlled by prostitutes, pimps, gamblers and thieves, but also inhabited by more respectable citizens. The model for these films was Karl Grüne's *The Street* [*Die Strasse*] (1923). In that film, a restless man leaves his wife and their orderly middle-class home to seek excitement. He becomes entangled in the underworld, which seeks to implicate him in a murder. He returns home shaken and only too happy to stay in his safe environment thereafter. *Tragedy of the Street* uses essentially this same plot structure.[29]

While this plot synopsis highlights two conventions of the street film—the function of the street as setting and the drama of male symbolic defeat—it is remarkable how it elides the theme of social and sexual mobility which, in *Dirnentragödie*, centers on a female protagonist. Indeed, although Grüne's film might be said to trace the middle-class male's descent into corruption and moral chaos (where chaos, corruption, and descent are associated with a particular vision of woman, who alternates between being viewed as an object of desire and as a figure of death), *Dirnentragödie* is best described as a female version of *Der Letzte Mann*: like Jannings's character in *Der Letzte Mann*, the aging prostitute in *Dirnentragödie* engages in a fantasy of social and economic mobility, only to find herself in the position of the "last woman," one who is unable to get beyond the barriers which define her identity according to class, age and, most strikingly, gender difference.

While more than one critic has assumed that the drama of the middle-class male bears the weight of *Dirnentragödie*'s represented meanings,[30] at least two others have offered different assessments of the film. "It is undeniable," writes Lotte Eisner, "that this film's extraordinary quality is principally due to the presence of

---

[29] Anthony K. Munson, "Dirnentragödie," in *Film and Politics in the Weimar Republic*, ed. Thomas Plummer et al., 63.

[30] See, for example, Murray, "*Mutter Krausens Fahrt ins Glück*."

Asta Nielsen,"[31] whose performance in *Dirnentragödie* marked the end of her screen career. Kracauer likewise refers to the presence of Nielsen and is forced to concede that even though the street film is the "master narrative" of male rebellion and submission, *Dirnentragödie* is not merely a derivative of Grüne's film. Describing Nielsen's persona and performance, Kracauer writes: "Asta Nielsen, emerging from the spheres of Ibsen and Strindberg, portrayed the prostitute incomparably: not a realistic one, but that imaginary figure of an outcast who has discarded social conventions because of her abundance of love, and now, through her mere existence, denies the questionable laws of a hypocritical society."[32]

Although he tends to romanticize the representation of the prostitute-woman, Kracauer's suggestion that Nielsen's performance was "not a realistic one" may be usefully read in terms of Eisner's remarks that open this analysis—"It was impossible to put a label on this great actress: she was neither 'modernist' nor 'Expressionist.'" Not realistic, not modernist, not expressionist, Nielsen's portrayal of the prostitute is profoundly melodramatic. Of course, it is not simply the figure of the prostitute, or Nielsen's acting style of inarticulate cry and expressive gesture, that leads me to define *Dirnentragödie* as a melodrama. It is also the unambiguous social and psychic functions assigned to various character types (the old prostitute, the young prostitute, the pimp, and the middle-class son) which suggest a reading of the film as a melodrama. Furthermore, while *Dirnentragödie* retains the convention of the middle-class male's venture into the street and his resigned return home, it renders this convention peripheral to the drama of the prostitute's efforts to liberate herself from an assigned social and sexual identity. The prostitute's fantasy of social mobility, moreover, allows us to speculate on *Dirnentragödie* as a film that addresses a female spectator. Indeed, because the fantasy of social mobility is inseparable from a shifting representation of female gender identity, *Dirnentragödie* can be seen as an expression of the ambitions and frustrations of its female audience—an audience perhaps most keenly aware of the precariousness of Weimar's much vaunted economic and sexual liberation.

---

[31] Eisner, *The Haunted Screen*, 263.
[32] Kracauer, *From Caligari to Hitler*, 158.

Dirnentragödie opens with a series of abstract and elliptical images: the camera tracks a woman's legs as they move cautiously across a cobblestone pavement until they meet a man's legs, at which point both pairs enter a doorway and disappear out of sight. Once off the street and in a dimly-lit room, the figures are identified as a prostitute and her pimp. He shakes her violently, insisting on his share of her earnings. She resists, screams out of the window for help, and attracts the attention of the people on the street below. He pulls her back inside and, while forcing her to the floor, he demands: "Have you found someone you like better?!" In effect, *Dirnentragödie* begins with an unsuccessful exchange, although the relationship between sexuality and economics extends beyond what the title's reference to prostitution might at first suggest. To be sure, the narrative depiction of sexuality as exchange literally establishes a relationship between women and men as a relationship between prostitutes and pimps. But the interchange between the anonymous prostitute and pimp in the opening sequence already introduces a disturbance into the symmetry of exchange, and foreshadows the film's particular version of tragedy: the tragedy of the woman who dares to defy the system which defines value, sexuality, and ultimately the terms of class and gender identity.

"In the form which prostitution took in the great cities," writes Walter Benjamin, "woman appears not merely as a commodity but as a mass-produced article. This is indicated in the artificial disguise of the individual expression in favor of a professional one, such as is brought about by the application of make-up."[33] These remarks are vividly illustrated in *Dirnentragödie*, for intercut with the scene of the anonymous prostitute's cry for help are shots of two other female figures: the old prostitute, Auguste (Asta Nielsen), and the young prostitute, Clarissa (Hilda Jennings). Preparing herself for an evening's work, Auguste constructs her image in a self-conscious fashion: using her teeth to pull the cork on a bottle of black hair dye, she touches up her grey hair and surveys her appearance in a cracked mirror that divides and doubles her image (figure 34). Sprawled on a couch, Clarissa indulges in momentary laughter but becomes visibly disturbed by the sound of the anon-

---

[33] Walter Benjamin, "Central Park," trans. Lloyd Spenser, *New German Critique*, no. 34 (Winter 1985): 52–53.

Figure 34. Divided image, divided perception
(*Dirnentragödie*, 1927)

ymous prostitute's voice. To calm her, Auguste assures Clarissa that she will "get used to it," for such violence is an everyday occurrence.

Although defined in relation to Clarissa (Auguste is older and more experienced, Clarissa is younger and more naive), Auguste is also defined in relation to her own image. Her gaze into the mirror symbolizes the problem of the aging prostitute: to be of value means to be desirable, and to be desirable means to be young. While the image of Auguste at the mirror could be read as inscribing the woman as the passive object for an ideal male gaze, it is significant that Auguste is seen actively to construct the image of female desirability—in other words, that she is seen to control that image rather than be controlled by it. However, the interplay of control over the image and its loss is not only rendered visually in Auguste's doubled mirror image; it also resurfaces throughout the film as a doubling or an oscillation between masculinity and femininity in the representation of her identity. Not unlike *Die Dame*'s New Woman, Auguste wears her hair cropped short, smokes cigars, and appropriates connotatively masculine styles and gestures. In a number of images, and especially when she is viewed from behind,[34] Auguste's body appears formidable and overpowering, without an explicitly erotic dimension. This is not to say, however, that she is represented as thoroughly "masculinized." When shot in close-up, for example, she retains a strikingly feminine appearance: her immense blazing eyes, the curls around her face, and the style of her dress all contribute to the softening of her image. In purely iconographic terms, Auguste may be said to represent a figure of sexual mobility—an unstable, composite figure who connotes both masculinity and femininity. This vision of mobility, moreover, is not only rendered iconographically, but in narrative terms, particularly in Auguste's relation to the male characters.

For example, Auguste's relationship to her pimp, Anton (Oskar Homolka), indicates a slippage in traditional female and male gender roles. During the scene in which Auguste prepares for work, Anton is introduced as part of the crowd gathered on the street to witness the confrontation between the anonymous prostitute and pimp. When the police arrive, Anton flees to Auguste and Clarissa and informs them—with an expression of surprise mixed with glee—that the anonymous prostitute actually turned her pimp over to the authorities. Anton's barely concealed pleasure as he relates the story of the pimp's fate seems to confirm the masochism of his character. Indeed, Anton not only appears helpless and passive (with a childlike curl on his brow); he also seems to enjoy submitting to Auguste's control.

If Auguste's relationship to Anton suggests a slippage in traditional definitions of gender, it is Auguste's relationship to the middle-class male, Felix (Werner Pittschau), that reveals a temporary release of class definitions and anticipates Auguste's full-blown fantasy of class rise. Represented as the highly conventional prodigal son, Felix returns home drunk and argues with his father. Much to

[34] Janice Solomon has provided a detailed analysis of framing, camera movement, and point of view in contributing to the "masculinization" of Nielsen's character in her essay, "Gender and Economics: Asta Nielsen in Rahn's *Dirnentragödie*," which was read at the 1985 scs Conference, New York University, June 1985.

his mother's sorrow and dismay, Felix claims his right to freedom and dramatically takes his leave of the middle-class home. While Auguste is working the streets, she finds Felix collapsed in a doorway. Instead of concluding the transaction with a potential customer, she takes Felix inside her apartment, provides him with food, and listens sympathetically to his story. Auguste's overtures toward Felix are, in one sense, profoundly maternal. (This is further reinforced by the frequent crosscutting between Felix's mother and Auguste and by the parting remarks of Felix's father, who predicts that his son will return home "as soon as he is hungry.") But Auguste's desires nevertheless prove far from maternal: she invites Felix to stay with her as long as he likes, and when Anton returns later that evening, she informs him that he must move out forever. Shocked and upset, Anton finally accepts Auguste's decision (and the money she offers to pay him off) and Auguste joins Felix, who beckons to her from the bedroom.

The next morning, Auguste engages in domestic chores, cheerfully preparing breakfast for Felix. Recognizing that Clarissa's youth presents a threat to her newfound happiness, she makes Clarissa promise never to take Felix away from her. Clarissa, who grudgingly agrees, assumes that Auguste's attachment to Felix is merely temporary—simply a passing fancy. Yet it is not only Clarissa who poses a threat to Auguste's happiness. Upon waking, Felix informs Auguste that he must go. In the morning light, he sees Auguste with profound apprehension, with an ambivalence mixed with horror and disgust. Misreading the source of Felix's apprehension in her class identity, Auguste tells him that things will be different, that she plans to buy a *Konditorei* and thus escape her economically dependent and socially dubious position.

At this point in the narrative, intertitles are all but absent and significant relationships are rendered solely through mise-en-scène, gestures, emblems, and symbols; in other words, through conventions typically associated with the *Kammerspielfilm*. Auguste goes to make a downpayment on the *Konditorei* and, in the meantime, Anton returns to the apartment to reclaim his "rightful" position. No longer represented as passive or helpless, Anton looms over Felix, his physical bulk traversing the frame. Warning Felix that he will become a kept man if he remains with Auguste, Anton emphasizes the symbolic threat Auguste represents by un-

Figure 35. Choreographed seduction
(*Dirnentragödie*, 1927)

derscoring his remarks with repeated jabs of a sausage knife. Once Felix's fear and revulsion are unmistakable, Anton stabs the knife into one of the sausages on the breakfast table. What follows is a carefully choreographed seduction: Anton brings Clarissa from her room, introduces her to Felix, turns on the record player, and puts a male doll on the spinning turntable. Standing behind the couple seated at the table, Anton engineers the seduction, forcing the couple into an embrace and then showering them with confetti and streamers (figure 35). Throughout this scene, the textual play of signs—the knife in the sausage, the spinning male doll, the streamers, the confetti, and, indeed, the looming presence of Anton himself—serve to make redundant the literal content of narrative action.

If the seduction scene clarifies meaning through exaggeration, the scene of Auguste's return home intensifies meaning through heightened emotional and melodramatic expression, thus permitting the evocation of meanings which exceed the narrative action. Concluding the deal on the *Konditorei*, Auguste walks home filled with a sense of accomplishment and control. She passes a former customer, who grabs her as she enters her apartment building, and she pushes him away with an expression of contempt. In the hallway, she meets Herr Kauzke, a pianist, and asks him to play something to suit her mood, "something from the heart." Sitting with Herr Kauzke at the piano, she envisions her future with Felix at the *Konditorei*: literalized as an image superimposed over the piano, her fantasy of social mobility is visualized for the spectator in a fixed representation (figure 36). While Herr Kauzke continues playing her chosen tune ("If It Weren't for Love"), Auguste makes her way upstairs. Upon entering the apartment and recognizing the signs of the seduction, Auguste's face registers an emotion which proves ineffable. Following the path of the streamers from the kitchen into the bedroom, she puts her ear to the locked door, begins knocking, then pounding, until finally she collapses on the floor (figure 37). An elaborate and frenetic montage bears the burden of expression, where gliding letters spelling "Stop!" (*Aufhören!*) are intercut with a rapid series of images: the piano keys, the sheet music, Felix's face, an ad for the *Konditorei*, and Auguste's fantasy image of a once possible economic and romantic future. The montage ends abruptly on a single, static image: Auguste sits motionless on the couch and alone in the dark.

The narrative now proceeds swiftly to its conclusion. Emerging from the bedroom, Felix encounters Auguste and his facial expression indicates his complete and utter revulsion at her presence. "Stay with me," Auguste implores, "I will forget everything" (figures 38 and 39). Unmoved by her pleas, Felix offers to pay for her services and departs to make plans to take Clarissa away with him. Although profoundly uninterested in accompanying Felix, Clarissa perceives Auguste's despair as laughable: "You look horrible, Guste," she quips, and with that remark reveals that she sees Auguste through Felix's eyes. Auguste's despair is then transformed into a desire for revenge. Enticing Anton with promises of co-ownership of the *Konditorei* (in a seduction scene staged similarly to the one staged by Anton himself), she persuades him to kill Clarissa. A series of abstract and elliptical images renders the murder in exactly the same way as the images that began the narrative: the

Figure 36. The fantasy of social mobility
(*Dirnentragödie*, 1927)

Figure 37. Locked doors and expressive anxiety
(*Dirnentragödie*, 1927)

Figure 38. Male ambivalence
(*Dirnentragödie*, 1927)

Figure 39. Excessive desire
(*Dirnentragödie*, 1927)

172

camera tracks Anton's legs until they meet Clarissa's, and the murder is implied by their shadows cast upon a wall. When Felix returns to the apartment, he reveals to Auguste that his interest in Clarissa has nothing to do with love. Auguste's face registers a mixture of guilt and panic and, oblivious to Felix's condemnation of her "bestiality," she frantically attempts to stop the killing. The image of the frenetic movement of her high-heeled shoes across the cobblestone pavement serves to emphasize the futility of her efforts: the deed has been done, Anton is arrested, and Felix returns home to his mother, resting his head on her lap.

The final scene brings us back to the street, where a crowd reacts to Clarissa's murder and to the newspaper account of Auguste's consequent suicide. Two anonymous prostitutes, iconographically marked as doubles for Clarissa and Auguste, provide the spectator with a summary of the conflicts and issues of the narrative. "Poor Auguste!" exclaims the young prostitute, while the older one laments, "That is how we will all end one day." The final image of a woman posting a notice of a room for rent returns the narrative to the beginning; the story of Auguste and Clarissa is over, but their place will soon be filled by other prostitutes.

Dirnentragödie has often been interpreted as a conservative film that offers no way out, no possibility to escape a closed circuit of violence. "In its fundamentally deterministic attitude towards social problems," writes one critic, "[*Dirnentragödie*] aligns itself with a conservative ideology. . . . It sympathizes with Auguste's middle-class ideals . . . [but] affirms that Auguste is destined to remain what she is. Though the film suggests through frequent cuts to Felix's mother (and vice versa) that the two are to be compared, the prostitute-mother is hopelessly unfit to provide for Felix's needs. She is subject to the bestial criminality of her surroundings. Felix recognizes this in the end, and this is certainly one of the reasons for his return to his natural mother."[35] This reading of *Dirnentragödie* places emphasis on the street film convention of male symbolic defeat and bases its assessment of conservatism on the failure of Auguste's attempt at class rise. Strikingly, it also adopts Felix's assessment of Auguste's inadequacy; "the prostitute-mother is unfit to provide for Felix's needs" and "is subject to the bestiality

---

[35] Munson, "Dirnentragödie," 64.

of her surroundings." If this reading is unconcerned with iconography and modes of identification, it unwittingly reveals its alignment with the textual inscription of Felix's point of view, and hence with a fundamental ambivalence toward the erotic and yet profoundly "masculine" figure of Auguste.

While it is thus tenable to view Felix's look as opening up a space for male spectator identification, an entirely different response is possible, even probable, when we consider *Dirnentragödie*'s status as a melodrama that addresses a female audience. *Dirnentragödie* charges certain conventions with an intensified, exaggerated meaning—with meaning in excess of what the narrative can comfortably support. Auguste's fantasy of class rise, for instance, dominates the narrative and yet comes to suggest desires and states of being beyond the immediate context of narration. The fantasy of class rise, in other words, is itself imbued with a desire that remains unexpressed in the narrative but strikingly apparent in the images. Recalling the highly celebrated image of Weimar's New Woman, the figure of Auguste may indeed fail to provide an adequate reflection of male desire but would hardly elicit the horror or revulsion of a female viewer. Instead, the very pathos surrounding Auguste's futile attempts at class rise would appear to address directly a female audience whose desire for mobility was not only similarly frustrated but also repressed in ordinary psychic and social circumstances. To be sure, the overlay of the iconography of the New Woman with melodramatic conventions of representation does produce a quality of excess, a certain disturbance in classical modes of visual pleasure and identification. While this excess may account for some critics' uneasiness with the film, it also suggests to me that *Dirnentragödie* is neither conservative nor entirely implicated in masculine visual pleasure.

Hintertreppe: MODES OF LOOKING AND FEMALE SPECTATOR IDENTIFICATION

One day, while rehearsing a very subtle play in which the characters' psychical relationships had to be brought out discreetly, Reinhardt sighed: "Of course I saw you. But I'm on the stage. Will the spectators in the back rows and, above all, those in the Gods be able to do the same?"[36]

Prefacing her discussion of *Hintertreppe* (*Backstairs*, 1921) with this quote from Max Reinhardt, Eisner aims to suggest how the interplay of gesture and movement is central to the look of the *Kammerspielfilm*. In order for psychical relationships to be brought out discreetly, she explains, Reinhardt demanded that the characters' look and gestural support be visible and unambiguous to the audience. Quoting from Heinz Herald, one of Reinhardt's collaborators, Eisner points out that "If an actor needs to lift his whole arm at the Grosses Schauspielhaus, he need only move his hand at the Deutsches Theater; and at the Kammerspiele it is enough if he moves his finger."[37] Eisner contends that it was this interest in physical and gestural support that inspired the production of the *Kammerspielfilm* or "intimate film drama" in which the spectator "could feel all the significance of a smile, a hesitation, or an eloquent silence."[38]

When Eisner comes to analyze *Hintertreppe*, she nevertheless detects a fundamental opposition at work in the film which makes it "rather disappointing" as a *Kammerspielfilm*. In her view, the violent contrast between expressionism and naturalism (particularly in the very different acting styles of Fritz Kortner and Henny Porten) remains the source of the film's confusion and the reason for its failure as a *Kammerspiel*. Following from Eisner's assessment, I argue that *Hintertreppe* is disappointing as pure *Kammerspiel* because it is more accurately understood as melodrama. The stark contrast between visual styles and gestural support not only provides *Hintertreppe* with a melodramatic "look" but also with a contemplative mode of looking almost demanded of the spectator.

Often described as a film organized by an "excess of simplicity," *Hintertreppe* comprises a limited number of characters living in an everyday milieu: a maid (Henny Porten), her lover (William Dieterle), and a postman (Fritz Kortner). Like *Dirnentragödie*, *Hintertreppe* centers on a female protagonist who acts out the frustration of endless repetition and waiting. Employed in a middle-class

---

[36] Eisner, *The Haunted Screen*, 177.

[37] Ibid., 177.

[38] Ibid., 177.

household, the maid's primary source of pleasure comes from the moments spent with her lover. When the lover is unexpectedly called away, she waits anxiously for a letter from him. After what seems like endless days of waiting, the maid comes to believe that she has been abandoned. A postman, who has watched the maid repeatedly from his basement window, sympathizes with her despair. He forges a letter from the lover and delivers it to her late one evening. In her joy and relief, the maid goes to the postman's apartment to thank him, only to discover him in the act of forgery. While her first reaction is one of anger, she comes to sympathize with the postman's attempt at kindness. She returns to the postman's apartment for dinner: he dresses in his uniform for the occasion, the two sit down for dinner, and then suddenly the lover returns. The narrative culminates in violence and suicide: the postman brutally slays the lover, the maid discovers that the postman had in fact intercepted her lover's letters and, when she is fired from her job, the maid moves trancelike to the rooftop and throws herself down to the cobblestone pavement below.

It is significant that the characters in *Hintertreppe* have no names. In keeping with conventions of melodrama, they are assigned primary psychic and social roles which allow them to be instantly recognizable as types and deployed in such a manner that the central conflicts of the drama are visible to the spectator. Furthermore, because these characters are denied any illusion of depth or psychological complexity, *Hintertreppe* stages a drama that exists primarily on the plane of representation. To borrow from Peter Brooks, *Hintertreppe* remains fundamentally "a drama of shapes rather than substances."[39]

It is not merely the symbolic function of characters that serves to externalize conflict in the film. From the very first shot of *Hintertreppe*, it is obvious that the mise-en-scène will also give, like an illustrative painting, a visual summary of overdetermined meaning. The hollow and cavernous stairwell, introduced in the opening shot, realizes an architectural approximation of the film's concern with themes of claustrophobia and confinement. In later scenes, the exterior spaces of the courtyard appear no less claustrophobic

---

[39] Peter Brooks, *The Melodramatic Imagination* (New Haven: Yale University Press, 1976), 104.

Figure 40. Architectural surveillance
(*Hintertreppe*, 1921)

than the cluttered interior spaces where the maid engages in various domestic chores. Furthermore, just as the maid is surveyed by the postman who gazes voyeuristically at her from his basement window, so too does she appear to be surveyed by the stylized facade of the *Hinterhaus* that towers above her. Indeed, when she goes to meet her lover or visit the postman, the brightly lit windows of the *Hinterhaus* seem to follow her movements with a vacant, glaring stare (figure 40).

The sense of claustrophobia and confinement is also created by the very slowness of narrative pace and by the recourse to narrative and visual repetition. The opening sequence, for example, represents the events of the maid's day in such a way as to suggest that this day is in fact a repetition of many others. From the moment she wakes until she meets her lover in the evening, the maid is seen performing a series of routine domestic chores: she sweeps the floor, polishes shoes, makes beds, and meets the mail. As if further to emphasize how repetition organizes the maid's experience of time, the narrative introduces her as she wakes to the sound of a ringing alarm clock. The maid's first impulse is to set the clock back five minutes and thus to escape the demands of routine. An iris-in and -out elliptically links this scene to the next. The maid is awakened a second time by the alarm clock, only now, as her frenetic and hurried movements suggest, she has overslept and must make up for lost time. This opening sequence orients the spectator to a very specific sense of time. The repeated scenes, the static camera positioning, and the very slow and deliberate narrative pace establish repetition as the distinguishing feature not only of the maid's but also of the spectator's experience of time.

Rather than "give the impression of a progressive movement towards an end which is significantly different from the beginning," writes Tania Modleski, "much melodrama gives the impression of a ceaseless returning to a prior state."[40] This assessment is vividly exemplified by *Hintertreppe*, since repetition organizes not only the spectator's perception of time but also the narrative sequencing of events. The first day shows the maid as she wakes up and performs routine domestic chores. Intercut with these scenes are shots of the postman, who gazes at the maid from his basement window (figures 41 and 42). The maid continues her work, the postman ascends the stairs with the mail, and then an iris-in and -out takes us to an evening sequence. The maid prepares to go out, and meets her lover in the courtyard; again, the postman's gaze follows her movements. Then a title announces "The Next Day." The morning sequences are elided and yet we may assume that they are similar to the first day, given the virtual repetition of the maid's activities from the point she prepares to meet her lover in the courtyard onward. The sets, the lighting, the camera positioning, and even the postman's gaze are exactly repeated, only this time the lover fails to appear.

In the lover's absence, even minimal narrative development is suspended and the most important events in the film are now rendered in the interplay of gesture, movement, and mise-en-scène. To be sure, the maid's chores persist and the postman still ascends

---

[40] Tania Modleski, "Time and Desire in the Woman's Film," *Cinema Journal* 23, no. 2 (Spring 1984): 23.

Figure 41. The maid's domestic routine
(*Hintertreppe*, 1921)

Figure 42. Male voyeurism
(*Hintertreppe*, 1921)

and descends the stairs. Nevertheless, a subtle variation is introduced as the postman comes to identify with the maid's growing sense of frustration and despair. Having witnessed the lover's failure to appear in the courtyard, the postman approaches the maid's apartment with a certain apprehension, and his delivery of the mail takes on a heightened significance (figure 43). The first time the postman arrives without a letter for the maid, her face expresses bewilderment and his gaze appears curiously fixated yet strangely sympathetic. The second time he comes to the door, the sense of pathos and anguish is further externalized; it is raining and the maid anxiously watches the postman make his rounds, meeting him at the door just as he arrives. She motions for the letters, but he turns his head away. She desperately rifles through his bag, her breathing becomes heavy and she finally, and quite emphatically, slumps her shoulders and places her head against the wall. The static composition of this scene is transformed into a tableau: the postman mimes the maid's slumped posture and the scene lingers on their shared gestures of despair (figure 44).

In both narrative and spatial terms, the postman's isolation and social inferiority seem similar to the maid's; he, too, performs repetitious tasks in a routine manner and also occupies claustrophobic and confining interior spaces. The staging of the postman's identification with the maid nevertheless reveals a fundamental difference in their experiences of repetition and frustration—their experiences of time and desire. The third time the postman arrives at the maid's apartment, now with a letter from the lover, the symmetry of their gestures is disturbed. The maid reads the letter eagerly while the postman cowers as he watches her expression of joy and relief. As the postman slowly moves to leave, the maid clutches his arm to show him the letter. She smiles broadly at having received the letter and he smiles, too, at the touch of her hand.

What follows are paired scenes of their reactions to the arrival of the letter. The maid reads and examines the letter several times, pours a glass of wine, and becomes inspired to write a letter to her lover. In the meantime, the postman moves slowly through his apartment, then sits at the table, and begins to compose a letter of his own. Pouring more wine, the maid picks up two glasses and goes to the postman's apartment to celebrate. Bursting through the door, she takes the postman by surprise, and he desperately tries

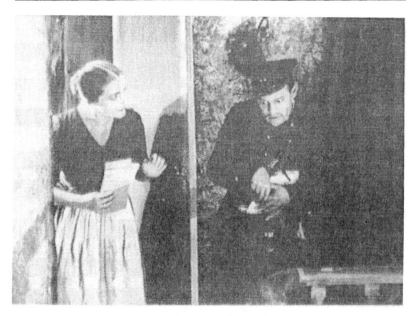

Figure 43. The postman's apprehension
(*Hintertreppe*, 1921)

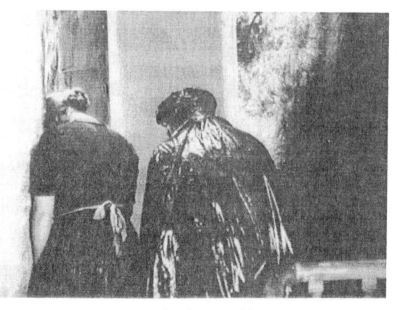

Figure 44. Shared gestures of despair
(*Hintertreppe*, 1921)

Figure 45. Disturbance of symmetry
(*Hintertreppe*, 1921)

to conceal what he is writing. Seeing the letter in his hand, she playfully attempts to snatch it from him, offering him a glass of wine in exchange. His hand suddenly forms a clawlike fist. She offers him a glass of wine once more, but her expression reveals her fear of his threatening gesture (figure 45). Slowly realizing that his barely controlled aggression may have something to do with what he has written, she takes the letter from him, only to find that he has forged the letter from her lover. Her exuberance turns to anguish and she looks at the postman accusingly. But when she recognizes his powerlessness and fear of reproach, her anger turns to sympathy and she looks at him with compassion. Holding the letter in one hand, she tenderly caresses the postman's head with the other.

The contrast between gestures and acting styles not only shapes the emotional resonance of this scene but also makes legible the fundamental conflicts and issues of the film. The postman's erratic and expressionistic gestures, for example, give an indication of the latent violence in his character. Indeed, when the lover reappears and confronts the postman with his deception, it hardly seems surprising that the postman's repressed anger finally flares in violence, in a mixture of destruction and self-tormenting despair. Similarly, the maid's expressive and melodramatic gestures reveal the compassionate, yielding side of her character. When she later discovers that the postman has not only forged but also withheld the letters for which she so desperately waited, her actions reproduce the force of an emotion we have already seen pass from the heights of joy to the depths of despair. The dramatic interplay of gestures that arrests our attention in *Hintertreppe*, however, has less to do with reading through character psychology than with discerning the subtle differentiation of gestures and recognizing important emblems. Significantly, the final moments of the film consist of a series of tableaux: the postman stands above the lover's body with a hatchet, a crowd gathers in the courtyard, and the maid's fall to death is registered by a group of women who look up, then down, and dramatically turn their heads away.

Hintertreppe provides a remarkable illustration of at least two very different modes of looking which are inscribed in the text: the voyeuristic, strangely sympathetic, and ultimately sadistic look of the postman and the compassionate and seemingly passive gaze of the maid. To claim that *Hintertreppe* is a melodrama that makes an appeal to a female spectator is thus to raise crucial questions. Given the textual inscription of male voyeurism, how does *Hintertreppe* engage a female spectator and position a mode of looking that provides the woman with the space for a reading? Are we to assume that the female spectator can only have a masochistic relationship to this voyeurism, or that she "sees" in the same way as the maid and therefore identifies with self-destruction and despair? To answer these questions, I would like briefly to discuss the way in which masochism has been taken up in feminist film theory, and then go on to suggest how *Hintertreppe* inscribes a third look—a contemplative look associated neither with (male) voyeurism nor (female) masochism—so as to provide the female spectator with a way in which to read the significance of the suffering that seeks expression in the text.

The relationship between masochism and film spectatorship has recently been analyzed by several feminist scholars.[41] In her book *The Desire to Desire: The Woman's Film of the 1940s*, however, Mary Ann Doane takes up the issue of masochistic identification as it relates specifically to the look of the female spectator, and therefore her observations provide a useful place to begin an analysis of *Hintertreppe*. Posing the question "How can the notion of female fantasy be compatible with that of persecution, illness, and death?" Doane turns to Freudian psychoanalysis for a provisional answer. As Doane points out, Freud initially linked paranoia and masochism to the subject's assumption of a "feminine" position, regardless of whether the subject was male or female. "The masochism which Freud assigns to the classical sexual pervert (usually male)," Doane writes, "is labelled 'feminine' precisely because the fantasies associated with this type of masochism situate the subject in positions characteristic of womanhood, i.e., they mean he is being castrated, is playing the passive part in coitus, or is giving birth."[42] Doane goes on to point out that while Freud made no distinction between male and female masochism in his early writings, his later analyses of clinical cases—most notably, his 1913 essay "A Child is Being Beaten"—forced him to make crucial distinctions along the lines of gender:

> It is not accidental that a certain ease of interpretation characterizes [Freud's reading of] the female masochistic fantasy . . . which takes the form of a three part transformation of a basic sentence: (1) My father is beating the child whom I hate; (2) I am being beaten (loved) by my father; (3) A child is being beaten. In the construction of the male fantasy, Freud can isolate only two sentences: (1) I am being beaten (loved) by my father; (2) I am being beaten by my mother. Although both

[41] See, for example, Kaja Silverman, "Masochism and Subjectivity," *Framework* 12 (1982): 2–9; Gaylyn Studlar, "Masochism and the Perverse Pleasures of the Cinema," *Quarterly Review of Film Studies* 9, no. 4 (Fall 1984): 267–82; and Miriam Hansen, "Pleasure, Ambivalence, Identification: Valentino and Female Spectatorship," *Cinema Journal* 25, no. 4 (Summer 1986), 6–32.

[42] Mary Ann Doane, *The Desire to Desire: The Woman's Film of the 1940s* (Bloomington, In.: Indiana University Press, 1987), 17. Doane's discussion of the woman's film in *The Desire to Desire* expands on her earlier essay, "The 'Woman's Film': Possession and Address," in *Re-Vision: Essays in Feminist Film Criticism*, ed. Mary Ann Doane, Patricia Mellencamp, and Linda Williams, The American Film Institute Monograph Series, vol. 3 (Frederick, Md.: University Publications of America, 1983), 63–82.

the female and male instanciations stem from the same origin, an incestuous attachment to the father, their psychical meaning-effects are necessarily quite different.[43]

In her explanation of the difference between male and female masochism, Doane draws attention to the relationship between fantasy and sexuality and the presence or absence of spectatorship as a possible role in male and female scenarios. For the male subject, she points out, the erotic implications of the masochistic fantasy assume paramount importance: he retains his own role and identity whether the father or the mother takes the place as agent of the beating. For the female subject, however, the erotic implications of the fantasy are displaced by the third sentence—"A child is being beaten"—and this sentence is significantly absent from the scenario of male masochism. The woman becomes a spectator to an event where the child who is being beaten is transformed into an anonymous boy or group of boys who serve to represent the woman in the fantasy. For this reason, Doane concludes that the scenario of female masochism reveals how the woman's assumption of the position as spectator necessarily entails her loss of identity and the desexualization of her gaze.

The difference between male and female masochism as described by Doane would seem to be illustrated in *Hintertreppe* with unusual clarity. The postman's voyeurism, for example, is seen to grant him a masochistic identification with the maid. While male masochism reveals itself in the postman's identification with and assumption of a "feminine" position, it is also transformed quite easily into sadism or, perhaps more precisely, into sadomasochistic fantasy. When the lover returns, the postman's identification with the maid brings about his realization of an imagined situation of being beaten by the lover. In what appears to be an unmotivated attack on the lover, the postman acts out his latent aggression that now erupts in uncontrollable violence (figure 46). The maid's assumption of a masochistic position similarly suggests the transformations Doane describes. In her experience of repetition and waiting, the maid comes to identify with the postman's sense of powerlessness and frustration. When the lover returns and is brutally slain by the postman, the maid literally assumes the po-

---

[43] Ibid., 17–18.

sition of spectator, outside the event. Standing outside the locked door to the postman's apartment, the maid is barred access to the scene of the murder, and thus the scenario of violence is withheld from the maid's (and the spectator's) sight (figure 47). Almost inexorably, the narrative returns to the place where it began: with a trancelike passivity, the maid willingly accepts death as the means of escape from the experience of time as repetition and endless waiting.

The fantasy of female masochism in films addressed to women leads Doane to claim that the woman's film "functions in a rather complex way to deny the woman a space of a reading." Although films that center on a female protagonist and anticipate a female viewing audience usually complicate the relationship between sexuality and the female body established by the classical narrative cinema, Doane nevertheless contends that they also deeroticize and disembody the gaze of the female spectator. "In a patriarchal society," Doane writes, "to desexualize the female body is ultimately to deny its very existence. . . . For, a bodyless woman cannot see."[44]

In contrast to this assessment, it seems to me that *Hintertreppe* resituates issues of voyeurism and masochistic identification and in fact provides a very specific place for a female reading. To be sure, *Hintertreppe* does inscribe a voyeuristic gaze associated with a male-spectator-in-the-text. It would nevertheless be difficult to assume that either a female or male spectator shares this voyeuristic gaze, since the film's emphasis on repetition, static composition, and gesture make impossible any simple equation of a controlling, voyeuristic gaze with the gaze of the spectator. This is not to say that the spectator is therefore aligned with a passive, disembodied gaze—with the kind of looking one might be tempted to associate with the maid. Instead, the simplicity of the plot, the stylized gestures, and the very slowness of narrative pace would suggest the existence of a third look—a look that must contemplate the significance of relationships as they are staged in gestures and mise-en-scène. This contemplative gaze is analogous to the kind of looking Laura Mulvey associates with von Sternberg's films, but in *Hintertreppe*, it is the interplay of gestures and movements rather than

[44] Ibid., 19–20.

Figure 46. The resolution of male masochism
(*Hintertreppe*, 1921)

Figure 47. Woman as spectator, outside the event
(*Hintertreppe*, 1921)

the female body that functions to freeze the narrative action in moments of contemplation. *Hintertreppe*, in other words, displaces visual pleasure from the female body onto a more generalized mise-en-scène of figures and scenery, but it does not thereby de-eroticize the woman's gaze.

In arguing for a contemplative look in *Hintertreppe*, I do not mean to imply that it inscribes an erotic fascination that is somehow separate from the construction of sexual difference in the cinema or in culture more generally. As I argued in chapter 2, to speak of a look, even a contemplative look, is necessarily to speak of those unconscious and intellectual processes that are inseparable from a conceptualization of a historically specific and gendered spectator. In this regard, it is important to underscore that the contemplative look in film melodrama typically turns less on problems of vision than on problems of expression: the slowness of pace, the hyperbolic gestures, the studied compositions all elicit a mode of looking attuned to the subtleties of visual style and narrative meaning.

As I suggested at the beginning of this analysis, *Hintertreppe* remains a drama of shapes rather than substances, and therefore we are not asked to plumb the depths of character psychology. Instead, the very simplicity and exaggeration of character types allows for the interplay of gesture and movement, where disguises and enigmas are exposed and made legible to the spectator. In the paired scenes and gestures of the postman and the maid, the spectator is invited to identify a shared sense of sorrow and despair. The postman's erratic, clawlike gestures, however, introduce a disturbance into this symmetry and reveal the perversity of his attempt to insinuate himself, under the mask of sympathy, in the maid's experience of frustrated desire. It is therefore inaccurate to define the repetition which organizes the temporal, narrative, and visual structure of *Hintertreppe* as a form of "repetition compulsion" or a desire that issues primarily from the reexperiencing of pleasure in pain. In *Hintertreppe*, as in other melodramas addressed to a female audience, repetition provides clarification in situations where recognition cannot be fully assured, where it must be repeatedly dramatized. As if to make emphatic the fundamental difference between the maid's and the postman's experience of time and desire, *Hintertreppe* continually repeats scenes, gestures and compositions and, in this way, underscores the need for the spectator to recognize and confront the implications of the drama, to apprehend the threat of mistaken identity in a world of significant shadows.

That *Hintertreppe* anticipates the presence of a female spectator is perhaps made most explicit by the final tableau. A group of women gathers in the courtyard and, for the very first time, the maid's experiences of pain and suffering are seen to elicit the sympathetic gaze of a textually inscribed female audience. The maid's fall to death is registered by their look; the women bear witness to the maid's suicide, and only then do they dramatically turn their gaze away. If the final tableau thus establishes female identity and female identification in the moment of their dissolution (i.e., the maid dies, the narrative ends), it also opens up a reading for the female spectator. Accustomed to a very specific experience of frustration and unfulfilled desire, the female spectator of *Hintertreppe* is invited to contemplate the difference between male and female powerlessness and therefore to recognize how the regime of isolation and repetition produces two utterly opposed conceptions of time and desire.

Zuflucht: MALE IDENTITY AND FEMALE VISUAL PLEASURE

To make the fabric of vision into a document, to make the document lurid enough so that it releases a vision, to make vision document and document vision, and to persuade us that they cannot be distinguished, that they are necessarily interconnected through the chain of spiritual metaphor, that resonances are set up, electrical connections established whenever we touch any link in the chain, is to make the world we inhabit one charged with meaning, one in which interpersonal relations are not merely contacts of the flesh but encounters that must be handled carefully, nurtured, judged, handled as if they mattered.[45]

What Peter Brooks so lucidly describes as the melodramatic impulse to make the "fabric of vision" into a document which is then "lurid enough" to release a vision provides an amazingly accurate

[45] Brooks, *The Melodramatic Imagination*, 22.

description of a film like *Zuflucht* (*Refuge*, 1927). Unlike *Dirnen-tragödie* and *Hintertreppe*, where documentary and expressionist modes are interconnected through gesture and mise-en-scène, *Zuflucht* evidences a more pronounced split between documentary realism and expressionist representation. Documentary scenes of various outdoor locations (the train station, the street market, the construction of the Berlin underground) are intercut with patently stylized scenes of domestic interiors. An "electrical connection" is nevertheless established between exterior and interior spaces, and this connection is not only the result of film editing. Indeed, it is the image of the passive, eroticized male that sets up resonances between documentary realism and expressionism—between what Brooks refers to as the "lurid document" and the "fabric of vision." *Zuflucht*, like *Hintertreppe*, aims to persuade us that documentary reality and expressionist representation are ultimately interrelated. In contrast to *Hintertreppe*, however, it is not the interplay of gestures and movement that arrests our attention in *Zuflucht*. Instead, it is the image of passive male eroticism that releases a vision capable of freezing the narrative action and encouraging a contemplative mode of looking.

Zuflucht begins with a series of documentary images and a title which announces, "On the East German Border." Crowds of poor people are seen disembarking from a train from Russia; once they are on the platform, a policeman approaches a working-class man and asks, "How long have you been over there?" We soon learn that this working-class man is Martin (Franz Lederer), a factory owner's son who renounced his upper-class background by joining the workers' movement, and who is only just returning to Berlin after having spent nine years in the Soviet Union. A montage of Martin's journey across the German countryside follows this brief introduction, and underscores the distance he must travel to reach the city, as well as his extreme state of exhaustion. We are then introduced to two "Berlin agrarians," Hanne (Henny Porten) and Frau Schurich, who till a vegetable garden on the outskirts of the city. As if out of nowhere, the police arrive at the garden to apprehend a man who has been sleeping in an abandoned farmhouse. Suddenly, another man leaps over a fence and diverts the attention of the police from the first man, who turns out to be Martin. While the police chase this second man, Hanne looks at Martin, recognizes his hunger and exhaustion, and offers him a temporary place to stay.

Returning to the city, Hanne, Martin, and Frau Schurich approach a dilapidated apartment building. The camera tilts to reveal the expanse of the building, and to emphasize the pervasive poverty of the working-class milieu. Once the three enter the apartment, Herr Schurich greets them by demanding, "Where did you uncover this one?" Herr Schurich's scrutinizing gaze is revealed in a point-of-view shot: in much the same way as the expanse of the apartment building is visually rendered, so the camera surveys Martin's body from foot to head. In spite of Herr Schurich's persistent questioning, Hanne offers Martin water with which to wash, and a plate of food. Within minutes, Martin falls asleep, still holding his plate in his hands. Taking the plate from him, Hanne brings Martin a blanket and lets him sleep. Before long, the Schurichs' son returns home drunk, throws his things on the couch where Martin sleeps and, in his inebriated state, pulls the blanket off Martin for his own use. Hanne bursts in the room, recovers the blanket, and forcefully pushes the younger Schurich away when he attempts to caress her. The scene ends with a close-up of Martin's face, shot with a soft-focus filter and relayed from Hanne's point of view. Hanne gazes lovingly at Martin and the image of male eroticism breaks through the documentary quality of the scene to become the site of a powerful visual attraction (figure 48).

As I hope my description of these opening sequences demonstrates, it is the visual presence of Martin in *Zuflucht* that charges the documentary images with an intensified significance. From the very moment Martin is introduced, he attracts the attention of almost everyone who sees him: the policeman, who picks him out of the crowd on the train platform, Herr Schurich, who surveys him with reproach and contempt, and Hanne, who looks at him with compassion and desire. Whatever the narrative meaning attributed to these various looks at Martin, no other character in the film can compete with his visual presence. To be sure, Martin's physical exhaustion provides narrative justification for the display of a nonthreatening male sexuality. But in both narrative and visual terms, Martin is continually arranged as a figure for us to see: not only is he frequently isolated in the frame (for instance, when he sits alone

on the couch), but the film also constructs his image *as* an image—
as the object of the characters' and the spectator's gaze.

For example, when Martin sleeps on the couch, he elicits
Hanne's attention as she prepares for work (figure 49). Seeing
Hanne's desiring gaze, the younger Schurich also looks at Martin
but, out of jealousy, he splashes the sleeping figure with water.
When the Schurichs' daughter returns early in the morning from
her night out on the town, she, too, looks at Martin and the camera
pans his body to underscore the pleasure of her gaze. Martin's status as image is literalized when his mother sits at her desk and
gazes at the collage of photographs she has collected of Martin over
the years (figure 50). Although her son, Otto, tells her that Martin
is dead, she looks at the photographs and insists, "He lives! A
mother feels that."

It is not only the visual construction of Martin as image but also
the narrative construction of Martin's character that distinguish
him as a special kind of male figure. Most obviously, Martin's
gentle and undemanding manner provides a striking contrast to the
younger Schurich, who continually taunts and makes passes at
Hanne, and to Herr Schurich, whose harshness is perhaps most
blatant when he tells his son to "kick Martin in the teeth." In addition, we learn (in a vivid and excessive nightmare vision) that
Martin has not only rejected his upper-class identity in favor of
socialist commitment, but that he has also rejected the avarice of
his brother, Otto, who aims to inherit the entire family fortune.
Most important, however, it is Martin's relationship to Hanne
which indicates the significance the film assigns to a different kind
of male identity. For example, when Hanne returns home from
work, only to be ridiculed by the Schurichs' daughter and then
confronted by the younger Schurich's drunken rage, she decides to
leave the working-class apartment forever. Martin, who has not
only witnessed but also provoked the jealousy of this family scene,
agrees to leave with her, and the two venture into the street, in
search of a place of refuge.

Walking through the city, Hanne and Martin pass by several
places where they could find shelter for the night, notably, a cheap
hotel lit up by neon lights, and the Phoebus Palast, equally lit up
to attract potential moviegoing customers. Choosing neither the
hotel nor the cinema, they finally wander into the waiting room of

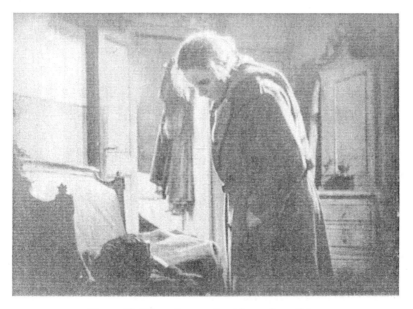

Figure 48. Woman's gaze at passive male eroticism
(*Zuflucht*, 1927)

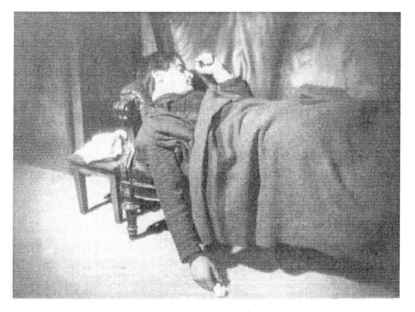

Figure 49. Passivity as exhaustion
(*Zuflucht*, 1927)

Figure 50. Literalizing the male image
(*Zuflucht*, 1927)

a train station. It is here, in a place of continuous departures and arrivals, that Martin begins to tell Hanne about his family, about the death of his father and the problems with his brother. Within minutes, Hanne falls asleep, and once he recognizes that he no longer has an audience, Martin falls asleep too.

The next evening, Hanne arranges to stay with Martin at the apartment of her best friend, Marie Janowsky, who lives with her two young daughters, and whose husband is out of town indefinitely. Hanne and Martin find temporary shelter in this all-female environment. When Martin arrives at the apartment with news of his job working on the construction of the Berlin underground, he immediately attracts the attention of Marie's two daughters. Again, Martin's presence claims the visual field. Shot with a soft-focus filter, Martin plays with the children, and this image is relayed from Hanne's and Marie's shared point of view. While, in one sense, this image serves to connote Martin's childlike innocence, Hanne's and

Marie's gaze is not simply—or not exclusively—maternal. For Hanne, Martin represents a figure on whom she can project her desires for a relationship based on an ideal of erotic reciprocity.[46] In a striking series of shots, Martin is seen looking out the window to his room in Marie's apartment. In the first shot, his face casts a reflection on the window and it appears as if Martin is gazing at his own likeness. In the second shot, however, we see that Martin is resting his hand on Hanne's shoulder as she sits on a chair near the window. He looks out into the darkness and she looks toward the camera; both appear thoughtful, even apprehensive, about their future together. This second shot remains on the screen for some time and so becomes a tableau, where the narrative action is arrested in order to offer a fixed and carefully composed representation. Significantly, this tableau serves not only to suggest the depth of Martin's and Hanne's passion, but also to foreshadow the precariousness of their relationship.

The following sequence underscores this precariousness and makes explicit the themes of motherhood and self-sacrifice which will dominate the duration of the narrative. Opening with a close-up of a Sunday newspaper, this sequence is marked as a day of rest. We see a static shot of the construction site where Martin labors; there are no workers, no obvious signs of activity and, for the first time, the construction site appears relatively peaceful. There is a cut to Martin, deeply asleep on the couch. This shot is followed by a series of images of Marie's daughters washing themselves at a washbasin. The pictorial quality of these images provides perhaps the only match for the image of Martin and, significantly, the editing of this sequence implies a relationship between the beauty of childhood and the beauty of the passive, eroticized male. We next see Hanne, who enters Martin's room, looks at him, and then urges him to get up and prepare for an afternoon in the Berlin Grünewald. Several images of Hanne and Martin, shot with a soft-focus filter, render this time in the Grünewald idyllic (figure 51). But when they take the streetcar home, the pleasure of their afternoon is threatened: Martin's mother, who happens to drive by the streetcar, sees her son even though he tries to hide his face. Martin ex-

---

[46] I borrow this formulation of "erotic reciprocity" from Hansen, "Pleasure, Ambivalence, Identification."

Figure 51. Documentary expressionism
(*Zuflucht*, 1927)

plains to Hanne that he can never go home, that he can never face his brother again. "But mother remains mother," Hanne laments, to which Martin responds, "To you I belong and with you I will stay."

Although this declaration of love seems to ensure the couple's future, the narrative makes it increasingly apparent that their future is not to be. They decide to marry, Martin returns to his job on the construction site, and Hanne confides to Marie that she is pregnant. While Hanne tries on her wedding gown, she receives word that Martin has physically collapsed under the pressure of heavy labor. Hanne goes to the hospital, but finds the doors locked since visiting hours are over. The next day, she leaves work early and speaks to the doctor, who tells her that Martin needs rest and should be moved to a resort in the south. Unable to afford this herself, Hanne calls Martin's mother and tells her to come for her son. Following the arrival of Martin's mother at the hospital, there is a seemingly unmotivated cut to Marie's apartment. In the foreground of the image, one of the daughters constructs a house of blocks and, in the background, Marie's husband emerges through the door. At the sound of her father's return, the daughter demolishes the building and, with that gesture, the collapse of Martin and Hanne's alternative family is figured with a dramatic finality.

Martin's illness nevertheless serves a complex narrative function which ultimately provides Hanne with a permanent place of refuge. Martin's illness facilitates his reunion with his mother. Indeed, because he requires the constant care that Hanne has neither the time nor the financial resources to give him, Martin returns to his mother's home (where his brother is noticeably absent). Martin's illness also makes tragically apparent his devotion and attachment to Hanne. On his deathbed, he implores his mother to find Hanne, to bring her to the house and to his side. Acceding to her son's wishes, Martin's mother journeys to Marie's apartment and the scene of her arrival there emphasizes the profound distance she travels from her opulent Grünewald home to Marie's lower-middle-class environment. The meeting of Hanne and Martin's mother is yet another effect of Martin's illness. When she learns of Hanne's pregnancy, Martin's mother suggests that Hanne and Martin marry right away. But Hanne explains that if they were to marry immediately, Martin would surely know that he was dying. Hanne's virtuous self-sacrifice moves Martin's mother to tears; she kisses Hanne and the two women agree to bring up the child together.

The final images of *Zuflucht* forge a visual alliance between the two women and emphasize their shared experience of loss (figure 52). While male passivity is associated with illness on the level of narrative, Martin continues to elicit a desiring gaze. The visual construction of male eroticism, in other words, is not transformed from a site of sexuality to a site of illness and pain, but remains the stylized object of a powerful visual attraction (figure 53).[47] In one of

[47] Mary Ann Doane makes this point in relation to the representation of woman in *The Desire to Desire*. Significantly, a woman's film like *Zuflucht* seems to recognize female subjectivity by reversing what Doane locates as central to so many "paranoid" women's films: it is the male body—and not the female body—that is associated with illness and death. Furthermore, because the representation of female desire is so central to *Zuflucht*, the image of the passive male remains the site of an erotic gaze.

Figure 52. Self-sacrifice and visual alliance
(*Zuflucht*, 1927)

Figure 53. The stylization of illness
(*Zuflucht*, 1927)

the film's most emotionally charged images, Hanne and Martin are framed in an extremely tight close-up. "When you will be my wife," Martin whispers, and then kisses Hanne passionately. He lies back in bed, his mother calls the doctor, but it is too late. Hanne closes his eyes, then goes to embrace his mother, and this image of the two women's solidarity and shared sense of sorrow closes the film.

The pervasive discourse on motherhood and self-sacrifice links *Zuflucht* to the tradition of the maternal melodrama in the Weimar years—to such films as *Mutter Krausens Fahrt ins Glück* (1929) and *So ist das Leben* (1929). And no doubt one of the reasons for *Zuflucht*'s enormous popularity with female audiences in the 1920s lies in the fact that it illustrates, in successive sequences, alternative visions of class identity and family life: from the oppressive male working-class apartment where Hanne and Martin first meet, to the all-female lower-middle-class household at Marie's, to the upper-class home of Martin's mother which presents the possibility of child-raising outside the institution of marriage. While the fantasy of social mobility and alternative family life certainly accounts for part of the appeal of *Zuflucht*, it would seem that the visual presence of Martin also explains the particular fascination that the film held for female audiences in the 1920s. Indeed, because an eroticized male figure claims attention within the visual field, *Zuflucht* opens up to female desire and to an alternative conception of visual pleasure. The pleasure in contemplating male passivity, moreover, is inseparable from the narrative depiction of the precariousness of a relationship based on erotic reciprocity. This suggests yet another reason for *Zuflucht*'s appeal to female viewers— viewers who perhaps most strongly felt the absence of that ideal in their own lives and who therefore sought refuge in the cinema.

Die freudlose Gasse: CENSORSHIP AND THE FEMALE SPECTATOR

In the scenes of misery in *The Joyless Street* the cliché is dominant—everything is too studied, too arranged, too emphatic. The back-alleys are too disreputable, the staircases too enigmatic, the counterpoints of shadow and light too discordant and too obvious. The face of Werner Krauss (the butcher with the twirly moustache) is too prominent, the parting of his hair too oily and his brutality excessive. The prostitutes on the alley-corner, the nobly fallen bourgeoisie and the insinuating madam all look too much like a Victorian print entitled, "Poverty and Human Depravity."[48]

Employing the critical vocabulary of emphasis and exaggeration, Eisner offers a perfect description of *Die freudlose Gasse* (*The Joyless Street*, 1925) as a melodrama. Her references to the "excessive brutality" of the butcher and to the film's pictorial, even mannered visual style, serve to support her assessment that everything in the film is too clichéd, too arranged and emphatic. In Eisner's estimation, *Die freudlose Gasse* lacks the "restraint and humanity" demanded by its subject matter, German inflation. "The picturesque triumphs over the tragic," she writes, "and this is why many passages in the film are now disappointing."[49]

Eisner's uneasiness with an aesthetic of excess and stark ethical conflict may be said to derive from what Peter Brooks calls melodrama's refusal of censorship and repression; its desire to say all, to stage and utter the unspeakable. As Brooks points out, the recourse to cliché, overstatement, and overemphasis is not accidental but actually intrinsic to the melodramatic mode. "The melodramatic utterance," he contends, "breaks through everything that constitutes the 'reality principle,' all its censorships, accommodations, tonings-down. Desire cries aloud its language in identification with full states of being. . . . Desire triumphs over the world of substitute-formations and detours; it achieves a plenitude of meaning."[50]

I have had occasion to refer to Brooks's study of melodrama in my analyses of *Dirnentragödie*, *Hintertreppe*, and *Zuflucht*. Each of these films, I have argued, employs melodramatic conventions so as to explicate, clarify, and heighten the terms of the depicted drama. Yet *Die freudlose Gasse* remains perhaps the most exemplary melodrama of all: like *Dirnentragödie*, it is a street film, but it has virtually nothing to do with male symbolic defeat; like *Hin-*

[48] Eisner, *The Haunted Screen*, 256.
[49] Ibid., 256.
[50] Brooks, *The Melodramatic Imagination*, 41.

tertreppe, it stages a drama of violent contrast in gestures and mise-en-scène, but villainy remains overt and obvious from the very opening sequence; like *Zuflucht,* it opens up to female desire, but there is no attempt to feminize, complicate or in any way destabilize male identity. *Die freudlose Gasse,* in other words, offers the clearest example of a melodrama that not only appeals to a female audience but also insists on dealing with unambiguous identities and relationships: villainy in the film is unrelenting and virtue stands opposed to what seeks to "discredit it, misrepresent it, silence, imprison or bury it alive."[51]

In this regard, it is crucial to underscore that *Die freudlose Gasse* structures two separate if interrelated dramas: the drama of Grete Rumfort (Greta Garbo) which traces the eventual recognition and reward of virtue, and the drama of Maria Lechner (Asta Nielsen) which ultimately functions to expose a social order. Critics of *Die freudlose Gasse* have often suggested that Grete's story reveals the influence of Hollywood filmmaking on the German cinema, whereas Maria's story highlights the definitive and consummate concerns of German expressionism.[52] What I will suggest, however, is that *Die freudlose Gasse* reflects both American melodrama and German expressionism, and fundamentally realigns the relationship between them. Although the film never names the connection between the two dramas, it postulates their relationship by referring to conditions, forces, and states of being which exceed the depicted narrative action.

Die freudlose Gasse opens with a static tableau—a sketch of a street scene depicting several figures either alone or in conversation—which is then transformed into an extended cinematic tableau (figure 54). The street scene is rendered in almost exactly the same manner as it was in the opening sketch, only now it is the camera that remains static as four figures move in and out of the frame. In an extreme long shot, we first see a man with a cane who walks through the street; he is followed by a woman who joins him, and the two engage in conversation as they walk together. Another woman enters the street; she is followed by a man with a peg leg. Suddenly, she turns around, sees this man behind her, and flees to

[51] Ibid., 33.

[52] See, for instance, Kracauer's analysis of the film in *From Caligari to Hitler,* 167–70.

Figure 54. Opening tableau
(*Die freudlose Gasse*, 1925)

hide behind a wall on the street. On her movement, there is a cut
to a medium shot of the four figures as they walk along the street.
The first man and woman still engage in conversation and the second woman persists in keeping her distance from the man with the
peg leg. There is another cut, this time to a close-up of the street
sign, "Melchiorstrasse." The camera again returns to a static position and the four figures move in and out of the frame in a slow,
dreamlike fashion. The camera remains fixed on the street sign until the second woman passes by. There is then a cut to a different
view of the street, where crowds of people emerge and, at this
point, the narrative proper begins.

Although this opening tableau at first appears peripheral to the
narrative action, it serves to establish basic relationships among
characters. As we soon discover, the four figures represented in the
tableau are the major characters in the fictional world of the film:
Grete and her father, Maria and her father. The familial structure
that the narrative later explores is thus suggested from the very

Figure 55. Male villainy
(*Die freudlose Gasse*, 1925)

beginning: Grete and her father move through the street together
while Maria tries desperately to elude her father's menacing presence. The dreamlike quality of the images intensifies the weight of
character action and interaction and, simultaneously, externalizes
psychic identities and relationships; the figures are strongly characterized but they have no psychological complexity. What we retain from this tableau is the sense of dramatic interplay between
highly conventionalized figures, and this interplay and clash will
organize the rest of the narrative.

Following this tableau, we are introduced to the butcher, Josef
Geringer (Werner Krauss), whom the title identifies in no uncertain terms as "the tyrant of Melchior Street." Twirling his moustache, the butcher personifies a threat that hardly needs justification; as a figure of villainy, his evil quite simply exists (figure 55).
After this, the double focus of the narrative is established through
the juxtaposition of two distinct class and familial structures. A title
announces the basement apartment, where the Lechner family

lives, and relays what seems to be a conventional scene from nineteenth-century melodrama: as the mother scrubs clothing on a washboard, the father hobbles into the apartment on his peg leg, screams at her, and physically threatens his daughter Maria for failing to bring meat from the butcher's (figure 56). There is then a cut to the first-floor apartment, where the Rumfort family lives (figure 57). Seated at a table are Grete, her young sister, and her father, and when Grete serves cabbage instead of meat, the father's expression registers his sense of powerlessness and defeat. Despite the pathos surrounding this family drama, the environment lacks both visual and dramatic intensity: brightly lit and furnished in middle-class style, it offers a stark contrast to the shadowy and claustrophobic working-class milieu only one floor below.

"The fundamental manichaeism of melodrama," Brooks explains, "should alert us to the fact that further analysis must be directed to the bipolar relation of its signs and their presentation."[53] *Die freudlose Gasse* offers several notable examples of polarized conflicts and violent contrasts in narrative tone and visual style. (In a striking series of shots, for instance, a millionaire's toast to the "gay ladies of Vienna" is followed by images of poverty-stricken women waiting outside the butcher's shop.) However, *Die freudlose Gasse* structures polarization in a much more fundamental way, since the juxtaposition of two separate dramas becomes the very basis for the divided mode of perception which governs our response to the film. In fact, once the narrative has introduced the conventional class environments of Grete and Maria, it proceeds to explore their separate stories as they exist at a moment of crisis and act out exemplary destinies. While the two stories frequently intersect, the two characters never actually meet. (Outside the butcher's or at Frau Greifer's, Maria's and Grete's paths cross, but the narrative makes it clear that they are strangers to one another.) Rather than establish an explicit relationship between the two characters, the narrative implies a connection between them by situating one story as the formal and, indeed, the dramatic counterpoint to the other.

Grete's story is most fundamentally about the temporary misrecognition and eventual reward of virtue. Throughout the narrative, she becomes increasingly implicated in prostitution, and al-

---

[53] Brooks, *The Melodramatic Imagination*, 10.

Figure 56. The working-class family
(*Die freudlose Gasse*, 1925)

Figure 57. The middle-class family
(*Die freudlose Gasse*, 1925)

though the film spectator knows full well that Grete is not only virtuous but self-sacrificing, her virtue continually goes unrecognized by the characters within the fiction. For example, because Grete stands long hours outside the butcher's shop, she collapses of exhaustion and so arrives late to work the next morning. Her boss calls her into his private office, where he comments on how tired she looks, puts his hand on her thigh, and suggests with a leer that she "must have had a long night." As Grete stands up to leave, the boss places money in the pocket of her dress and offers her further assistance if she should ever need it. The scene closes as Grete returns to her desk, completely oblivious to the insinuating glances of her co-workers, who see the bills in her pocket. That evening, Grete discovers that her father has cashed in his pension in order to invest in apparently lucrative stocks. Euphoric with his newfound wealth, he urges Grete to go to Frau Greifer's to buy a new coat. Frau Greifer, the madam of the local brothel, entices Grete to buy an expensive fur coat on credit. When Grete shows off her new purchase at work the next morning, the boss again calls her to his office. In a rapid series of shots, he grabs her and she struggles to break free from his grip. With righteous anger, she resigns. He follows her down the stairs and announces to the entire staff that Grete is fired, since he will not permit a whore in his office.

These scenes offer a vivid demonstration of how *Die freudlose Gasse* allows the spectator privileged knowledge that the characters do not have; we know that Grete is virtuous, but we must witness how her virtue is continually obscured or misconstrued. The remainder of the narrative therefore works to clarify and to assert Grete's "true" identity, yet the complex structuring of recognition and misrecognition persists and is extended to include a number of characters whose interests initially do not and cannot coincide. When Grete learns that her father's gamble on the stock market has failed, for example, she lies to him in order to alleviate his anxiety. She reminds him that she still has a job and then suggests that they rent out a room in the apartment. When Davy, an American Red Cross worker, agrees to take the room in the Rumfort house, the threat of abject poverty seems averted. He gives her sixty dollars, which she must immediately pay out on her father's overdrawn account, but the promise of future payments, as well as Davy's presence in the house, alleviate Grete's apprehension about financial and family matters. Grete's father's sense of inadequacy, however, becomes heightened with another man in the house. And when one of Davy's friends accuses Grete's sister of stealing, the father's barely controlled jealousy erupts and he orders Davy from the house. Grete discovers that her sister is indeed guilty of theft, but it is too late: Davy has gathered his things and her father has collapsed from a heart attack.

From this point on, Grete's innocence is made even more apparent to the spectator, precisely because Grete remains unaware of the threat to her virtue. With her father's illness, Grete is left with no choice but to seek help from Frau Greifer. On Frau Greifer's suggestion, she agrees to meet a wealthy man, who turns out to be the butcher, now dressed in his Sunday best. The scene of their meeting is presented in a highly elliptical fashion, so that the spectator is made to experience the slow passage of time and the tense exchange of glances which render the seduction impossible. Frau Greifer expresses her disappointment that things did not work out and invites Grete to her birthday party, where prospects might be better. While Frau Greifer goes to get the money which will ensure Grete's presence at the party, a manservant approaches Grete to warn her about the terms of Frau Greifer's generosity. But Grete accepts what she assumes to be a loan and ignores the manservant's warnings.

On the night of the birthday party, the play of recognition and misrecognition receives its most heightened and theatrical expression. Grete arrives at Frau Greifer's and is led to a dressing room behind a stage, where she is asked to prepare for the evening. Shots of women dressing and undressing, relayed from Grete's point of view, register her shock and her horror. There is a cut to an audience anxiously waiting for the performance to begin, which is followed by a shot of Grete's look from behind the curtain at the sight of Davy in the audience. Frau Greifer's assistant takes Grete from the curtain, strips her down, and forces her to wear a gown that exposes her breasts. In the meantime, Grete's father receives a letter from the bank, informing him that sixty dollars has been paid on his account. He suddenly recognizes his daughter's self-sacrifice and fears that she may be in danger. With a rapid montage of stomping feet and piano playing, we are taken back to Frau Grei-

Figure 58. The threat to virtue
(*Die freudlose Gasse*, 1925)

fer's, where audience anticipation has reached a fever pitch. Sticking her head through the stage curtains, Frau Greifer announces that the performance is about to begin. Significantly, the performance that follows is not Frau Greifer's elaborate revue (which we do, in fact, see part of later) but rather the spectacle of Grete's victimization and the final reward for her virtue.

Dressed in the revealing gown, Grete sits in front of a three-faced mirror which triples her image; a silhouette of a man appears, also threefold, and we gradually identify him as the manservant who approached Grete earlier (figure 58). The manservant chases Grete through the room and out onto the stage, where she is seen by Davy, who comes backstage and demands an explanation for her presence at the brothel. With an expression of contempt, Davy stomps out, and when the manservant attempts to tell him that Grete is innocent, he exclaims, "I have seen enough!" But Davy has not seen quite enough yet: on his way out, he meets Grete's father, who takes the blame for Grete's predicament. Showing

Davy the letter from the bank, the father goes to find Grete. The scene ends with all three men—the father, Davy, and the manservant—gathered in the room where Grete sits alone in despair. The father embraces her, Davy brings her coat, and the manservant looks on sympathetically. Quite significantly, the artifice and theatricality of this resolution is commented on by the shot which immediately follows it: a shot of an audience composed of men who vigorously applaud.

In contrast to Grete's story, Maria's story is marked by an unrelenting pessimism. In successive scenes, Maria is represented as the victim of male oppression: she is tyrannized by her father, betrayed by her lover, and exploited by the butcher. Maria's story, like Grete's, structures a complex play of recognition and misrecognition which grants the spectator privileged knowledge about the agony that Maria must undergo and act out. But where Grete's story deals with innocence and the reward of virtue, Maria's story is fundamentally about processes of guilt, desire, and repression. In the opening sequence, for example, Maria escapes her father's wrath by retreating to her bedroom, where she writes a letter to her lover, Egon, explaining that he is her only hope for the future. She looks at a wilted flower and her desire materializes in the mise-en-scène: an image of Egon's face, superimposed on the flower, externalizes the depth of her passion. Maria's reverie is interrupted when her mother appears at the door and implores her to hurry to the butcher's before the father returns. As Maria prepares to leave, her mother—dishevelled and truly powerless—watches her daughter from the doorway: situated precariously on the boundary between the street and the apartment, the mother is framed by the hanging laundry which seems to beckon her back inside. This image of Maria's mother serves to comment on the futility of Maria's aspirations for escape from the excesses of male authority. This is made especially clear when we are introduced to Egon in an elaborate sequence that shows him to be a womanizer and a social climber. Not quite a part of the upper-class milieu, Egon nevertheless successfully seduces Lia Leid, the wife of a wealthy lawyer; when he arranges to meet her at Frau Greifer's the following evening, the spectator comes to recognize that Maria has been deceived and that her relationship with Egon is fundamentally doomed.

Figure 59. The terms of exchange
(*Die freudlose Gasse*, 1925)

Maria's encounters with prostitution serve to emphasize the extent to which she is willing to sacrifice herself for Egon. Soon after
the butcher announces that his supplies have run out, Maria confides to her friend that if she returns home without meat, she will
certainly be beaten by her father. The friend suggests that they
knock on the butcher's window, since she (and, indeed, the spectator) previously witnessed two women approach the butcher in
this way. Although the butcher's voyeuristic gaze at Maria and her
friend reveals an initial hesitation, once he invites them inside, his
look is far less ambivalent. In a shot relayed from the butcher's
point of view, the camera pans the friend's body and draws attention to the simplicity of her dress and the nervousness of her gestures. The friend follows the butcher to the storage vault and when
she reemerges, she accepts the slab of meat he offers her with an
expression of resignation and shame (figure 59). As the friend
slowly takes her leave, the butcher holds out meat for Maria, who
immediately turns and flees. We next see Maria at Egon's apart-

ment and she pleads with him to take her in. Although he explains that her request is impossible, he hints that he needs three hundred dollars for an investment, and thus implies that things might be different if he were financially solvent. Promising to obtain the money for him, Maria goes to Frau Greifer's and willingly prostitutes herself to a millionaire so as to assure her future with Egon. Momentarily left alone in the room, Maria hears voices next door. Standing on the bed, she peers through the smoked-glass window and sees Egon with Lia Leid. The image of her gaze through a flower motif in the window links this scene to the earlier one in her bedroom, but now it is betrayal and anger rather than desire that materialize in the mise-en-scène. Pushing the bed to one side, Maria enters the room, and a close-up of her hands at Lia's neck allows us to infer a murder we never actually see.

After the murder, significant messages are profoundly externalized as Maria becomes the virtual sign of the repressed anger that seeks expression in the text. The millionaire takes Maria as his mistress and she accedes to his company with a stony silence. Exasperated by her coldness, he demands to know what it is she wants; barely moving her lips, she asks to go back to Frau Greifer's so as to liberate herself from a "horrible memory." The scene of Maria's return to the site of the murder vividly demonstrates the melodramatic impulse for redramatization, for an "acting out." No longer dressed in the simple black shift, Maria appears in an extravagant white gown and an excessively full blond wig (figure 60). As if to literalize this scene as the staging of the return of the repressed, Maria replays the events leading up to the murder and then slowly turns to the millionaire and begins to strangle him. He gasps for breath and she gradually releases her grip. "I know who the murderer is," she exclaims, "Egon Stirner!" On the narrative level, Maria's violence is thus meant to suggest the depth of her obsession—she is "lost" in the reenactment of her own crime. But Maria's violence also acts out a fantasy that the narrative can barely articulate.

Indeed, after this scene Maria's story comes to an abrupt conclusion. Reading about Egon's conviction in the newspaper, Maria is overcome with guilt: she leaves a letter for her mother, asking forgiveness, and goes to the police to confess her crime. Upon hearing her confession, Egon bends down to kiss Maria's hand but the cam-

Figure 60. Melodramatic excess and female identity
(*Die freudlose Gasse*, 1925)

era remains fixed on her motionless, impassive expression. Although Maria's story ends here, the narrative continues, ending
with a series of images that seem unrelated to what has gone before. I would like briefly to consider these concluding images, for
it is an operation of textual displacement that allows us to discern
the processes of desire and repression which find only indirect
expression in the narrative.

Following the theatrical resolution of Grete's story, there is a cut
to an angry crowd of women who gather outside the brothel. At
first, the appearance of this crowd seems somewhat confusing; not
only does the women's anger at Frau Greifer seem narratively unmotivated, but they are also cast as anonymous, symbolic extras.
(Significantly, Maria's mother does appear briefly in this sequence,
but her aggressive stance makes it somewhat difficult to identify
her as the character introduced earlier in the film.) There is then
another cut to the butcher's shop, where a crowd has also gathered,
only now we are reintroduced to a clearly recognizable character—
Maria's friend whose presence invokes Maria's absence. The friend

pleads with the butcher for meat for her child, but he dismissively responds, "I have meat, but not for your child" (figure 61). Banging on the door to his basement apartment (figure 62), she finally pushes her way through and murders the butcher with his own ax. In a series of elliptical images, the friend escapes on to the street, the butcher's dog seems to chase her, and when the butcher's bloody face briefly appears in the window (figure 63), a crowd of women gathers at the window to gaze at his demise. The frenzied pace of these images comes to a sudden halt: in the final shots, we see the empty rooms of the brothel and the vast expanse of the now deserted street.

In its movement toward this apocalyptic conclusion, *Die freudlose Gasse* offers a remarkable illustration of the melodramatic refusal of censorship and repression—the desire to express all, to get past the barriers established by a censoring agency. For this reason, it is hardly surprising that the film was subjected to intense scrutiny and revision by the German Film Censorship Board (Filmoberprüfstelle), by that "agency" which recognized that the film melodrama addressed issues of primary concern to women and encouraged a particular kind of spectator identification. In their report of March 29, 1926, the censors explain why they demand revisions in the film, and why they are concerned with its potentially detrimental effects on a female spectator:

> The essential content of the film consists of showing how Viennese girls are forced to sell their moral honor and to earn their bread in brothels as a result of need and the misery of inflation. In the center of the plot stands a butcher, who seduces girls by giving out illegal rations of meat. . . . At the end of the film, according to the customary moral recipe, the good are rewarded and the evil are punished, since the butcher's skull is split with his own ax. . . . The entire motif of this film and the way this motif is played out in the plot, however, is demoralizing and partially brutalizing. In the whole film, only one girl—the daughter of Commissioner Rumfort—resists the temptation to sell her honor for money or meat. But even this girl ends up in the brothel, because the commissioner is ruined after having invested in worthless stocks. . . . Through this forced situation, in which the girls are brought

213

Figure 61. Theatrical resolution: the butcher's refusal
(*Die freudlose Gasse*, 1925)

Figure 62. Knocking down the door
(*Die freudlose Gasse*, 1925)

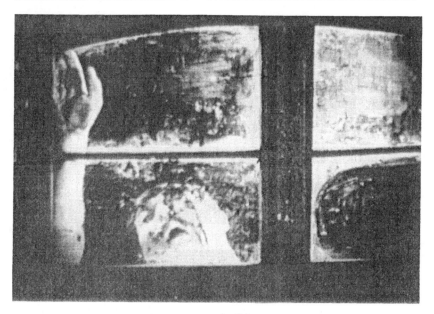

Figure 63. Death of the tyrant
(*Die freudlose Gasse*, 1925)

without exception into depravity, the impression must emerge that the girls' action is the necessary consequence of misery and need. This must have a demoralizing effect on the female viewer.[54]

Although the censors do not explicitly call *Die freudlose Gasse* a melodrama, they nevertheless demonstrate their familiarity with melodrama's polarization of good and evil and its recourse to the conventional "moral recipe." They find this *moral* recipe *demoralizing* for the female viewer and contend (at least in this initial statement) that the film's deterministic attitude toward social problems may induce female viewers to emulate the behavior on the screen.

The censors did not revoke the entire film, however, and therefore much of their report is devoted to defending their decision to release a revised version of it. "According to the legal position of the Control Board," they explain, "a film is considered to have a demoralizing effect if it can be determined with far reaching prob-

---

[54] "Die freudlose Gasse," Filmoberprüfstelle (Berlin den 29. März 1926); original in Stiftung Deutsche Kinemathek.

ability that there is an immediate danger of it worsening the moral feelings and thoughts of the normal, average viewer." Pointing out that much of *Die freudlose Gasse* "appears neither to have a demoralizing nor brutal effect," the censors maintain that the revised version of the film may "encourage the female viewer's sympathy but it will not provide an allurement for her to do the same as the fallen women." Grete Rumfort, they explain, "defends her innocence to the end and succumbs neither to the seductions of her boss nor to the allurements of Frau Greifer. . . . Even in the salon she refuses to put on the whorish dress or let her clothes be torn from her body." If Grete's story seems to offer incontestable proof of the film's moral value, the censors recognize that a female viewer may sympathize with Maria's story and, as they note, Maria "is a far less stable character." In order to account for the multiple spaces for identification afforded by the film and to defend their decision to release a revised version of it, the censors provide a reading which emphasizes how all the female characters are brought to depravity out of their abundance of love: Grete out of love for her father, Maria out of her love for Egon, and Maria's friend out of love for her starving child.

While the censors fail to mention that Maria and her friend act as much out of anger as they do out of love, the specific amendments they make to the film suggest that the representation of this anger lurked behind their concerns with female spectators "over-identifying" with the film. In fact, of the scenes they revised, two deal specifically with the representation and effects of female aggression: the scene where Maria strangles the millionaire, and the shot of the butcher's bloody face. With these revisions, the censors imply that Grete's obvious virtue will offset Maria's "unstable" moral character. And yet, what emerges from the contradictory messages of their report is the lingering suspicion that female spectators would identify with both female protagonists.

The censors' attempt to contain some of the more obvious excesses of *Die freudlose Gasse* may shed light on the reasons for the different versions of the film still in circulation today.[55] Although

---

[55] I have seen the German version of *Die freudlose Gasse* at the Stiftung Deutsche Kinemathek (Berlin), and it is markedly different from the version of the film currently in distribution in the United States. In the American version, a number of key scenes are missing; notably, the scene of Maria and her friend at the butcher's, and the stran-

they did not call for any changes in the scene in which Maria strangles Lia Leid, this scene was reedited in the American version of the film and the effect of the reediting is to stabilize Maria's character temporarily. In the German version, the strangulation scene occurs near the beginning of the film, after Maria has prostituted herself to the millionaire to assure her future with Egon. In the American version, by contrast, the strangulation scene occurs near the end of the film and is relayed in a flashback when Maria confesses her crime to the police. While the German version thus establishes Maria's guilt early on so as to explore processes of desire and repression, the American version delays attributing guilt to Maria in order to obfuscate the identity of the murderer and highlight enigma and suspense.

The existence of two versions of *Die freudlose Gasse* might be seen to indicate the difference between films addressed to German and American audiences; where the German version stages an intense inner drama, the American version dispenses with inwardness and exploits narrative suspense. While such an interpretation is certainly plausible, it is crucial to recognize how the structuring of a double drama in *Die freudlose Gasse* actually recasts any simple opposition between conventions associated with the American and the German cinema. For a start, both versions of the film reveal the marks of film censorship and yet neither version is so incoherent as to efface completely the discontinuity and clash produced by the dramatic juxtaposition of two types of melodrama. Furthermore, if Grete's story introduces issues of Americanism in

gulation of Lia Leid. A number of new scenes and characters have also been added: there are more shots of the upper-class hotel; a new character, Regina, is introduced into the love triangle of Egon, Maria, and Lia Leid; and the narrative suggests that Maria dies of a fatal illness at the end. Most striking, however, is the happy ending tacked onto the American version of the film, in which Grete and Davy embrace. According to Douglas Gomery, these changes were the result of the film's American re-release in 1935, after Greta Garbo had achieved stardom in the United States. "Assuming that audiences would be drawn to *Joyless Street* only to see what Garbo looked liked a decade earlier," Gomery explains, "distributors excised Asta Nielsen's role entirely— nearly 40 percent of the original film. It is this mutilated 1935 version that is still being rented as 'Pabst's *Joyless Street*' by a major distributor of films to college cinema classes and television stations." See Douglas Gomery's chapter, "Researching Film History," in Robert C. Allen and Douglas Gomery, *Film History Theory and Practice* (New York: Alfred A. Knopf, 1985), 34. While I have not been able to locate any other information on the amendments made to the film for foreign distribution, the difference between the American and German versions is interesting and merits further research.

the figure of Davy and concludes with the triumph of virtue, the very theatricality of this triumph undercuts any simple optimistic resolution. Maria's story, moreover, concludes with an undeniable pessimism, but the representation of her inwardness and repression erupts in hyperbolic expression in the film's final images. *Die freudlose Gasse*, in other words, takes up conventions associated with American melodrama and German expressionism and reconstitutes them both in an address to a female spectator where no amount of censorship—short of withdrawing the film entirely—can contain the force of the anger and desire which seeks expression in the text.

In this respect, *Die freudlose Gasse* is remarkably similar to the other film melodramas I have analyzed in this chapter which also address a female audience. Indeed, *Die freudlose Gasse* shares with *Dirnentragödie*, *Hintertreppe*, and *Zuflucht* the singular motif that allows us to understand the appeal of the film melodrama to female audiences in Weimar, to women previously positioned outside the gates of official culture: a female figure stands outside a locked or closed door and begins knocking, then pounding, as if to express the force of an ineffable desire and anger. That this singular gesture of frustration and defiance reappeared, almost unchanged, in various film melodramas of the 1920s, indicates that the contours of female subjectivity and desire were markedly different from those typically associated with the male subject in Weimar. We should recall that Kracauer draws attention to another textual motif—the motif of male regression—to establish the central obsession of mass cultural audiences in Weimar. As Kracauer suggests, the mass cultural spectator's desire to return to the maternal womb, revealed in the gesture of the male figure resting his head on the woman's lap, is symptomatic of an "instinctive reluctance to attempt emancipation" which he considers to be "a typical German attitude." In direct contrast to this assessment, which makes no distinction between male and female subjectivity in the 1920s, I have argued that the film melodrama in Weimar compels us to acknowledge a more complex notion of "emancipation," since the existence of a patriarchal power structure rendered the very choice of rebellion or submission highly problematic for women, and necessarily different than it must have been for men. Whether the dilemma of female emancipation was addressed in fantasies of stark ethical conflict (*Die freudlose Gasse*) or social mobility (*Dirnentra-gödie*), in depictions of endless repetition (*Hintertreppe*) or in images of passive male eroticism (*Zuflucht*), the appeal of the film melodrama derived from its attempt to speak to the promises and failures of sexual and economic liberation in Weimar, and thus to the fundamental contradictions in women's lives.

FEMINISM AND FILM HISTORY —JOYLESS STREETS CIRCA 1988

·

The German woman in the truly palmy days of
German life has no need for emancipation any
more than in those same good days need the man
fear that he may be wrenched out of his place by
woman. Only when there was a lack of absolute
certainty in the knowledge of her task did the eternal instinct of self and race preservation begin to
revolt in woman, then there grew from this revolt
a state of affairs that was unnatural and which
lasted until both sexes returned to their respective
spheres which an eternally wise Providence pre-
ordained for them.
—ADOLF HITLER
Speech to the Women's Party Congress
at Nüremberg (1934)[1]

It would be misleading to draw a direct parallel between the illustrated press and the cinema in the late Weimar years, just as it
would be wrong to insist on an absolute continuity between Weimar and Nazi Germany. Nevertheless, continuities do exist, and a
certain similarity in the photographic and cinematic representation
of female gender identity immediately suggests itself. In 1933, for

---

[1] Excerpted from Robert A. Brady, *The Spirit and Structure of German Fascism*
(London: Left Book Club Edition, 1937), 188; and quoted in Michèle Mattelart,
Women, Media, Crisis: Femininity and Disorder (London: Comedia Publishing Group,
1986), 123, fn. 11.

example, Henny Porten was featured in a film melodrama entitled *Mutter und Kind* (*Mother and Child*). Not unlike the illustrated magazines of the period, *Mutter und Kind* offers a romantically stylized image of rural life, exalting the simple virtues of the German *Hausfrau* and the pains and joys of motherhood. Significantly, this film was directed by Hans Steinhoff, an important director during the Nazi years who was entrusted with making some of the most lavish film melodramas of the 1930s and early 1940s.

While the shape of the future was becoming strikingly apparent in the films of Steinhoff and others, changes in the cinematic representation of women were already well underway as early as the mid–1920s. In 1927, for instance, the image of female bisexuality achieved its most heightened and tragic expression in *Dirnentragödie*, a film that served to mark the end of Asta Nielsen's career in the German cinema. By the late 1920s, Elisabeth Bergner assumed roles similar to Nielsen's, but the image she projected was less one of sexual mobility than one of female adolescence on the verge of sexual awakening and maturity. If, as I have argued, the pathos surrounding Nielsen's screen persona reveals both a desire for sexual mobility and an acknowledgment of its impossibility, the pathos surrounding Bergner's screen roles translates this impossible desire into a kind of nostalgia for an earlier stage of sexual development.

This is not to imply that the melodramatic impulse I have analyzed as central to the Weimar cinema was completely abandoned in the 1930s; neither is it to suggest, if only rhetorically, some sort of teleology in the historical development of the German film. Instead, it is to emphasize the persistence of a melodramatic aesthetic despite the shift away from androgyny and sexual mobility in the Nazi cinema, and thus to argue for both the continuities and discontinuities in the development of the German film. The Weimar cinema, in other words, must be seen as integral to what preceded and what came after it, just as it must be recognized as constituting a privileged aesthetic and cultural moment.

The Weimar cinema was neither mass cultural nor modernist, since that very distinction tends to encourage an understanding of the German silent film as *either* popular or avant-garde, realist or experimental. As I have attempted to suggest through reference to various institutional and textual practices, the Weimar cinema was undeniably mass cultural, and yet it actively encouraged experimentation and artistic collaboration. What remains especially interesting about this period of filmmaking for us today, however, is the manner in which aesthetic experimentation was accompanied by an experimentation with gender roles and a concerted effort to address a highly profitable female audience. While the play with gender roles in the German silent cinema has fascinated a number of contemporary theorists and historians, I have endeavored to show that this play with the representation of sexual identity can only be understood in relation to a gendered spectator. The particular combination of female bisexuality and melodramatic expression, I have argued, goes a long way toward explaining the popularity of the film melodrama with female audiences, since the extreme pathos attributed to female bisexuality bears witness to the imaginative life of Weimar women, who struggled with two mutually opposed facts: that the definitions of female gender identity must be changed, and that this change was becoming increasingly impossible.[2]

"It is an irretrievable image of the past," wrote Walter Benjamin in 1937, "which threatens to disappear in any present which does not recognize its common relation with that image."[3] As if to extend Benjamin's remarks, Edward Said has recently asked the following questions of contemporary cultural theorists:

> Who writes? For whom is the writing being done? In what circumstances? These, it seems to me, are the questions whose answers provide us with the ingredients for making a politics of interpretation. But if one does not wish to ask and answer these questions in an abstract and dishonest way, some attempt must be made to show why they are questions of some importance to the present time.[4]

[2] For a discussion of melodrama in relation to this notion of irreversibility, see Franco Moretti's *Signs Taken for Wonders* (London: Verso, 1983), which is discussed in detail in Steve Neal, "Melodrama and Tears," *Screen* 27, no. 6 (November–December 1986): 6–22.

[3] Walter Benjamin, "Eduard Fuchs, der Sammler und der Historiker," *Zeitschrift fur Sozialforschung* 6 (1937): 346–80; reprinted in translation as "Eduard Fuchs: Collector and Historian," trans. Knut Tarnowski, *New German Critique*, no. 5 (Spring 1975): 27–58.

[4] Edward Said, "Opponents, Audiences, Constituencies, and Community," in *The Politics of Interpretation*, ed. W.J.T. Mitchell (Chicago: University of Chicago Press, 1983), 7.

It is, I believe, especially urgent today for cultural theorists to engage with the questions so eloquently posed by Said: who writes,
and for whom, and in what circumstances? Indeed, these questions
have taken on a particular importance for the writing of history,
since history is, as Benjamin suggests, inescapably bound up with
structures of anticipation and memory in the present. The need for
a specifically feminist interpretation of history, moreover, has assumed a crucial significance given the current intellectual climate
in which, as Alice Jardine has explained, most critics "continue to
either ignore gender or else to incorporate it into an untransformed
reading system, with an ironic wink of the eye, a guilty humanistic
benevolence, or a bold stroke of 'male feminism.' "[5] In these circumstances, it has become increasingly clear that questions of who
writes for whom are not only inseparable from a politics of interpretation, but are also of the utmost importance to the manner in
which we choose to respond to both the past and the present time.

Feminist theory has repeatedly drawn attention to the difference
between agency and address (for instance, to the difference between speaking and being spoken as a subject in language), and
feminist theory continues to raise the most urgent questions for any
politics of interpretation. As this study of Weimar film history
serves to suggest, the problems involved in sorting out identity and
difference become particularly acute in the theorizing and writing
of history, since so many documents preserved from the past offer
few traces of women's presence, and overwhelming evidence of
their absence, marginality, and repression. What is fundamentally
at issue here, however, is not a lack of adequate documentation. In
fact, because women have long been excluded from the texts and
the documents of history, the process of feminist interpretation—
of posing new relations between the visible and the invisible, the
representable and the unrepresentable—necessarily entails a critical or transformed history and not a history predicated on the (illusory) fullness of empirical detail. From the outset of my research
on women in Weimar, I understood my project to be one of rereading and rewriting: a revision of our thinking about the past rather
than a "filling out" or completion of the historical record.[6] In recon-

---

[5] Alice Jardine, *Gynesis: Configurations of Woman and Modernity* (Ithaca, N.Y.: Cornell University Press, 1985), 53.

[6] I borrow this formulation from Mary Ann Doane in her essay, "The 'Woman's Film':

sidering the historical traces of the Weimar years, I became acutely aware of the need to propose new directions in the writing of film history, to show how questions relating to spectatorship and gender can only be answered within history and understood as defined by the historical representation of sexual difference, and to suggest ways in which to conceptualize national identity without subordinating female subjectivity to the familiar model of male subjectivity in crisis.

The Weimar cinema provides a particularly useful place to begin reconsidering the writing of film history, especially given the manner in which the Weimar cinema has been interpreted in the past and the ways in which it continues to be interpreted in the present. Kracauer's study of the Weimar cinema, for example, is clearly a product of the time when it was written. (Indeed, his emphasis on authoritarianism, and the link he establishes between personality structure and male identity, seem to refer as much to post–World War II Europe as to Weimar Germany.) A historical and theoretical revision of Kracauer's interpretation has long been overdue. I share with contemporary theorists the desire to complicate and extend Kracauer's reading so as to open up discussions about spectatorship and representation during the 1920s.

Much of my approach to Weimar film history has in fact involved what may be considered the major impulse of contemporary thought: the process of deconstructing the binary logic which valorizes the single term, and which consequently assures the repressive subordination of difference.[7] Thus, in chapter 1, I show how the opposition between mass culture and modernism in Weimar film histories merely conceals an overriding concern with male subjectivity and identity; then, in chapter 2, I suggest how concepts of proximity and distance in theories of perception have traditionally placed the female spectator on the side of passivity and spectacle, and the male spectator on the side of activity, vision, and knowledge; finally, in chapters 3 and 4, I show how the simple

Possession and Address," in *Re-Vision: Essays in Feminist Film Criticism*, ed. Mary Ann Doane, Patricia Mellencamp, and Linda Williams, The American Film Institute Monograph Series, vol. 3 (Frederick, Md.: University Publications of America, 1983), 67.

[7] For an excellent discussion of deconstruction and feminism, see Shoshana Felman, "Women and Madness: The Critical Phallacy," *Diacritics* 5, no. 4 (Winter 1975): 2–10.

equation of femininity with femaleness in artistic and scientific discourses in Weimar aimed to suppress women's bisexuality so as to
assure the "proper" development of female sexuality. While a great
deal of my critical revision of Weimar film history has therefore
involved an attack on binary oppositions and repressive dichoto-
mies, there is one opposition I have deliberately not submitted to
a deconstructive reading: male and female spectatorship. Indeed,
in my desire to theorize female subjectivity in Weimar outside of
familiar oppositions and time-honored frameworks, I have endeavored to conceptualize female spectatorship not in simple opposition
to male spectatorship but as necessarily—because historically—different.

It is this insistence on gendered spectatorship, moreover, which
serves to underscore what I believe to be the particular relevance
of this study to the present time, to a time when a number of cultural critics have not only proclaimed the "historicization" (or
death) of feminism as a movement, but have also inaugurated a
"postfeminist" approach to questions of gender so as to get beyond
the supposed blind spots and excesses of feminist interpretation.[8]
Interestingly enough, feminism and history have shared a similar
fate in postmodern criticism; in fact, both have frequently been
declared anachronistic, or merely symptomatic of an older mode of
thinking beyond which we are rapidly moving. While I agree that
the fate of feminist and historical analysis in the 1980s is indeed a
symptom of wider currents within intellectual thought, I find it
highly revealing that Weimar culture has been one of the privileged sites where these symptoms have recently been manifested.

As I suggested in chapter 1, contemporary theorists of the Weimar cinema have clearly taken up the postmodern challenge to
break away from the logic of polar oppositions, to call all forms of
duality into question, and to insist on the fundamentally bisexual
nature of gender definition and identification. In this view, the formal and narrative instability of Weimar films is said to mark the
site of an ambiguity, beyond the fixed identities of male or female
spectatorship. While this new approach aims to challenge the exclusive emphasis on male subjectivity that has characterized so

[8] See Alice Jardine's discussion of "postfeminism" in *Gynesis*.

225

many histories of the Weimar cinema in the past, it succeeds in revising previous interpretations only by abandoning any consideration of the historical moment to which the films refer. In a gesture remarkably similar to Heidegger's in the 1920s and 1930s, there thus returns in the 1980s yet another attempt to get beyond gender (and, indeed, beyond feminism) by moving from the masculine to the "neutral" term. Not surprisingly, it is this critical move which ultimately serves to confirm the contours of male subjectivity and desire more profoundly.

It is significant, however, that issues of sexual ambiguity in the Weimar cinema have also attracted the attention of feminist theorists who, while less inclined to dissociate questions of ambiguity completely from questions of gendered spectatorship, nevertheless insist on a fluidity in structures of identification and spectatorial response. This insistence on the bisexual nature of male and female subjectivity is absolutely central to theorizing representation and spectatorship in the Weimar cinema. And yet unless one considers how bisexuality is figured differently for men and for women within a patriarchal culture, the analysis of sexual ambiguity and instability in the cinema will necessarily remain limited and incomplete. In chapter 2, for example, I showed how a number of discourses in Weimar testify to a male identification with femininity, but also reveal the processes of repression and projection that typically accompany such identification. Furthermore, as I pointed out in chapter 3, scientists and sex-reformers in the 1920s frequently acknowledged women's predisposition to bisexuality, but only to insist on women's need to renounce masculinity so as to ensure the proper development of their femininity (and thus their "natural" place within society). A truly nonreductive description of identification and sexual orientation in the cinema, in other words, must not confuse the play with gender *identity* with a transformation of gender *identities*, for to do so is to lose sight of the ways in which male and female spectatorship are figured differently within a patriarchal power structure.[9]

While my analysis of the Weimar cinema has thus insisted on the

[9] On this point, see Kaja Silverman's essay, "Lost Objects and Mistaken Subjects: Film Theory's Structuring Lack," *Wide Angle* 7, nos. 1–2 (1985): 14–29.

necessity of theorizing spectatorship in history and in relation to a gendered subject, it has also attempted to modify existing theories of the female spectator within feminist film criticism. For a theorist like Mary Ann Doane, with whose work I have engaged throughout this study, questions of visual pleasure and spectatorship cannot be understood by referring to the bisexuality of human subjectivity, since male and female spectatorship are necessarily rendered asymmetrical within the logic of cinematic representation. Doane recognizes, moreover, that issues of power remain central to any deconstructive reading of gender and spectatorship—and it is to her credit to have insisted on the sexual politics of representation and interpretation, particularly given the current attempt to merge deconstructive criticism with postfeminist approaches to questions of gender. Doane's repeated emphasis on the impossibility of female spectatorship—on women's inability to see, to know, or to derive pleasure in the cinema—nevertheless serves to confirm what Kracauer posits, in a different register and from a different point of view, as central to Weimar film history: namely, that male subjectivity is paramount, and that woman exists only in absence or in opposition to a fundamentally male imaginary.

In contrast to this assessment, I have attempted to suggest the *difficulties* of female spectatorship in Weimar but not its *impossibility*. Through close analysis of illustrated magazines and film melodramas, I have argued that it is a mistake to see male subjectivity or patriarchal power as absolute or unassailable in the 1920s, just as it is wrong to valorize Weimar culture as somehow beyond gender or the repressive subordination of difference. The Weimar years, I believe, have much to tell us about representation and sexual difference, but only when we consider these issues historically and in relation to a gendered subject. Whatever the risks involved in attempting to theorize female subjectivity today—and the risks are high—the Weimar years serve to illuminate the stakes for feminism in rethinking gendered spectatorship within history, for it is indeed the contradictory image of female subjectivity in the past which now threatens to disappear in a present which fails to recognize its common relation with that image. I have attempted to locate the contours of female subjectivity within a history and a representational practice long assumed to be the sole preserve of

227

male desire and male subjectivity in crisis. In my view, it is this kind of theoretical and historical approach to questions of representation and spectatorship that alone allows us to discern what Lotte Eisner deems the peculiarly "haunting" quality of the German silent cinema—a quality I have analyzed as haunted precisely by the traces of a different vision and a different desire.

· BIBLIOGRAPHY ·

Allen, Robert C., and Douglas Gomery. *Film History Theory and Practice*. New York: Alfred A. Knopf, 1985.

Altenloh, Emilie. *Zur Soziologie des Kino: Die Kino-Unternehmung und die sozialen Schichten ihrer Besucher*. Jena: Eugen Diederichs, 1914. Reprinted in facsimile by Medienladen, Hamburg, 1977.

Balázs, Béla. *Theory of the Film: Character and Growth of a New Art*. Trans. Edith Bone. New York: Dover, 1970.

Bathrick, David, Thomas Elsaesser, and Miriam Hansen, eds. Special Issue on Weimar Film Theory. *New German Critique*, no. 40 (Winter 1987).

Belach, Helga, et al. *Asta Nielsen*. Berlin: Stiftung Deutsche Kinemathek, 1973.

———. *Henny Porten: Der erste deutsche Filmstar*. Berlin: Hände und Spener, 1986.

Benjamin, Walter. *Charles Baudelaire: A Lyric Poet in the Era of High Capitalism*. Trans. Harry H. Zohn. London: New Left Books, 1973.

———. "Eduard Fuchs, der Sammler und der Historiker." *Zeitschrift fur Sozialforschung* 6 (1937): 346–80. Reprinted in translation as "Eduard Fuchs: Collector and Historian." Trans. Knut Tarnowski. *New German Critique*, no. 5 (Spring 1975): 27–58.

———. *Illuminations*. Trans. Harry Zohn. New York: Schocken Books, 1969.

———. *Reflections: Essays, Aphorisms, Autobiographical Writings*. Trans. Edmund Jephcott. New York and London: Harcourt Brace Jovanovich, 1978.

———. "Über einige Motive bei Baudelaire." In *Gesammelte Schriften*, vol. 1, part 2, ed. Rolf Tiedemann and Hermann Schweppenhäuser, 605–54. Frankfurt am Main: Suhrkamp, 1974.

———. *Ursprung des deutschen Trauerspiels. Gesammelte Schriften*, vol. 1, part 1, ed. Rolf Tiedemann and Hermann Schweppenhäuser, 203–430. Frankfurt am Main: Suhrkamp, 1974. Reprinted in English translation as *The Origin of German Tragic Drama*, trans. John Osborne. London: New Left Books, 1977.

———. "Zentralpark." In *Gesammelte Schriften*, vol. 1, part 2, ed. Rolf Tiedemann and Hermann Schweppenhäuser, 655–90. Frankfurt am Main: Suhrkamp, 1974. Reprinted in translation as "Central Park," trans. Lloyd Spenser. *New German Critique*, no. 34 (Winter 1985): 32–55.

Bergstrom, Janet. "Sexuality at a Loss: The Films of F. W. Murnau." *Poetics Today* 6, nos. 1–2 (Spring 1985): 185–203.

Bovenschen, Silvia. *Die imaginierte Weiblichkeit*. Frankfurt am Main: Suhrkamp, 1979.

Brennicke, Ilona, and Joe Hembus. *Klassiker des deutschen Stummfilms 1910–1930*. Munich: Goldmann, 1983.

Bridenthal, Renate. "Beyond *Kinder, Küche, Kirche*: Weimar Women at Work." *Central European History* 6, no. 2 (June 1973): 148–66.

Bridenthal, Renate, and Claudia Koonz. "Beyond *Kinder, Küche, Kirche*: Weimar Women in Politics and Work." In *Liberating Women's History: Theoretical and Critical Essays*, ed. Berenice A. Carroll, 301–29. Champaign, Il.: University of Illinois Press, 1976.

Bridenthal, Renate, Atina Grossmann, and Marion Kaplan, eds. *When Biology Became Destiny: Women in Weimar and Nazi Germany*. New York: Monthly Review Press, 1984.

Brooks, Peter. *The Melodramatic Imagination: Balzac, Henry James, Melodrama and the Mode of Excess*. New Haven: Yale University Press, 1976.

Buci-Glucksmann, Christine. "Catastrophic Utopia: The Feminine as Allegory of the Modern." *Representations* 14 (Spring 1986): 220–29.

Buck-Morss, Susan. "Benjamin's Passagen-Werk: Redeeming Mass Culture for the Revolution." *New German Critique*, no. 29 (Spring–Summer 1983): 211–40.

Budd, Michael. "Retrospective Narration in Film: Rereading the Cabinet of Dr. Caligari." *Film Criticism* 4, no. 1 (Fall 1979): 35–43.

Bürger, Peter. *Theory of the Avant-Garde*. Trans. Michael Shaw. Minneapolis, Mn.: University of Minnesota Press, 1984.

de Lauretis, Teresa. *Alice Doesn't: Feminism, Semiotics, Cinema*. Bloomington, In.: University of Indiana Press, 1984.

Derrida, Jacques. "Geschlecht: différence sexuelle, différence ontologique." *L'Herne* (September 1983): 419–30.

Doane, Mary Ann. *The Desire to Desire: The Woman's Film of the 1940s*. Bloomington, In.: Indiana University Press, 1987.

———. "Film and the Masquerade: Theorizing the Female Spectator." *Screen* 23, nos. 3–4 (September–October 1982): 74–87.

———. " '. . . when the direction of the force acting on the body is changed.': The Moving Image." *Wide Angle* 7, nos. 1–2 (1985): 42–58.

———. "The 'Woman's Film': Possession and Address." In *Re-Vision: Essays in Feminist Film Criticism*, ed. Mary Ann Doane, Patricia Mellencamp, and Linda Williams, 63–82. The American Film Institute Monograph Series, vol. 3. Frederick, Md.: University Publications of America, 1983.

———. "Woman's Stake: Filming the Female Body." *October* 17 (September 1981): 23–36.

"Dossier on Melodrama." *Screen* 18, no. 2 (Summer 1977): 105–19.

Draper, Hal, and Anne G. Lipow, "Marxist Women versus Bourgeois Feminism." In *The Socialist Register 1976*, ed. Ralph Miliband and John Saville, 179–226. London: The Merlin Press, 1976.

Eisenschitz, Bernard. "Who Does the World Belong To? The Place of a Film." *Screen* 15, no. 2 (1974): 65–73.

Eisner, Lotte. *L'Ecran Démoniaque*. Paris: Le Terrain Vague, 1952. Translated with new material as *The Haunted Screen: Expressionism in the German Film and the Influence of Max Reinhardt*. Trans. Roger Greaves. Berkeley and Los Angeles: University of California Press, 1969.

Elsaesser, Thomas. "Film History and Visual Pleasure: Weimar Cinema." In *Cinema Histories/Cinema Practices*, ed. Patricia Mellencamp and Philip Rosen, 47–84. The American Film Institute Monograph Series, vol. 4. Frederick, Md.: University Publications of America, 1984.

———. "Lulu and the Meter Man: Louise Brooks, Pabst, and *Pandora's Box*." *Screen* 24, nos. 4–5 (July–October 1983): 4–36.

Elsaesser, Thomas. "Social Mobility and the Fantastic: German Silent Cinema." *Wide Angle* 5, no. 2 (1982): 14–25.

———. "Tales of Sound and Fury: Observations on the Family Melodrama." *Monogram* 4 (1972): 2–15.

Engberg, Marguerite. *Asta Nielsen*. Trans. into German from the Danish by Børge Trolle and Erik Ziese. Bad Ems: Verband der deutschen Filmclubs E. V., 1967.

Evans, Richard J. *Comrades and Sisters: Feminism, Socialism and Pacifism in Europe 1870–1945*. New York: St. Martin's Press, 1987.

———. "Feminism and Female Emancipation in Germany, 1870–1945: Sources, Methods, and Problems of Research." *Central European History* 9, no. 4 (December 1976): 323–51.

———. *The Feminist Movement in Germany 1894–1933*, vol. 6. London: Sage Studies in Twentieth Century History, 1976.

Felman, Shoshana. "Women and Madness: The Critical Phallacy." *Diacritics* 5, no. 4 (Winter 1975): 2–10.

Fiedler, Leonhard. *Max Reinhardt: in Selbstzeugnissen und Bilddokumenten*. Hamburg: Rowohlt, 1975.

Filmoberprüfstelle. "Die freudlose Gasse." Berlin den 29. März 1926. Original in Stiftung Deutsche Kinemathek.

Freud, Sigmund. *Civilization and Its Discontents*. Trans. James Strachey. New York: Norton, 1962.

Freund, R., and M. Hanisch, eds. *Mutter Krausens Fahrt ins Glück. Filmprotokoll und Materialien*. Berlin, 1976.

Gadamer, Hans Georg. "Heidegger's Later Philosophy." In *Essays in Philosophical Hermeneutics*. Trans. David E. Linge. Berkeley and Los Angeles: University of California Press, 1976.

Gallagher, Catherine, and Thomas Laqueur, eds. *The Making of the Modern Body: Sexuality and Society in the Nineteenth Century*. Berkeley and Los Angeles: University of California Press, 1987.

Ganschow, Uta Berg, ed. *Berlin: Aussen und Innen—53 Filme aus 90 Jahren*. Berlin: Stiftung Deutsche Kinemathek, 1984.

Gay, Peter. *Weimar Culture: The Outsider as Insider*. New York: Harper and Row, 1970.

Gidal, Tim N. *Modern Photojournalism, Origin and Evolution, 1910–1933*. New York: Collier Books, 1973.

Gledhill, Christine, ed. *Home Is Where the Heart Is*. London: British Film Institute, 1987.

Grafe, Frieda. "Doktor Caligari gegen Dr. Kracauer." *Filmkritik* 5 (May 1970): 242–44.

Gramann, Karola, and Heide Schlüpmann. "Unnatürliche Akte: Die Inszenierung des lesbischen im Film." In *Lust und Elend: Das erotische Kino*. Munich: Bücher, 1981.

Grossmann, Atina. "Abortion and Economic Crisis: The 1931 Campaign Against Paragraph 218 in Germany." *New German Critique*, no. 14 (Spring 1978): 119–38.

———. "*Girlkultur* or Thoroughly Rationalized Female: A New Woman in Weimar Germany?" In *Women in Culture and Politics: A Century of Change*, ed. Judith Friedlander et al., 62–80. Bloomington, In.: Indiana University Press, 1986.

———. "The New Woman and the Rationalization of Sexuality in Weimar Germany." In *Powers of Desire: The Politics of Sexuality*, ed. Ann Snitow, Christine Stansell, and Sharon Thompson, 153–71. New York: Monthly Review Press, 1983.

Gruber, Helmut. "Willi Münzenberg's German Communist Propaganda Empire, 1921–1933." *Journal of Modern History* 38, no. 3 (September 1966): 278–97.

Hansen, Miriam. "Early Silent Cinema: Whose Public Sphere?" *New German Critique*, no. 29 (Spring–Summer 1983): 147–84.

———. "Pleasure, Ambivalence, Identification: Valentino and Female Spectatorship." *Cinema Journal* 25, no. 4 (Summer 1986): 6–32.

Hardt, Hanno, and Karin Becker. "The Eyes of the Proletariat: The Worker Photography Movement in Weimar Germany." *Studies in Visual Communication* 7, no. 4 (Fall 1981): 72–82.

Heath, Stephen. "Joan Riviere and the Masquerade." In *Formations of Fantasy*, ed. Victor Burgin, James Donald, and Cora Kaplan, 45–61. New York and London: Methuen, 1986.

Heidegger, Martin. *Being and Time*. Trans. John Macquarrie and Edward Robinson. New York: Harper and Row, 1962.

———. *Discourse on Thinking*. Trans. John M. Anderson and E. Hans Freund. New York: Harper and Row, 1966.

———. *Poetry, Language, Thought*. Trans. Alfred Hofstader. New York: Harper and Row, 1972.

Heidegger, Martin. *The Question Concerning Technology*. Trans. William Lovitt. New York: Harper and Row, 1974.

Hirschbach, Frank D., et al. *Germany in the Twenties: The Artist as Social Critic*. New York: Holmes and Meier, 1980.

Hodann, Max. *History of Modern Morals*. Trans. Stella Browne. London: William Heinemann Medical Books Ltd., 1937. Reprinted in facsimile by AMS Press, New York, 1976.

Hogenkamp, Bert. "The Proletarian Film and the Weimar Republic: A Comment." *Historical Journal of Film, Radio and Television* 2, no. 2 (1982): 177–79.

———. "Workers' Newsreels in the 1920s and 1930s." *Our History* 68 (n.d.): 1–36.

Horak, Jan Christopher. "*Mother Krause's Trip to Happiness*, Kino-Culture in Weimar Germany, Part 2, 'Tenements Kill Like an Ax.'" *Jump Cut* 27 (July 1982): 55–56.

Huaco, George. *The Sociology of Film Art*. New York: Basic Books, 1965.

Huyssen, Andreas. *After the Great Divide: Modernism, Mass Culture, Postmodernism*. Bloomington, In.: Indiana University Press, 1986.

———. "Mass Culture as Woman: Modernism's Other." In *Studies in Entertainment: Critical Approaches to Mass Culture*, ed. Tania Modleski, Theories of Contemporary Culture, vol. 7, 188–207. Bloomington, In: Indiana University Press, 1986.

———. "The Vamp and the Machine: Technology and Sexuality in Fritz Lang's *Metropolis*." *New German Critique*, nos. 24–25 (Fall–Winter 1981–1982): 221–37.

Irigaray, Luce. *Speculum de l'autre femme*. Paris: Les Éditions de Minuit, 1974. Reprinted in translation as *Speculum of the Other Woman*. Trans. Gillian C. Gill. Ithaca, N.Y.: Cornell University Press, 1985.

Jacoby, Russell. *The Repression of Psychoanalysis: Otto Fenichel and the Political Freudians*. New York: Basic Books, 1983.

Jaeger, Klaus, Horst-Diether Kalbfleisch, and Helmut Regel, eds. *Der Weg ins Dritte Reich: Deutscher Film und Weimars Ende*. Oberhausen: Verlag Karl Maria Laufen, 1974.

Jameson, Fredric. *The Political Unconscious: Narrative as a Socially Symbolic Act*. Ithaca, N.Y.: Cornell University Press, 1981.

Jardine, Alice. *Gynesis: Configurations of Woman and Modernity.* Ithaca, N.Y.: Cornell University Press, 1985.

Jenkins, Stephen. *Fritz Lang: The Image and the Look.* London: British Film Institute, 1981.

Johnston, Claire. "Femininity and the Masquerade: *Anne of the Indies.*" In *Jacques Tourneur,* ed. Claire Johnston and Paul Willeman, 36–44. London: British Film Institute, 1975.

Kaes, Anton. "The Debate about Cinema: Charting a Controversy (1909–1929)." Trans. David J. Levin. *New German Critique,* no. 40 (Winter 1987): 7–33.

———, ed. *Kino-Debatte: Texte zum Verhältnis von Literatur und Film, 1909–1929.* Tübingen: Max Niemeyer Verlag, 1978.

———. "Mass Culture and Modernity: Notes Toward a Social History of Early American and German Cinema." In *America and the Germans: An Assessment of a Three Hundred Year History,* vol. 2, 317–31. Philadelphia, Pa.: Pennsylvania Press, 1985.

Kaplan, E. Ann. "Theories of Melodrama: A Feminist Perspective." *Women and Performance: A Journal of Feminist Film Theory* 1, no. 1 (Spring–Summer 1983): 81–85.

Kearns, Martha. *Käthe Kollwitz: Woman and Artist.* Old Westbury, N.Y.: The Feminist Press, 1976.

Kepley, Vance. "The Workers' International Relief and the Cinema of the Left." *Cinema Journal* 23, no. 1 (Fall 1983): 7–23.

Kerbs, Diethart. "Die Epoche der Bildagenturen." In *Die Gleichschaltung der Bilder: Pressefotografie 1930–1936.* Berlin: Frölich und Kaufmann, 1983.

Koch, Gertrud. "Why Women Go to the Movies." *Jump-Cut* 27 (July 1982): 51–53.

Kofman, Sarah. *The Enigma of Woman: Woman in Freud's Writings.* Trans. Catherine Porter. Ithaca, N.Y.: Cornell University Press, 1985.

Koonz, Claudia. *Mothers in the Fatherland: Women, the Family, and Nazi Politics.* New York: St. Martin's Press, 1987.

Korte, Helmut, ed. *Film und Realität in der Weimarer Republik.* Munich: Carl Hanser Verlag, 1978.

Kracauer, Siegfried. *Das Ornament der Masse.* Frankfurt am Main: Suhrkamp, 1977.

———. *From Caligari to Hitler: A Psychological History of the*

German Film. Princeton, N.J.: Princeton University Press, 1947.

————. *Kino*. Ed. Karsten Witte. Frankfurt am Main: Suhrkamp, 1974.

————. "Kult der Zerstreuung." In *Das Ornament der Masse*, 311–17. Frankfurt am Main: Suhrkamp, 1977. Reprinted in translation as "Cult of Distraction: On Berlin's Picture Palaces." Trans. Thomas Y. Levin. *New German Critique*, no. 40 (Winter 1987): 91–96.

————. "The Mass Ornament." Trans. Jack Zipes and Barbara Correll. *New German Critique*, no. 5 (Spring 1975): 67–76.

————. *Von Caligari zu Hitler*. Trans. Ruth Baumgarten and Karsten Witte. Frankfurt am Main: Suhrkamp, 1979.

Kühn, Gertraude, Karl Tümmler, and Walter Wimmer, eds. *Film und revolutionäre Arbeiterbewegung in Deutschland 1918–1932*, 2 vols. Berlin, DDR: Hochschule für Film und Fernsehen der DDR, 1975.

Kurtz, Rudolf. *Expressionismus und Film*. Berlin: Verlag der Lichtbildbühne, 1926.

Lacqueur, Walter. *Weimar: A Cultural History, 1918–1933*. New York: G. P. Putnam's Sons, 1974.

Ludecke, Willi. *Der Film in Agitation und Propaganda der revolutionären deutschen Arbeiterbewegung, 1919–1933*. Berlin: Oberbaumverlag, 1973.

Lukács, Georg. "Gedanken zu einer Äesthetik des Kino." Reprinted in translation as "Thoughts on an Aesthetic for the Cinema." Trans. Barrie Ellis-Jones. *Framework* 14 (Spring 1981): 2–4.

Lunn, Eugene. *Marxism and Modernism: An Historical Study of Lukács, Brecht, Benjamin and Adorno*. Berkeley and Los Angeles: University of California Press, 1984.

Manvell, Roger, and Heinrich Fraenkel. *The German Cinema*. New York: Praeger, 1971.

Marckwardt, Wilhelm. *Die Illustrierten der Weimarer Zeit: Publizistische Funktion, Ökonomische Entwicklung und inhaltliche Tendenzen*. Munich: Minerva Publikation, 1982.

Mason, Tim. "Women in Germany, 1925–1940: Family, Welfare and Work." *History Workshop: A Journal of Socialist Historians* 1 (Spring 1976): 74–113; 2 (Autumn 1976): 5–32.

Mattelart, Michèle. *Women, Media, Crisis: Femininity and Disorder*. London: Comedia Publishing Group, 1986.

Meier, Gerd. "Materialien zur Geschichte des Prometheus Film-Verleih und Vertriebs GmbH, 1926–1933." *Deutsche Filmkunst*, nos. 1–8, Berlin, DDR (1962): 12–16; 57–60; 97–99; 137–40; 177–80; 221–24; 275–77; 310–12.

Mellencamp, Patricia. "Oedipus and the Robot in *Metropolis*." *Enclitic* 5, no. 1 (Spring 1981): 20–42.

Metz, Christian. *The Imaginary Signifier: Psychoanalysis and Cinema*. Trans. Celia Britton, Annwyl Williams, Ben Brewster, and Alfred Guzzetti. London: The MacMillan Press, 1982.

Miller, D. A. "*Cage aux folles*: Sensation and Gender in Wilkie Collins's *The Woman in White*." In *The Making of the Modern Body*, ed. Catherine Gallagher and Thomas Laqueur, 107–36. Berkeley and Los Angeles: University of California Press, 1987.

Modleski, Tania. "The Terror of Pleasure: The Contemporary Horror Film and Postmodern Theory." In *Studies in Entertainment: Critical Approaches to Mass Culture*, ed. Tania Modleski, Theories of Contemporary Culture, vol. 7, 155–66. Bloomington, In.: Indiana University Press, 1986.

———. *The Women Who Knew Too Much: Hitchcock and Feminist Theory*. New York and London: Methuen, 1988.

———. "Time and Desire in the Woman's Film." *Cinema Journal* 23, no. 3 (Spring 1984): 19–30.

Monaco, Paul. *Cinema and Society: France and Germany During the Twenties*. New York, Oxford, and Amsterdam: Elsevier, 1976.

Mörchen, Helmut. "Reportage und Dokumentarliteratur." In *Deutsche Literatur: Eine Sozialgeschichte*. Ed. Horst Albert Glaser. Hamburg: Rororo, 1983.

Morris, Meaghan. *Upward Mobility*. Bloomington, In.: Indiana University Press, forthcoming 1989.

Mulvey, Laura. "Afterthoughts on 'Visual Pleasure and Narrative Cinema' Inspired by *Duel in the Sun*." *Framework*, nos. 15–17 (Summer 1981): 12–15.

———. "Visual Pleasure and Narrative Cinema," *Screen* 16, no. 3 (Autumn 1975): 6–18.

Münzenberg, Willi. *Programm und Aufbau der Sozialistischen Jugend-Internationale*. Stuttgart: Internationaler Sozialistischer Verlag, 1919.

Murray, Bruce. "*Mutter Krausens Fahrt ins Glück*: An Analysis of the Film as a Critical Response to the 'Street Films' of the Commercial Film Industry." *Enclitic* 5–6, nos. 1–2 (1981–1982): 44–54.

Neal, Steve. "Melodrama and Tears." *Screen* 27, no. 6 (November–December 1986): 6–22.

Nicolson, Harold. "The Charm of Berlin." *Der Querschnitt* (May 1929) (originally in English). Reprinted in *Der Querschnitt: Das Magazin der aktuellen Ewigkeitswerte, 1924–1933*, 261–63. Berlin: Ullstein Verlag, 1980.

Nowell-Smith, Geoffrey. "Minnelli and Melodrama." *Screen* 18 (Summer 1977): 113–18.

Petro, Patrice. "Mass Culture and the Feminine: The 'Place' of Television in Film Studies." *Cinema Journal* 25, no. 3 (Spring 1986): 5–21.

Pettifer, James. "Against the Stream—*Kuhle Wampe*." *Screen* 15, no. 2 (1974): 49–64.

———. "The Limits of Naturalism (On *Mutter Krausens Fahrt ins Glück*)." *Screen* 16, no. 4 (1975–1976): 5–15.

Place, Janey. "Women in film noir." In *Women in Film Noir*, ed. E. Ann Kaplan. London: British Film Institute, 1978.

Plummer, Thomas G., et al. *Film and Politics in the Weimar Republic*. New York: Holmes and Meier, 1982.

Potamkin, Harry M. "The Rise and Fall of the German Film." *Cinema* 1 (April 1930): 24–25.

Quataert, Jean. *Reluctant Feminists in German Social Democracy, 1885–1917*. Princeton, N.J.: Princeton University Press, 1979.

Rentschler, Eric, ed. *German Film and Literature: Adaptations and Transformations*. London and New York: Methuen, 1986.

Rich, B. Ruby. "From Repressive Tolerance to Erotic Liberation: *Maedchen in Uniform*." In *Re-Vision: Essays in Feminist Film Criticism*, ed. Mary Ann Doane, Patricia Mellencamp, and Linda Williams, 63–82. The American Film Institute Monograph Series, vol. 3, Frederick, Md.: University Publications of America, 1983.

Riviere, Joan. "Womanliness as a Masquerade." Originally published in *The International Journal of Psychoanalysis* 10 (1929). Reprinted in *Formations of Fantasy*, ed. Victor Burgin, James Donald, and Cora Kaplan, 35–44. London: Methuen, 1986.

Rose, Jaqueline. *Sexuality in the Field of Vision*. London: Verso, 1986.

Rosenberg, James L. "Melodrama." In *The Context and Craft of Drama*, ed. Robert W. Corrigan and James L. Rosenberg, 195–218. San Francisco: Chandler Publishing Co., 1964.

Said, Edward. "Opponents, Audiences, Constituencies, and Community." In *The Politics of Interpretation*, ed. W.J.T. Mitchell, 7–32. Chicago: University of Chicago Press, 1983.

Schiller-Nationalmuseum, Marbach. *Hätte ich das Kino! Die Schriftsteller und der Stummfilm*. Catalogue to an exhibit in the Schiller-Nationalmuseum, Marbach a.N., 1976.

Schivelbusch, Wolfgang. *The Railway Journey: Trains and Travel in the 19th Century*. Trans. Anselm Hollo. Oxford: Basil Blackwell, 1980.

Schlüpmann, Heide. "The Bordello as an Arcadian Site? G. W. Pabst's *Diary of a Lost Girl*." In *The Films of G. W. Pabst*, ed. Eric Rentschler. New Brunswick, N.J.: Rutgers University Press, forthcoming 1989.

————. "The First German Art Film: Rye's *The Student of Prague (1913)*." In *German Film and Literature: Adaptations and Transformations*, ed. Eric Rentschler, 9–24. New York: Methuen, 1986.

————. "Kinosucht." *Frauen und Film* 33 (October 1982): 45–52.

Schönlank, Bruno. "Kino." In *Deutsche Arbeiterdichtung 1910–1933*, ed. Günter Heintz, 293–94. Stuttgart, 1974.

Schulte-Sasse, Jochen. "Foreword: Theory of Modernism versus Theory of the Avant-Garde." In Peter Bürger, *Theory of the Avant-Garde*. Minneapolis, Mn.: University of Minnesota Press, 1984.

Sedgwick, Eve Kosofsky. *Between Men: English Literature and Male Homosocial Desire*. New York: Columbia University Press, 1985.

Seydel, Renate, and Allan Hagedorff. *Asta Nielsen: Ihr Leben in Fotodokumenten, Selbstzeugnissen und zeitgenössischen Betrachtungen*. Munich: Universitas Verlag, 1981.

Silverman, Kaja. "Lost Objects and Mistaken Subjects: Film Theory's Structuring Lack." *Wide Angle* 7, nos. 1–2 (1985): 14–29.

Silverman, Kaja. "Masochism and Subjectivity." *Framework* 12 (1982): 2–9.

———. *The Subject of Semiotics*. New York: Oxford University Press, 1983.

Simmel, Georg. *Georg Simmel: On Women, Sexuality, and Love*. Trans. Guy Oakes. New Haven: Yale University Press, 1984.

———. "Die Grossstadt und das Geistesleben." in *Die Grossstadt: Jahrbuch der Gehe-Stiftung*, 187–206. Dresden, 1903. Reprinted in translation as "The Metropolis and Mental Life." In *The Sociology of Georg Simmel*, ed. Kurt H. Wolff, 409–24. New York: The Free Press, 1950.

Sloterdijk, Peter. *Kritik der zynischen Vernunft*. 2 vols. Frankfurt am Main: Suhrkamp, 1983. Reprinted in translation as *Critique of Cynical Reason*. Minneapolis, Mn.: University of Minnesota Press, 1987.

Solomon-Godeau, Abigail. "Reconstructing Documentary: Connie Hatch's Representational Resistance." *Camera Obscura*, nos. 13–14 (1985): 113–48.

Staiger, Janet, and Douglas Gomery. "The History of World Cinema: Models for Economic Analysis." *Film Reader* 4 (1979): 35–44.

Stoos, Toni. " 'Erobert den Film!' oder Prometheus gegen UFA & Co." In *Erobert den Film! Proletariat und Film in der Weimarer Republik: Materialien zur Filmgeschichte*, West Berlin: Neue Gesellschaft für Bildende Kunst und Freunde der deutschen Kinemathek, 1977.

Studlar, Gaylyn. "Masochism and the Perverse Pleasures of the Cinema." *Quarterly Review of Film Studies* 9, no. 4 (Fall 1984): 267–82.

Suleiman, Susan Rubin, ed. *The Female Body in Western Culture: Contemporary Perspectives*. Cambridge and London: Harvard University Press, 1986.

Taylor, Ronald, ed. *Aesthetics and Politics: Debates Between Ernst Bloch, Georg Lukács, Bertolt Brecht, Walter Benjamin, Theodor Adorno*. London: New Left Books, 1977.

Theweleit, Klaus. *Männerphantasien*. 2 vols. Frankfurt: Verlag Roter Stern, 1977, 1979. Reprinted in English translation as *Male Fantasies*. Trans. Stephen Conway. 2 vols. Minneapolis, Mn.: University of Minnesota Press, 1987, 1988.

Thönnessen, Werner. *The Emancipation of Women: The Rise and*

Fall of the Women's Movement in German Social Democracy 1863–1933. Trans. Joris de Bres. London: Pluto, 1976.

Tudor, Andrew. *Image and Influence*. New York: St. Martin's Press, 1974.

Vicinus, Martha. "Helpless and Unfriended: Nineteenth Century Domestic Melodrama." *New Literary History* 13, no. 1 (Autumn 1981): 127–43.

Weininger, Otto. *Geschlecht und Charakter*. 1903. Reprinted in English translation as *Sex and Character*. New York: A. L. Burt Company, 1906.

Welch, David. "The Proletarian Cinema and the Weimar Republic." *Historical Journal of Film, Radio and Television* 1, no. 1 (1981): 3–18.

Whitford, Frank. "Expressionism in the Cinema." *Studio International* 179, no. 918 (January 1970): 24–27.

Willet, John. *The New Sobriety: Art and Politics in the Weimar Period*. London: Thames and Hudson, 1978.

Williams, Linda. "Something Else Besides a Mother: *Stella Dallas* and the Maternal Melodrama." *Cinema Journal* 24, no. 1 (Fall 1984): 2–27.

———. "When the Woman Looks." In *Re-Vision: Essays in Feminist Film Criticism*, ed. Mary Ann Doane, Patricia Mellencamp, and Linda Williams, 83–99. The American Film Institute Monograph Series, vol. 3. Frederick, Md.: University Publications of America, 1984.

Willmann, Heinz. *Geschichte der Arbeiter-Illustrierten Zeitung 1921–1938*. Berlin: Dietz Verlag, 1975.

Witte, Karsten. "Introduction to Siegfried Kracauer's 'The Mass Ornament.' " Trans. Jack Zipes and Barbara Correll. *New German Critique*, no. 5 (Spring 1975): 59–66.

Wollenberg, Hans H. *Fifty Years of German Film*. London: Falcon Press, 1948.

Wuss, Peter. "Film Concepts in the Brechtian Era." *Filmwissenschaftliche Mitteilungen* 6, no. 1 (1965): 39–48.

Zuckmayer, Carl. *Als Wär's ein Stück von mir*. 1966. Reprinted in translation as *A Part of Myself*. Trans. Richard and Clara Winston. New York: Harcourt Brace Jovanovich, 1970.

Printed in the United States
1299200006B/120